Ethnic Minority Identity

Ethnic Minority Identity

A Social Psychological Perspective

NIMMI HUTNIK

Reader,
Lady Shri Ram College,
(University of Delhi)
Lajpat Nagar,
New Delhi

CLARENDON PRESS · OXFORD
1991

Oxford University Press, Walton Street, Oxford OX2 6DP

Oxford New York Toronto
Delhi Bombay Calcutta Madras Karachi
Petaling Jaya Singapore Hong Kong Tokyo
Nairobi Dar es Salaam Cape Town
Melbourne Auckland

and associated companies in
Berlin Ibadan

Oxford is a trade mark of Oxford University Press

Published in the United States
by Oxford University Press, New York

A catalogue record for this book is available from the British Library

Library of Congress Cataloging in Publication Data
Hutnik, Nimmi
Ethnic minority identity : a social psychological perspective / N. Hutnik.
Includes bibliographical reference and index.
1. Ethnicity—Great Britain.   2. Minorities—Great Britain.
3. Ethnic relations   4. Assimilation (Sociology)   5. Social
psychology—Great Britain.   6. Great Britain—Social conditions.
I. Title
GN585.G8H8   1991   305.8'00941–dc20   91-14317
ISBN 0–19–852193–6

Typeset by Cambridge Composing (UK) Ltd
Printed and bound in Great Britain by
Bookcraft (Bath) Ltd
Midsomer Norton, Avon

Always, for Ivan

Acknowledgements

I would like to thank Ivan Hutnik my friend of many years, for being the prime sounding-board of all my ideas. His empathy, encouragement, and support have been invaluable to me.

Thanks, too, to my mother, Clare Parambi and my little daughter Anna for giving me 'time off', so that I might write this book.

I would like to thank Lady Shri Ram College for temporarily freeing me from my duties as lecturer in order that I might study at Oxford.

I would like to thank Oxford University, and in particular the Department of Experimental Psychology, for three of the most stimulating and enlightening years of my life.

I would like also to thank the Charles Wallace Trust of India for financing a second trip to Oxford in order that I might enrich the book.

Finally, I would like to thank the many people who have brought this book to fruition. Thanks to Shanta and Sophie for typing the manuscript. Thanks to numerous friends whose ideas and lives have in many subtle ways influenced the direction of this book: Dave and Ange, Susie and Lawrie, Meera and Luke, Priya and Michael, Annie and Malay, and Mohan and Usha.

Above all, thanks to my Father, who has been the light upon this work.

New Delhi   N.H.
May 1991

Contents

I

Ethnic Minority Identity
in Britain: a Scenario

1.

Structural and functional constraints on ethnic minority individuals in Britain

I arrive at Heathrow (it is October 1982) and the woman who clears away my polystyrene cups and plastic tray is of Indian origin, hair tightly pulled back in the traditional *juda*, awkwardly dressed in trousers and an apron. Her eyes light up when I address her in Hindi. Outside, in the cold damp October air, there are buses waiting to take me—into London? to Oxford? to Southampton? The men in the drivers' seats are also Indian. They, too, respond warmly when I say, 'Oxford ke liye, ek ticket de dijiye' ('Please give me a ticket for Oxford').

I have heard that there is a little place behind Euston Station that serves *masala dosas* and another one in Marylebone. There are *ras malais* too and *jelebis* and *gulab jamuns*; they even have Kingfisher beer. Walking through Southall, or Handsworth, or any road in Bradford, Hindi film music blares into the street, intruding into my privacy. I could be in India.

I go to a school in Handsworth one morning, and the lady in the room marked 'Head Teacher' is Indian. She wears a dress but her accent is unquestionably *Andhra*. Later in the year, I watch her on 'Eastern Eye' dressed impeccably in a Kanjeevaram silk sari. She has learned to adapt to the demands of being an Indian in Britain. Her students all wear plaits; most of them oil their hair.

Gradually, I get to know people. The man shaking cocktails behind the bar at an Oxford University summer ball is Vinod, five foot ten inches tall, of Indian origin, but with a definite 'second generation' accent. He drops by to visit us. He has more in common with my friend (who is English) than with me, though racially we are from the same 'stock'. Three months later, Vinod announces that he has recently got married—to Vimla, who also is 'Indian', but very 'first generation': Vimla came to Britain first when she was 25. Today Vinod and Vimla have marital problems: Vimla had not anticipated marrying a man who is at heart an Englishman.

26 January. At the Oxford Centre for Community Relations there is a celebration for Republic Day. Indians from different parts of the city gather to celebrate the struggle for freedom from the British Raj and the declaration of India as a Republic. I learn that on Fridays the OCCR is used as a mosque for the Muslims in the city. On Hindu festivals it is used

as a temple. Nearby there is a church run by an Indian pastor for the Indian Christians. Such is the mosaic of contemporary British life.

As I get to know people, I become more and more intrigued by the fabric of ethnic minority life in Britain. So many questions, so many mysteries. I quickly learn, having been rudely snubbed on more than one occasion, that these second generation individuals do not like being called 'immigrants'. They are not, after all, immigrants: they are British born and British bred.

Had they ever visited India, their country of origin. Some had. What was their reaction to it?

Some were very positive:

I like India much better than I do England, it's much nicer, the people are more friendly there, I don't know, its just the atmosphere, I like it, I feel more 'at home' there. Whereas here, you know, when you go out in the streets you know you're a different colour from most people, and English people don't like Asians that much.

Some were ambivalent: another girl, when asked whether she had enjoyed her trip to India, said:

I don't think I would use the word 'enjoy'. It was a very important trip to me, I learnt a lot, some of it I liked, some of it I found very painful to take . . . like the poverty and the heat . . . there are an awful lot of people in one place—very difficult to 'enjoy', but very colourful, very interesting . . .

Others were decidedly negative:

I didn't really enjoy it. I found it really difficult to adjust to the climate and . . . I felt it was such a claustrophobic atmosphere. I was very aware of differences in attitudes amongst people and specially as all my relatives are really quite religious, I didn't have much in common with them. I think the main thing was their attitude towards women and the religious restrictions on women. I just can't put up with them: their restrictions on dress and socializing. And people (women) who go out and work are really a minority . . .

In my initial encounters, I talked in depth with eleven second generation South Asians. (In Britain the term South Asian is used to represent people of Indian, Pakistani, and Bangladeshi origin.) I was curious to know about their friendships. Did they have close friends who were white? What about their Asian friends? Who did they feel most 'at home' with?

Nine out of eleven people interviewed reported having close white friends; quite a large number (seven) reported having close Asian friends, and only one person said she had no South Asian friends at all. ('I can't relate to snotty Indian views, besides I've had no time and there weren't any Asians in my class'.) Six out of the eleven subjects reported having a greater proportion of white to Asian friends; two said that they had an equal number of friends from both backgrounds, one reported having a greater proportion of Asian to white friends, and two could not decide or did not know how to answer the question. However, when asked whom they felt most at home or most secure with, only one person said their English friends, two people indicated that race was unimportant, and the remainder were unequivocal about their choice of Asian friends. One young girl replied:

My Asian friends. They're much closer to me than my white friends, I can talk to them about personal things whereas with my friends at school, I can talk in a joking way or a serious way, but not about personal things.

Two of the girls I questioned were currently 'going out' with English boys and could not visualize getting married by the traditional arranged marriage system. None of the younger ones (18 years and below) was allowed by their parents to date. Three genuinely did not know what would happen with regard to marriage and the remainder could not see any way out of an arranged marriage. One boy said:

I keep telling my mum I won't have an arranged marriage, but she says, 'I want to choose you a nice bride'. I keep telling her, 'I'm not going to get married right, if it's going to be arranged', but she . . . well, you can't really fight against your own parents, can you?

All the subjects who expected to be married by arrangement indicated a preference for a British-born Asian over either an English person or even someone from their country of origin.

Compelled by curiosity and concern, I was keen to understand more about these people's ethnic identification. So much had been written about people from ethnic minority groups wanting to deny their ethnic origins, manifesting self-hatred. Did these young individuals wish sometimes that they were white? Perhaps because of the undisguised nature of the question, eight out of the eleven answered in the negative. Three people did, however, answer in the affirmative, but the reasons given were much of a pragmatic nature than an indication of any deep-seated doubt about ethnic dignity. One boy said:

Take like going out with girls for instance, that's when I wish I were white. Because white people are allowed to go out any time they like. It's just that Indians are stricter than white people. White people are not disciplined enough by their parents whereas Indian parents discipline their kids too much.

If they did not really care to be white, how then did they see themselves? This question produced a variety of responses. Some expressed a high level of assimilation or 'passing into' the majority group. One girl said:

I don't really think of myself as an Asian, or I don't think of myself as anything really, I don't feel different.

Others expressed a high level of dissociation. One boy claimed:

I'd rather *choose* to be Asian. Yes, I think it gives you a vantage point, makes you feel different in a way.

Still others were aware of the differences between the two communities and the value of building bridges between the two. A fifteen-year-old boy said:

I see the English community and the Asian community as two different communities where they shouldn't be, but I'm accepted in both communities. I go around with my Indian friends sometimes and I go around with my English friends . . . because I fit in with both communities.

What of racial discrimination, what was their experience of that? Three out of the eleven reported no experience of discrimination. Eight remembered incidents which they classified as discrimination. Six subjects mentioned name-calling ('Paki, go back to the jungle') as the worst offence. Some of the subjects responded to these incidents by brushing them off or ignoring them; others, particularly the young boys, responded with violence ('In school I beat them up'). One subject even felt these incidents were not a bad thing.

In a way it's quite a healthy thing, you *react* to it and it remotivates you. You get angry and then whatever you're trying to do, you do better. That's the impact it has on me. Quite a positive impact.

What hope then for the South Asians in Britain? One university student who had lived in Britain since the age of seven put it in this way:

I think there *is* a lot of discrimination in this society. But then again, this isn't a closed society and with hard effort, putting your heads down, Asians can and will make it in this country. They'll be a fairly dynamic community . . . it will get worse before it gets better, but in fifty years' time . . . there will be a lot more acculturation and that will have an impact. But also on the British side. I mean people who are forty or fifty years old now all had their primary socialization when Britain had an Empire, and it was an all-white society, right, and it was very affluent as well. Now, young people are being brought up today—it's a multi-racial society for them and it will seem totally unremarkable to them if an Asian moves into their street. It won't mean anything. So there will be acculturation on the Indian side but also in a certain way there will be an acculturation to a multi-racial society on the part of the British.

Thus, in spite of experiences of prejudice and discrimination, not one of them thought it likely that they would return to India permanently. Britain was 'home' to all these young people.

It struck me that each of them in different ways was making an effort to integrate. I use the term 'integration' in a broader sense than perhaps is normally used. Some of them, indeed, were concerned to shed their Indian ways and to become as English as possible. Yet this was by no means the dominant response. It seemed to me that many of them had achieved a healthy level of adjustment without a loss of their ethnic identity. They were competent in the ways of English life, they spoke English fairly well, in school they were not doing too badly at all. Yet at home they ate Indian food, watched Indian films, spoke the ethnic language, and used ethnic clothes. It was as if many of them had achieved a creative synthesis of the two, sometimes very disparate, cultures. It was not that this creative synthesis was some kind of compromise. It was more than that: it was the ability to be critical and affirmative about both cultures and an ability to find a secure identity in each. In some instances it involved working through very real conflicts. I had to know more.

Facts

Britain today is irrevocably multi-racial. With the influx of immigrants from the countries of the New Commonwealth in the 1950s and 1960s, a new dimension has been added to the tapestry of ethnic relations: that of racial visibility. No longer is Britain a 'white' society. The arrival of the Poles, the Ukrainians, and the Jews during the Second World War presented its own ethnic dilemmas. But the advent of large numbers of Indians, Pakistanis, and Bangladeshis from the Indian subcontinent, and Afro-Caribbeans from the West Indies has changed the colour of life in Britain.

It is estimated that ethnic minorities constitute 5 per cent of the total population of the United Kingdom today. Of these, almost 50 per cent are second generation i.e. they are British born (Anwar 1986). The 1981 census projected a population estimate of 2.6 million ethnic minority individuals in 1986 out of the total population of 53 million. In the 1981 census 2.2 million members of ethnic minorities were recorded. Of this 2.2 million, an estimated 1.2 million (55 per cent) were of Asian origin, about 0.55 million (25 per cent) are Afro-Caribbean, and the remaining 20 per cent have their origin in South East Asia, the Mediterranean, and other parts of the New Commonwealth.

The history of this wave of immigration lies in the fact that during the late 1940s and early 1950s, the United Kingdom embarked upon a strategy of rapid economic expansion. The main problem was an acute shortage of labour. Britain introduced the Polish Resettlement Programme, and 16 000 Poles, displaced by the Second World War took up residence in the United Kingdom. The labour provided by this programme was insufficient and the European Volunteer Workers scheme attracted another 100 000 workers of European origin to the country. This was still inadequate to fulfil Britain's labour requirements, and the United Kingdom turned to its colonies and ex-colonies in Africa, India, and the Caribbean (Parekh 1986). The coloured immigrants readily accepted the jobs that were offered to them. More often than not, these jobs were badly paid and scorned by white workers. Thus, coloured immigrants came to be associated with lower working class occupations 'They were seen and treated largely as factory fodder' (Parekh 1986, p. 2) They may not have been on the lowest rung of the pecking order; but they were certainly not the first choice of the British government.

Simultaneously with Britain's acute shortage of labour, the Indian Independence struggle had led to the Partition in 1947 of the Indian subcontinent into what are now India and Pakistan. In perhaps one of the greatest mass migrations of history, a large proportion of the Muslims resident in India travelled many hundreds of miles to take up residence in Pakistan. Likewise, Hindus and Sikhs left their homes to begin life again in the new 'India'. Partition had displaced hundreds of thousands of families along the border of the two countries. The loss of land and a familiar workplace plus a lump sum of compensation money provided the necessary impetus for migration to Britain. Many of those so disrupted were illiterate and from underdeveloped areas of India and Pakistan. Thus, their migration involved the telescoping of two major movements into one (Khan 1979a): the first was the migration from village life to big city life, an event that is traumatic enough even in developed countries such as the United Kingdom where discrepancies in wealth, technology, and style of life are not so pronounced. The second was the migration from the East to the West, where the time-frame, the system of social relationships among people, and countless other cultural factors are fundamentally different to those of the East. The psychological consequences of such a telescoping of migrations are almost beyond comprehension. Once in the United Kingdom these immigrants were left largely to their own devices, unlike the Polish settlers, for whom a co-ordinated effort was made to provide educational, housing, and welfare facilities (Parekh 1986).

It is hardly surprising then that these dislocated people chose at first to share households in order that they might establish the close supportive relationships which are vital to the fabric of village life (Dahya 1973). The pioneer migrants settled in industrial areas where there were job opportunities. Later arrivals settled where the first-comers had established micro-social networks. Thus, the ethnic minority population today is concentrated in a small number of areas: in the South East, especially in the Greater London area (56 per cent), in the Midlands (23 per cent), in the North and North West (16 per cent); and the remainder (5 per cent) in the South West, Wales, and Scotland (Anwar 1986).

Naturally, the age distribution of the ethnic minority population is somewhat skewed. According to the Office of Population Censuses and Surveys (1983), there are far fewer elderly people (only 3 per cent aged 65 plus compared with 12 per cent for the total population). More than half of the population of Asian and Afro-Caribbean origin is under 25, as compared with approximately 35 per cent of the general population. Nearly 40 per cent of Asians are under 16 years old, compared with 30 per cent of West Indians, and only 22 per cent of the general population. This skewed age distribution has social policy implications for education, employment, and service facilities for ethnic minorities and it becomes increasingly clear that an in-depth understanding of ethnic minority identity in the second generation is vital to the integration of these groups into the fabric of British life.

Prejudice and discrimination

Once arrived, the new immigrants were faced with the task of settling into Britain. Certainly many Afro-Caribbeans expected to assimilate, to be absorbed into the mainstream of British life (Tajfel and Dawson 1965). After all, their language was the same, their religion not different, and Britain had been the 'mother country' for many, many years. The Asians adopted a more cautious stance, less willing to 'let go' of the home culture but willing none the less to adapt, functionally at least, to the demands of everyday life in Britain. But the past dies hard in people's hearts. The British were scarcely prepared for the new wave of coloured guests. Ordinary people, brought up on the concept of Empire, the rightness of imperialism, the white man's burden, and a major role for Britain in world affairs, were shocked to find many of Britain's colonial subjects arriving in the country just at the very time Britain's power was in obvious decline. It was easy to confuse one with the other: somehow, they reasoned, the migrants caused the decline. Prejudice and discrimination became a common experience for these racially visible minorities. It is no less common today . . .

In a recent report on British social attitudes, Jowell and Airey (1984) present some telling statistics. Using a representative probability sample of 1761 adults aged 18 and above, in 114 parliamentary constituencies throughout the United Kingdom, they reported that nine out of ten people think that Britain is racially prejudiced and a third admit to being prejudiced themselves against Asians and black people. Only one in six thinks there is less prejudice today than five years ago and only one in six thinks there will be less prejudice five years from now.

Of the 35 per cent who admit that they themselves are racially prejudiced, 46 per cent are Conservative voters. For Labour and Alliance supporters, the figure is 28 per cent.

Asked whether they would object if a close relative married a black or Asian person, 54 per cent said they would; 78 per cent said most other white people would. However, among young adults prejudice is not so rampant; in the 18–34 age group a 2 to 1 majority reported that they would not mind.

Further, the report suggests that people in England are more prejudiced than people in Scotland or Wales and that white-collar workers are more prejudiced than blue-collar workers.

Stopes-Roe and Cochrane (1986) attempted to assess preceptions of prejudice in Britain. Asian parents and young people were asked to assess the levels of prejudice against themselves which were current in British society. These responses were then compared with those of white British parents and young people. Overall, there was no difference in perceptions of prejudice against Asians by either the British or the Asian groups of respondents ($\overline{X}$ Asian = 50; $\overline{X}$ British = 50.1)

However, Asians parents tended to make higher estimates of prejudice than their young people, whereas British parents in fact made lower estimates than their young people. The Asian subjects in this study were also asked several questions about their personal experiences of prejudice and discriminatory behaviour. The personal experience of prejudice of Asian parents and young people did not differ on the matter of contacts with the police, in employment, or in housing: the majority felt that they had encountered none, but many more young people than parents said they had experienced trivial harassment in public places.

A published, national survey however, (Brown 1984) revealed serious inequalities in employment, housing, education, and other services. In 1982, Anwar (Anwar 1982) found that almost 60 per cent of Afro-Caribbean people in the 16–20 age-group were unemployed as compared to 42 per cent of whites. In 1985, Anwar found (Anwar 1986) that the unemployment rate among ethnic minorities was 20.9 per cent, which is almost twice as high as the rate for whites. In 1984, the West Midlands County Council found that white school leavers are three times more likely than Afro-Caribbeans and two and a half times more likely than Asians to find jobs. In Bradford, only 7.5 per cent of 16-year-old ethnic minority applicants found work compared with 32 per cent of white applicants in the same age-group. In Sheffield, Drew and Clough (1985) found a similar trend: only 13 per cent of young blacks were employed compared with 47 per cent of whites. A study by Brennan and McGeevor (1986) reports that a greater proportion of ethnic minority degree-holders are unemployed 12 months after graduation than their white counterparts. In a survey conducted by the Policy Studies Institute in collaboration with the Commission for Racial Equality (Brown and Gay 1985), it was found that over one-third of the employers sampled discriminated directly against ethnic minority job applicants. This figure does not account for instances of indirect discrimination.

Statistics such as these are, to say the least, somewhat disheartening for members of ethnic minorities. Not merely are the doors of employment closed to a large number of ethnic minority individuals, it seems that certain occupations, particularly higher class ones, are more inaccessible than others. Ethnic minorities are seriously under-represented in the police force, in the teaching profession, amongst accountants and doctors, in spite of holding more than adequate qualifications for these posts.

Employment is one field in which ethnic minority individuals face prejudice and discrimination, and housing is another. Two separate research reports published by the Commission for Racial Equality (CRE 1984), which investigated council housing allocations in Hackney and in Liverpool, provided evidence of large-scale discrimination against both ethnic minority applicants and tenants. Because of a serious shortage of accommodation, large numbers of people are competing for limited numbers of houses. Within such a highly competitive set-up, racial visibility provides an all too simple criterion for decisions regarding housing allocations. Even rented accommodation is hard to come by. Often, the reason offered for such instances of direct discrimination is that the neighbours would not like it. More subtle rationalizations are an anticipated drop in house values, the fear of overcrowding, and the expectation that coloured immigrants will not maintain let alone improve their houses and gardens. Faced with such outright disadvantage, it becomes top priority with coloured immigrants to secure property for themselves. Yet even mortgages, for one reason or another, are hard to obtain for ethnic minority individuals. Building societies and estate agents are manifestly discriminatory, albeit in an indirect manner (CRE 1985), often granting inadequate mortgages at higher rates than for white people. In some local authority housing estates the level of prejudice runs so high that many people are afraid to go out even during the day. The number of racial attacks against Asians shows an alarmingly increasing trend.

In 1981, the Home Office reported that the rate of racial attacks against Asians was 50 times that for white people. For Afro-Caribbeans, it was 36 times as high. Another report published by the Home Office in 1986 confirms these findings: the most common form of racial attack was that of whites against Asians. Asians comprised 70 per cent of the victims (usually a woman or a child) of recorded incidents in London. The attackers were usually white teenagers, who occasionally had been encouraged by parents and more often than not were a member of a gang. The report further documents that in the Metropolitan Police area, of the 1877 racial incidents recorded in 1985 (of which 336 were cases of serious assault), only 15 per cent were solved. It is hardly surprising, then, that the Asian community has set up its own vigilante groups on some housing estates. Describing the trends in British racial violence, Lawrence (1987, pp. 156–7) says:

Brixton was in flames . . . over three days of violence, many hundreds of people were injured; over 200 vehicles (including ambulances and fire engines) were damaged or destroyed; 145 buildings were damaged and over 7000 police officers were used in an attempt to restore order. Rioting broke out on the streets of many towns and cities in Britain in July 1981. Aldershot, Balham, Battersea, Birkenhead, Blackpool, Bradford, Brixton, Cirencester, Derby, Ellesmere Port, Fleetwood, Fulham, Gloucester, Halifax, Handsworth, Huddersfield, Hull, High Wycombe, Knaresbrough, Keswick, Leeds, Leicester, Lewisham, Luton, Moss Side, Nottingham, Portsmouth, Preston, Reading, Sheffield, Slough, Southall, Southampton, Stoke Newington, Toxteth, Wolverhampton, and Woolwich all experienced episodes of violence. It varied enormously in its character, scale and political significance . . . so, although individuals may have become involved in this spate of riots for a variety of reasons, perhaps sometimes for fun or to take advantage of them as a cloak for simple theft, one important form of participation may have been tantamount to an expression of political solidarity with those involved elsewhere.

Coloured immigrants and legislation

The unplanned settlement of coloured immigrants has produced obvious strains and unnecessary stresses. When in the mid-1950s the British economy slowed down and the need for labour in the main industries began to decline, several white groups resorted to racial harassment and attack. Riots followed.

In 1962, the Commonwealth Immigrants Act was passed, permitting only those whose passports were issued in the United Kingdom free entry into Britain. Those British subjects with passports issued in the New Commonwealth were subject to controls administered by the Ministry of Labour. Then, in 1967, Kenya expelled African Asians holding British passports. Falling into the UK passport-holder category, they escaped the regulation controlling the entry of many other blacks, and many of them headed for Britain. The reaction of the government was immediate: the 1968 Commonwealth Immigrants Act was passed, restricting the right of entry to all but those whose parents or grandparents were born or naturalized in the United Kingdom or in the part of the old Commonwealth. This act thereby secured the right of free entry for most white UK passport-holders in East Africa, while restricting the African Asians to the same system of control as other black immigrants.

The Immigration Act of 1971 subsequently superseded the 1962 and 1968 Acts. This Act divided people into patrials and non-patrials, the non-patrials being subject to entry regulations. Patrials, that is, Commonwealth citizens who were connected by descent to Britain, were free from entry regulations. In effect with a few exceptions, this divided the Commonwealth into white Commonwealth citizens and non-white Commonwealth citizens. Under the 1971 Act, non-patrials were allowed into Britain only on a work-permit basis. This Act virtually ended primary immigration from the Indian subcontinent and the West Indies (Parekh 1986). Restrictions then came to be applied to the spouses and dependants of blacks and East African Asians already settled in Britain.

It should be clear from these statistics that many ethnic minority groups in Britain are required to endure many structural and functional constraints in everyday life. In other words, 'the space of free movement' (Lewin 1952) is restricted by prejudice and discrimination for members of such groups. Under these constraints then, what is the hope for integration, what expectations may the government and the public reasonably hold of ethnic minority groups in Britain, and what hope can ethnic minority groups nurture in their relations with the government and society at large?

In order to answer these and many more questions it will be necessary to look into the theoretical perspectives, both sociological and psychological, of ethnic minority identity and also to review the empirical work done on ethnicity. Part II of this book will first look at what constitutes an ethnic minority group. It will then go on to investigate the sociology of ethnicity from assimilationism to cultural pluralism. Next, we will look at the psychological theories of ethnic minority identity. In Part III, research issues on ethnicity will be examined, covering areas such as styles of cultural adaptation, strategies of self-categorization, and levels of self-esteem among members of ethnic minority groups. Finally, the implications of these findings will be examined in relation to the integration of ethnic minority groups in Britain.

II

Theoretical perspectives

2.

Definitions and concepts

Few would argue that there has been an unprecedented upsurge of ethnicity in the past two decades. In the United States, the 1960s saw the advent of the Civil Rights Movement, which has since gained credibility and achieved much in the way of rights for minority groups. In the early 1980s, Britain was rocked out of complacency by the Brixton riots. In India, recent attempts at secession by the Sikhs in the Punjab, the Gurkhas in Darjeeling, and the Mizos in the North East are witness to the fact that ethnicity is a powerful yet little understood motivating factor interwoven into the very fabric of everyday life. Certainly, the violence that is often consequent upon an awakening of ethnic identity, makes ethnicity no mean force to be reckoned with. Yet the concept is far more elusive than is immediately apparent.

Ethnicity and ethnic groups

Surprisingly, ethnicity is a term that has only recently come into popular parlance. It was first used by David Riesman in 1953; but, as Glazer and Moynihan (1975) point out, it makes its appearance in the *Oxford English Dictionary* only in 1972. The 1980 version of the *Shorter Oxford English Dictionary* bypasses the term altogether, merely defining the word 'ethnic' as pertaining to nations not Christian or Jewish, 'ethnicism' as heathenism or paganism, and 'ethnography' as the scientific description of nations or races of men, their customs, habits, and differences.

In some circles there has been only a begrudging acceptance of the term and its connotations. Authors often prefer to use terms such as 'basic group identity' or 'primordial affinities and attachments that derive from belonging to an ethnic group' (Isaacs 1974) rather than use the term itself. The ultra-reductionist analyses ethnicity into its several components, preferring always the 'skinny outline rather than the rich thicket of reality', because it is 'so much purer, clearer, nobler' (William James as quoted by Isaacs 1974). Yet it is this 'rich thicket of reality' that must be penetrated, acknowledging the possibility that the phenomenon of ethnicity may indeed be more global than may be captured by a scholar's pen, that the whole may indeed be more than the sum of its parts.

Many definitions of ethnicity emphasize a common cultural pattern which separates the ethnic group from other immediate groups. Narroll (1964) used the term 'ethnic group' to designate a population which:

(1) shares fundamental cultural values realized in overt unity in cultural forms; (2) makes up a field of communication and interaction; (3) is largely biologically self-perpetuating; and (4) has a membership which identifies itself and is identified by others as constituting a category distinguishable from other categories of the same order.

Milton Gordon (1964) referred to ethnicity as a sense of 'peoplehood' created by common race, religion, national origin, history, or some combination of these.

Theodorson and Theodorson (1969) defined an ethnic group as:

. . . a group with a common cultural tradition, a sense of identity which exists as a subgroup of a larger society. The members of an ethnic group differ with regard to certain cultural characteristics from the other members of their society.

Francis (1947), however, pointed out that although every ethnic group has a distinctive culture, a common cultural pattern does not automatically constitute an ethnic group.

Although these definitions make passing references to the subjective elements comprising ethnicity (such as a sense of 'peoplehood' or identity), it is fair to say that the central emphasis is the sharing of a common culture.

In 1969, Barth put forward a convincing argument highlighting the limitations of such an emphasis. If the culture-bearing aspect of ethnicity is the critical feature, then the classification of persons as members of an ethnic group must depend upon their exhibiting certain particular traits of the culture; differences between groups become differences in the possession of an array of traits and the attention is upon cultural content, not upon the structure of these groups. Might not, Barth asks, a group of people with the same values and ideas pursue different patterns of life and institutionalize different values in different environments? In other words, the cultural features of the ethnic group may change over time, due to contact and exchange of information with other groups, yet the sense of separateness, of distinctive ethnicity, often continues to persist. Barth (1969, pp. 14–15) suggests, therefore that the focus of investigation should shift from the cultural factors exemplified by the group to the process of persistence and maintenance of ethnic boundaries and the 'continuing dichotomization between members and outsiders'.

Barth's (1969) radical shift from cultural features to ethnic boundaries suggested an explanation for the failure of the 'Great American Dream' which had claimed that in time, perhaps over two or three generations, all ethnic groups would lose their cultural characteristics and disappear into the melting-pot of a common American identity. That this did not in fact occur was a matter of some puzzlement to American sociologists until Barth pointed out that although the ethnic markers (dress, language, house form, life-style, and even basic value orientations) used by members of ethnic groups to signal belonging may change with time, the process of self-ascription and identification need not necessarily undergo a similar change. Ethnic groups may thus become behaviourally assimilated while yet maintaining a strong sense of ethnic identity. In this light, ethnicity is not so much a product of common living, as a product of self-awareness of one's belonging in a particular group and one's distinctiveness with regard to other groups.

Shibutani and Kwan (1965) proposed an authoritative definition which subsequently established the lines of enquiry into ethnicity. They suggested that 'an ethnic group consists of a people . . . who conceive of themselves as being alike by virtue of their common ancestry, real or fictitious, and who are so regarded by others'.

This definition enjoys several advantages. It focuses on the ascriptive elements of ethnicity ('who conceive of themselves', and 'who are regarded by others') rather than upon cultural content. It also recognizes the fact that a sense of collective identity may, in extreme cases, have an almost wholly internal or external origin: minority groups in subordinate positions may develop a self-consciousness of a kind only because the dominant group perceives them as 'somehow different' and therefore erects barriers against complete assimilation. As Lyon (1972) points out, the Afro-Caribbeans in Britain are one such minority group.

Ethnic identity

The sense of personal identification with the ethnic group and the identification by others as being a member of the ethnic group defines, in part, but only in part, the concept of ethnic identity. The advantage of such a definition over previous definitions that have emphasized cultural similarities and differences is immediately obvious: by focusing on the psychological aspects of ethnic identity (subjective identification, or lack of it, with the ethnic group) it is now possible to embrace the second and third generation, whose overt manifestations of life-style may be identical with the dominant group but who may yet maintain varying degrees of identification with the ethnic group. Taylor and Simard (1979) define ethnic identity as 'that component of a person's self-definition which is derived from an affiliation with a specific group'. In the past, this process of self-definition in relation to one's group affiliation was an unproblematic issue for the individual. Self-definition was derived directly from what was given at birth: a race; a language; a culture; a tribe; a history of the group's relationship with other groups in society. However, with rapid modernization, technological advance, and increased mobility, it is now possible to choose one's ethnic identifications in a self-conscious way. Most people have multiple group affiliations which may be emphasized or minimized according to the situation. Thus, as Wallman (1983) points out, ethnic identity is not a fixed, inflexible commitment, steadfast, and once-for-all. Neither is it necessarily singular: multiple ethnic identities may coexist. Perhaps, most importantly, ethnic identity is only one of many identity options (Wallman 1983):

> No-one, not even members of visible (racial) or beleaguered ethnic minority groups, consistently identifies himself or is always identified by others in ethnic terms. Ethnicity is only one identity option . . . and the signficance of ethnicity to the individual must be taken into account.

Ethnic identity is necessarily an elusive and complex concept. The term often involves a variety of objective and subjective realities. The family's Indian heritage may be irrelevant to the ethnic minority individual if it is psychologically important for him/her to be British. Also, there may be little or no correspondence between the identity which is psychologically important for the individual and the way s/he is perceived by others: s/he may categorize him/herself as British, whereas in the eyes of others s/he is perceived as Indian. As Chun (1983) points out, individuals continually strive to place and define themselves in the world of relationships and meanings. The world of relationships and meanings consists, on the one hand, of social relations and, on the other, of persistent existential questions which may encompass social, political, philosophical, and cosmological perplexities. The sense of identity emerges as the individual clarifies for him/herself some of these issues and learns to place him/herself within the total configuration of social relationships and ontological questions. Thus ethnic identity is arrived at by a process of what Chun (1983) calls 'socioepistemic self-emplacement'.

Minority groups

Ethnic groups are often, though not always, minority groups. Schermer-horn (1971) points out that the definitions of ethnic groups proposed by the various authors do not specify their relative ranking in society. Ethnic groups may be therefore either dominant or subordinate. He argues, however, that because each society can have only one dominant group but a plurality of subordinate groups, it follows that a preponderance of ethnic groups are in subordinate rather than dominant positions, and it therefore seems justifiable to drop the adjective 'subordinate' as pragmatically unnecessary. Although seemingly convincing, this argument effectively shifts the spotlight from any consideration of what rank/position is held or given to the ethnic entity.

Most theorists (Morris 1968; Tajfel 1978) underline the fact that minority peoples not only *feel* themselves bound together by race, nationality, culture, common history, but also share a common fate, and common experiences of discrimination and social disadvantage—all of which serve to strengthen in-group cohesiveness and solidarity and to enhance self-consciousness of their minority group membership.

Wagley and Harris (1958) suggested five criteria which describe the essence of minority group membership:

1. Minorities are subordinate segments of complex state societies.
2. Minorities have special physical or cultural traits which are held in low esteem by the dominant segments of society.
3. Minorities are self-conscious units bound together by special traits which their members share and by the special disabilities these traits bring.
4. Membership in a minority is transmitted by rule of descent which is capable of affiliating succeeding generations even in the absence of readily apparent special cultural and physical traits.
5. Minority peoples by choice or necessity tend to marry within the group.

The essential difference between definitions of ethnic groups and minority groups lies in the implication of a serious imbalance in power and prestige: minorities are *subordinate* segments of complex state societies; they are bound together by common experiences of discrimination and social *disadvantage*; they have special physical or cultural traits which are held in low esteem by the *dominant* segments of society. By definition, then, membership in a minority group entails the many social consequences of being unlike the majority. It also means suffering the structural disadvantage of being relatively deficient in power and resources. This implies that members of a minority are excluded from taking a full share in the life of the society because they differ in certain ways from the dominant group. Often, this tends to develop attitudes of discrimination and prejudice against members of the minority, which in turn serves to strengthen the internal cohesion and structure of the minority group (Tajfel 1978, p. 312):

It is only when being assigned and/or assigning oneself to a particular social entity leads at the same time to certain perceived social consequences which include discriminatory treatment from others and their negative attitudes based on some common criteria (however vague) of membership that the awareness of being in a minority can develop.

The emphasis on 'perceived social disadvantage' being the hinge upon which minority identity swings, has meant that the numerical connotations of the term have been largely subsumed under its sociological implications. The social élite are immediately excluded from this definition, by virtue of their position of social advantage. So too, although the word 'minority' usually denotes a small part of a larger whole, a minority group in the sociological sense is not always a numerical minority in the population. To take a few examples: the Bantu population in South Africa is many times more numerous than the dominant white group. Nevertheless, their restricted mobility and very limited voting rights, amongst many other factors, classify them without question into the category of 'minority group'. In the United States blacks form a clear majority in many of the southern states, but they are none the less a minority in relation to the numerically smaller but powerful white group. Conversely, defining 'the majority' as the group which in any salient situation holds the balance of power and resources, does not necessarily mean that every majority group is a numerical majority: the whites in South Africa are a case in point.

From the above, it can be seen that ethnic groups are not always minorities, although most minority groups are ethnic groups defined in some instances by a shared culture (tribes and religious groups), in others by a shared ideology (some political groups), and in yet others simply by the persistence of group boundaries, but in most instances in suffering low status and a lack of power relative to the majority.

Ethnic and racial minorities

One further distinction remains to be made. Whilst focusing on the fact that both suffer minority status in society, there are certain dissimilarities between ethnic and racial minorities that need to be highlighted. Lyon (1972) points out that an ethnic minority is not always a racial minority— the French in Canada are racially indistinct from the majority—and that a racial minority is not always an ethnic one. Ethnic minorities are usually recognizable primarily because they maintain their cultural identity, whereas racial minorities (such as blacks in the United States and even West Indians, Lyon contends, in Britain) may scarcely have a distinctive culture. Their collective identity cannot, therefore, be maintained from within but is enforced from without by a racialist majority that uses mere racial visibility—black skin—to maintain the group's subordinate position in society.

The crucial difference then, between ethnic and racial minorities lies in the answer to the question: 'Who is being exclusive?' In the case of racial minorities, boundaries are drawn by the majority group such that the minority is excluded from full participation in the larger society. For ethnic minorities, however, boundaries are often drawn from within the group itself and are consequently maintained from within.

Let us look more closely at two groups in Britain: the Afro-Caribbeans and the Indians. According to Lyon (1973) the Caribbean people, who are a *racially* excluded category in Britain, possess only the sub-cultural differences developed under colonial race-slavery and now re-created within the context of contemporary British culture. Historically, too, for the Afro-Caribbeans, intermarriage with the British was positively valued, as a lightening of skin colour had many positive social benefits. Indians, on the other hand, came to Britain with a distinct cultural heritage and tradition, characterized by strong pressures against biological amalgamation with the British even to the extent that their members faced excommunication from the community if they contemplated intermarriage. In this sense, Indians are primarily an ethnic minority, and not a racial minority, although their racial visibility does contribute to a separation from the majority. The pulls of culture and tradition from within the group contribute at least equally if not more to the persistence and maintenance of ethnic boundaries. Thus the high endogamy rates of Indians in Britain are voluntary and ethnic, whereas similarly high rates amongst blacks may well be enforced and racial. Lyon (1972, p. 258) summarizes the argument well:

Ethnic minority identity can only be accounted for by adequately taking into account the organising activities of the minority collectively. By contrast, racial minorities may not possess any collective or communal organisation, for they are, by definition, a subjugate and often residual category possessing no more social separateness on matters of endogamy and occupational specialisation, special ideologies or valuations than the majority political–class alignment has forced upon them in the name of racial order.

Scholars have often confused the issue by failing to make this distinction. It is too easy to categorize what is essentially a racial minority as 'ethnic' by focusing upon the sub-cultural traits that have emerged as a consequence of racial exclusion. Rastafarianism among the Afro-Caribbeans in Britain is an attempt to redefine a negatively valued identity in positive terms, but it is not undergirded with the institutional completeness (Breton 1964) that characterizes an 'ethnic' community. So too, as Lyon rightly points out, all black people in America possess only American culture because their original culture was systematically destroyed. The social separateness of the racial exclusion has often led to (Lyon 1972, p. 258):

. . . the attempt to find cultural traits to fit the system of racial segregation and looks suspiciously like an attempt to justify racial exclusion on grounds of ethnic separateness. Such an attempted legitimation is particularly confusing and slippery because the ethnic 'sub-cultural' signs used to justify or 'explain' the structural separation are in themselves consequential upon the system of racial exclusion.

The political implications of the cleavage between ethnic and racial minorities becomes immediately clear. If, indeed, it is the direction from which exclusion is maintained that is the crucial feature of ethnic and racial relations, then racial minorities have less control and less power to change their position in society than do ethnic minorities.

The psychological implications of this distinction are also of paramount importance. If a racial minority is not also an ethnic collectivity then acceptance of the majority viewpoint pre-empts any group solidarity and assimilation becomes the logical and perhaps the only facility for coping with one's minority identity. If on the other hand, the group is organized on an ethnic basis then several options of coping with one's ethnic minority identity are available: one may wish to stay within the group in spite of its minority status in society and dissociate from the majority group culture completely, one may wish to leave the group altogether, or one may attempt to create a synthesis between the majority and the ethnic minority group, while being rooted within the ethnic minority. These options will be discussed in greater depth in Chapter 8.

It will be clear now that the title of this book is a deliberate, strategic choice. 'Ethnic minority identity' does not merely refer to 'ethnic identity' or only to 'minority identity'. It is meant to encompass the whole gamut of social psychological relations involved in being a member of a group that is subordinate or relatively disadvantaged in society, but which also has cultural mores and traditions that contribute to its maintenance.

3.

Sociological perspectives on ethnic minority identity

When the physical characteristics, and/or the cultural traditions of an ethnic or racial minority were unacceptable to the dominant group in society, even a brief historical review reveals that attempts were often made either to eliminate the group altogether or so assimilate it into the dominant group. In the seventeenth century, Protestants in France were banished or driven into hiding if they continued to remain Protestant. In the same century, Christians in Japan were exterminated. So, too, a large number of the Aborigines in Tasmania. In South-East Asia, particularly Indonesia and Thailand, the Chinese trading minority was seen as a threat to national interests and were therefore violently driven out of the country or, as in Indonesia, forced to adopt most aspects of the culture. Perhaps the most dramatic example of an attempt to eliminate a group that was considered an unacceptable ethnic minority group, was Hitler's mass extermination of the Jews under Nazi rule. Even as recently as the 1970s attempts at ejection continued: both Uganda and Kenya, perceiving the long-settled Indian traders to be a threat, physically ejected as many as they could and severely limited all spheres of activity to those who chose to remain. Thus, membership in an ethnic minority may carry with it far-reaching social and political consequences. Certainly, its influence upon the individuals' psyche may indeed be profound.

A more subtle form of elimination, more commonly used and more easily rationalized, is the attempt to assimilate the ethnic minority group by encouraging it to adopt the culture of the dominant group. Simpson (1968, p. 428) sees assimilation as:

a process in which people of diverse ethnic and racial backgrounds come to interact . . . in the life of the larger community. Wherever representatives of different racial and cultural groups live together, some individuals of subordinate status (whether or not they constitute a numerical minority), become assimilated. Complete assimilation would mean that no separate social structures based on racial or ethnic concepts remained.

Assimilation (often also termed acculturation) (The *New Encyclopaedia Britannica*, Vol. 12, 15th edn) is now defined as:

those phenomena that result when groups of individuals having different cultures come into continuous first-hand contact, with subsequent changes in the original culture patterns of either or both groups.

Simpson's (1968) definition construes assimilation as more of a one-way process, where the subordinate group *B* in interaction with the dominant group *A* is incorporated completely into *A* such that it becomes *A* with no significant changes in the structure or culture of *A*.

$$A \longleftrightarrow B = A$$

Such a view of assimilationism is best exemplified in the theory of Anglo-conformity.

The definition in use today sees assimilation as a two-way process, where the subordinate group *B* interacts with the dominant group *A* in such a way that both groups are changed by the interaction and the resultant is a homogeneous amalgam of both groups, *C*.

$$A \longleftrightarrow B = C$$

The 'melting-pot theory' is the best example of this. Both these theories will now be examined in some detail.

These theories, Anglo-conformity and the melting-pot, have been described by many theorists, and an appropriate strategy had to be worked out as to how best to portray the dominant themes embodied therein. It was finally decided to outline the key ideas as expressed by a selected number of 'key' people, one, at the most two, per theory. The selection of these 'key people' inevitably reflects the biases of the author.

The theory of Anglo-conformity

This, one of the earliest theories of ethnicity, originated in seventeenth-century America, where the English settlers had quickly and successfully established themselves as the dominant group in the New World. According to Postiglione (1983), who traces the development of American social theory in the context of ethnicity, the theory of Anglo-conformity was popularized in the late nineteenth century and avalanched into full strength in the early twentieth century, with the writings of Madison Grant (1916), Henry Pratt Fairchild (1926), Howard C. Hill (1919), and Ellwood P. Cubberly (1929). The theory of Anglo-conformity asserted that the culture of northern and western Europe was superior to that of southern and eastern Europe. Madison Grant (1916, p. 79) wrote that:

. . . the new immigration, while it still included many strong elements from the north of Europe, contained a large and increasing number of the weak, the broken and the mentally crippled of all races drawn from the lowest stratum of the

Mediterranean basin and the Balkans, together with hordes of the wretched, submerged populations of the Polish ghettos.

It was considered to be of paramount importance to keep America 'pure'. Cubberly (1929, pp. 15–16) suggested that the solution to the new wave of unwanted immigration was to break up ethnic settlements in order to:

. . . assimilate and amalgamate these people as part of our American race, to implant in their children so far as can be done, the Anglo-conception of righteousness, law and order, and popular government, and to awaken in them a reverence for democratic institutions and for those things in our national life which we as people hold to be of abiding worth.

Anglo-conformity was heavily under-girded by the theory of Social Darwinism, a rather unscientific offshoot of Charles Darwin's theory of evolution. In short, the theory was that one race, presumably that of northwestern Europe, must represent the most highly evolved of all races. To the Social Darwinists, differences between races were not accountable for by sociological analysis: they were merely biological facts due to race. Thus, the character of the southern and eastern European groups was thought to include dishonesty, poverty, uncleanliness, etc. They were, therefore, a threat to the purity and the unity of America.

One of the main proponents of the Anglo-conformity theory, Henry Pratt Fairchild, was an immigration official whose writing heavily influenced American immigration policy for many years. It is his theory that will be examined here in some detail.

The central theme running through much of Fairchild's work relates to the problem of how to maintain social unity. Unity, he says, is one of the essentials of stability, order, and progress (Fairchild 1926). Unity is threatened by the influx of immigrants with their foreign cultures, languages, and mores. Just as physical features such as skin colour and facial features are inherited, so too, and perhaps more importantly, psychological traits are hereditary. Each race has a distinctive configuration of psychological traits. Thus, the primary basis of group unity is seen to be racial. Every effort must therefore be made to preserve the unity of America (Fairchild 1926, p. 155):

If immigration is to continue, and if our nation is to be preserved, we must all, native and foreigner alike, resign ourselves to the inevitable truth that unity can be maintained only through the complete sacrifice of extraneous national traits on the part of our foreign nationals.

A self-sacrificial conformity to the Anglo-Saxon norm was expected of those races stationed on lower rungs of the evolutionary order (p. 155):

There can be no give-and-take in assimilation.

Fairchild's model of assimilation was built upon the metabolic metaphor. First, there was the assimilating organism, the Anglo-American type, the dominant, most highly evolved race. Fairchild divides American immigration history into two major phases: pre-1882 and post-1882. The pre-1882, immigration (p. 123):

produced a type with outstanding characteristics, . . . it is a type of peculiar excellence. This is in the English type and it is the American type . . . It is certainly a noble type with a remarkable record of achievement . . .

The post-1882 immigration, Fairchild labelled as being 'the new menace' (p. 107).

Secondly, only certain type of substances are easily assimilated and therefore it is wise that unassimilable substances, presumably immigrants of the post-1882 variety, 'are not admitted except in strictly limited quantities' (p. 137).

Thirdly, substances can only be assimilated to the extent that they come into contact with appropriate assimilating organs of the body. In other words, assimilation does not occur naturally or spontaneously. It requires a purposive, intentional effort on the part of the host nationality. Fairchild, therefore put much affirmative energy behind the Americanization movement. (The Americanization movement took the form of an education campaign, using night schools, worker training programmes, etc. to Americanize the immigrant.) Fairchild believed that the movement was indispensable but that it had largely failed due to an overemphasis on the cognitive elements of education to the almost complete neglect of the affective elements. It is not what you know, but how you feel that is the true test of nationality. Nevertheless the Americanization movement had provided, according to Fairchild, a cognitive framework, a knowledge of America, without which assimilation would have been impossible.

Returning to the metabolic metaphor, Fairchild observed fourthly, that all assimilated materials were totally incorporated into the body itself, that all traces of diverse origin are lost. True assimilation then requires a complete transformation (p. 154):

The traits of foreign nationality which the immigrant brings with him are not to be mixed or interwoven. They are to be abandoned.

The corollary to this assertion is, of course, that the assimilating organism undergoes no change whatsoever to correspond to different types of food. In other words, in order that America may remain unified, it on no account must dilute the quality of its natural character.

Finally, Fairchild reminds us that in order that the assimilative process may take place, the assimilative organism itself must be healthy and well-organized. The implication here is that adherence to the principles of group unity was of paramount importance and that it would be well to remember that (pp. 78–9):

> . . . the strongest possible group unity exists when national solidarity and racial identity are combined.

Critique

To present a critique of Fairchild's theory of assimilationism would be akin to presenting arguments against slavery or casteism. In the 1990s, such arguments little need to be rehearsed. Yet evidence of the continuing practice of slavery, in South Africa and, not so long ago, in Rhodesia, and casteism in India merit at least a cursory analysis of the inherent flaws of such an ideology.

The unashamedly racist nature of the theory is immediately apparent and to carry it to its logical conclusion, segregation and 'separate development' are the obvious solutions to the problem of maintaining the purity of group unity if complete assimilation does not occur. Thus, the segregation of the blacks in the early part of this century, and even today the homelands of South Africa, Swaziland, Transkei, etc.

As with any racist ideology, the theory is under-girded with a strong sense of cultural imperialism. This assumption is pervasive even in contemporary life although it is often found in a state that is 'functionally autonomous' from its racist roots. It manifests itself in a simple non-comprehension (or, to put it more accurately, a deliberate unwillingness to comprehend) practices that diverge from the commonly accepted norm. The phenomenon of the Indian arranged marriage often elicits this type of attitude. Cultural imperialism was, in Fairchild's day, rationalized on the basis of evolutionary superiority. Thus, it was entirely without contradiction that the early settlers, themselves, immigrants to the New World, subjugated the resident American Indians and quickly established their dominant status in society.

More specifically, the equation of group unity with identity is open to question. Unity does not require each to be like the other. The husband is not like his wife, yet they share a common unity. Unity may be achieved in diversity, it does not necessarily require a loss of identity or ethnicity.

Perhaps it is Fairchild's mistaken metaphor that must take the onus of the blame. The influx of immigrants can only under conditions of fertile imagination, and that too with many hazardous logical leaps, be likened to the process of metabolic assimilation. Food is taken to sustain and to maintain the body. Immigrants come for their own economic advantage, or because of political persecution in their home countries, or because they are exiled, or for a myriad other reasons; they do not arrive with the sole purpose of benefiting the country of their adoption. Thus, the metabolic metaphor breaks down immediately.

To be fair to Fairchild, although his theory was rigidly uni-directional, he was not unduly unsympathetic when newcomers were not assimilating to any significant degree. Although the Americanization movement directly blamed the immigrants for this non-assimilation, Fairchild rhetorically asks whether it would be realistic to expect an American, should he move to a foreign country, to forget his feelings and sentiments about his home country. Assimilation, Fairchild reminds us, is not entirely under voluntary control, and it would be unwise to adopt a 'holier than thou' attitude.

So, too, Fairchild never labels the non-Aryan, non-Nordic races as 'inferior', as do other writers of his time. His fear is merely that race mixture (through intermarriage) would lead to 'Mongrelization', or a loss of specialization, such that specialized genes (carrying specialized cultural traits) would neutralize or cancel each other out. However, given his sympathy and the careful way in which he uses his language, he never once stops to consider the devastating effects that a total denial of one's national heritage could have upon the individual. As Postiglione (1983, p. 91) points out:

The slightest appeal to the disciplinary matrix of psychology for such answers is totally absent from his analysis. It is as if some men had the ability to divorce themselves from the psychology of their being by virtue of the fact that they were immigrants.

The melting-pot theory

Contemporary to the theory of Anglo-conformity, was the melting-pot theory of American ethnicity. As is often the case, the symbol of the melting-pot, powerful and persuasive for many years to come, originated not with sociologists or psychologists but with a literary production by a Jewish immigrant, Israel Zangwill, whose play, *The melting pot*, was first performed in 1908. In the play, David, the Russian Jewish immigrant cries out (Zangwill 1929):

America is God's crucible, the great melting pot where all the races of Europe are melting and reforming. Here you stand, good folk, think I, when I see them at Ellis Island, here you stand in your fifty groups, with your fifty languages and histories, and your fifty blood feuds, hatreds and rivalries. But you won't be long like that brother, for these are the fires of God you've come to—these are the fires of God. A fig for your feuds and vendettas, Germans and Frenchmen, Irishmen and Englishmen, Jews and Russians—into the crucible with you all. God is making the American.

Central to the theory of the melting-pot is the idea that gradually all ethnic groups will inevitably become assimilated, not into some Anglo-Saxon image, but into a new identity which is essentially American. Unlike the theory of Anglo-conformity, it suggests that in the process of interaction both the dominant group and all other ethnic minority groups are changed into a homogeneous American identity that is neither A nor B. Hence, the equation $A \longleftrightarrow B = C$. C represents the all-American person who feels, not English, not German, not Italian, not Spanish, but quintessentially American. This variety of assimilationism expected a gradual but total loss of old ethnicities.

Although he used the term only once, Frederick Jackson Turner, of all the melting-pot theorists, is considered to be its strongest proponent. In contrast to Fairchild, whose mode of analysis was ideological and prescriptive, Turner a historian (rather than a maker of social policy) used a descriptive mode.

In *The frontier in American history*, first published in 1893, Turner details his observations of the immigration process and the stages of settling-in. Because he was writing about that period of history which corresponds roughly to what Fairchild termed the pre-1882 era of immigration, Turner stresses the importance of the reciprocal relationship between the European immigrants and American settlements. Two main stages are outlined: first, immigrants become 'Americanized', which refers to the effect of the frontier on the newly arriving European immigrant in America, where the environment modified and developed European life. The European is changed by his interaction with the frontier. Secondly, the immigrants in turn overcome and transform the wilderness (Turner 1920, p. 23):

In the crucible of the frontier, the immigrants were Americanized, liberated, and fused into a mixed race.

The pioneer experience, its essence and ideology is captured in Turner's concluding paragraph (p. 259):

This then is the heritage of the pioneer experience—a passionate belief that a democracy was possible which should leave the individual a part to play in free society and not make him a cog in a machine operated from above; which trusted in the common man, in his tolerance, his ability to adjust to differences with good humour, and to work out an American type from the contribution of all nations . . .

It is fairly obvious that Turner's sentiments towards diversity were generally positive. He uses the biological metaphor of organ differentiation (rather than assimilation) to explain that unity can be maintained in diversity: complex organs of the body are highly differentiated in order to perform specific functions, but are held together by the overall unity of the body. So, too, interpreting his metaphor, different ethnic groups may function together to produce a united America.

Critique

The symbol of the melting-pot drew strong reactions from many quarters. Fairchild wrote *The melting pot mistake* (Fairchild 1926), Kallen, 'Democracy versus the melting pot' (Kallen 1925), Glazer and Moynihan, *Beyond the melting pot* (Glazer and Moynihan 1970), and Feminella, 'The immigrant and the melting pot' (Feminella 1973).

To Fairchild, the melting-pot is anathema. Assimilation does not occur naturally, but only by dint of hard work and 'the complete sacrifice of extraneous national traits on the part of our foreign elements'. To Kallen and to the others, as we shall see later, the image of the homogenized all-American type is essentially against the true spirit of democracy: in any case, as Glazer and Moynihan point out, after the many years during which opportunities for complete assimilation have abounded, there is still no common American identity.

But perhaps it is Turner himself who is the best critic of his theory. Although he manifests an easy acceptance of diversity in his writing on immigrants from northern Europe, he is not so much in sympathy with 'tides of alien immigrants', 'the unfortunates of Southern and Eastern Europe', who are dull of brain and who serve to lower the standard of living (Turner 1920, pp. 271, 278). While we may excuse him for his condescension, his theory may have taken a somewhat different texture had he devoted his energies to the post-1882 era of immigration.

Perhaps more importantly, Turner expresses a residual doubt as to whether the melting-pot can truly produce a homogeneous America. Referring to particular ethnic groups, he says (Turner 1920, p. 349):

In the outcome, in spite of the slowness of assimilation, where different groups were compact and isolated from the others . . . there was the creation of a new type which was neither the sum of all its elements, nor a complete fusion in a melting pot.

This residual doubt, this observation that assimilation was not occurring was to be picked up and explored by the proponents of cultural pluralism. It came to light that the integration of ethnic minority groups into the larger society does not necessarily require a loss of ethnicity, and that integration should not be equated with assimilation.

Cultural pluralism

For several good reasons, both the theories advocating assimilation drew strong opposition. The Anglo-conformity theory was heavily criticized on ideological grounds: that the advocating of a 'pride of race' philosophy could hardly be justified in a nation that was centring itself upon the ideals of democracy. The melting-pot theory was shown to be inadequate by the observation that the many ethnic groups of America continued actively to maintain their ethnicity even beyond the third and the fourth generations, by which time they should have 'melted' into a common American identity. It became increasingly apparent that assimilationism, in whatever form, needed to be replaced by a theory that would: (1) attribute dignity and equality to people of all cultures; and (2) comprehensively explain and affirm the persistence and coexistence of ethnic minority cultures in spite of strong pressures towards assimilation.

In the mid-1960s, cultural pluralism became the new bandwagon upon which the sociology of ethnicity attached itself. Cultural pluralism advocated the coexistence and development of different ethnic groups with social and political equality for each under a common government. It may be represented by the equation (Postiglione 1983):

$$A \longleftrightarrow B = A + B$$

Here, A and B are cultures, not necessarily of the same status, which coexist peacefully within society and which retain their cultural identity over time. Each culture is thought to be able to contribute something positive to the fabric of society. Children, therefore, should be taught to be proud of their cultural heritage.

The theory was not a new one: John Dewey's notion of democratic pluralism had been debated for many years; the central author of *cultural* pluralism, however, was Horace Kallen. Kallen's writings were published contemporaneously with those of Fairchild, but the theory of cultural pluralism was slow in gaining acceptance. The great American dream of a single American identity was so much more attractive and the guidelines for social policy so much more clear and distinct that influence of assimilationism continued virtually unchecked for decades.

It was as early as 1925 that Kallen published his major treatise on American ethnicity in a book entitled *Culture and democracy in the United States* (Kallen 1925). The central theme is contained in a chapter entitled 'Democracy versus the melting pot' (Kallen 1925), in which Kallen proposes that the idea of the melting-pot was fundamentally against the spirit of democracy. In developing the argument, Kallen points out that the early settlers, particularly those who came from places such as The Netherlands, left their lands for the very fear of losing their ethnic identity. America was a place where they hoped to conserve their liberty and identity. For Americans of British ancestry, it was of paramount importance to counter the threat of the English monarchy. Thus, the Declaration of Independence unequivocally claimed equality for all and repudiated pride of race as an enemy of democracy.

It is this very pride of race, Kallen continues, that has resurfaced in the face of the threat of dilution of the 'old' stock by immigrants of an 'inferior' stock. It is necessary to declare all men unequal, where in 1776, it was necessary to declare all men equal (Kallen 1925, p. 98):

If this is not ethnic nationality returned to consciousness, what is it?

Thus Kallen subtly points out the inherent contradictions in the theory of assimilation; first that the 'pride of race' philosophy is one of mere convenience rather than sound ideology. Secondly, that in itself it constitutes evidence that ethnicity continues to persist and be maintained well beyond the third and fourth generations. He then outlines, for the first time, the process by which ethnicity resurges, is maintained, and continues to persist even over long periods of time. There are four phases through which immigrants pass in the process of settling in. The first phase may be likened to Gordon's phase of cultural assimilation (Gordon 1964), where prompted by a need to establish for themselves a secure economic future, and realizing that differences in speech, clothing, and manners are a handicap in the economic struggle, they assimilate or become superficially Americanized. To Kallen, the shedding of these cultural characteristics does not touch the core of one's ethnic minority identity, which is intrinsic and unalterable. It is exhibited in the psychological characteristics that group members share in common—a like-mindedness and a common group consciousness. Thus, out of economic necessity, a superficial commonality of culture is achieved. However, after economic independence is reached, the process of assimilation slows down and comes to a stop. This is the second phase (Kallen 1925, p. 114):

The immigrant group is still a national group, modified, sometimes improved, by environmental influence, but otherwise a solitary spiritual unit . . .

Why does assimilation slow down or come to a stop? Because in the struggle for economic independence, ethnic minority groups inevitably encounter prejudice, discrimination, and economic exploitation at the hands of other powerful groups in society (Kallen 1925, pp. 101–2).

It is the shock of confrontation with other ethnic groups and the natural feeling of aliency re-enforced by social discrimination and economic exploitation that generate in them an intenser group consciousness, which then militates against Americanization by rendering more important than ever the two factors to which the spiritual expression of the proletarian has been largely confined. These factors are language and religion.

A certain amount of conflict is unavoidable, then, when ethnic groups come into contact with each other. It is the conflict that generates a sense of ethnic identity and out of the conflict renewed attempts are made to rediscover those ethnic markers that will serve to preserve this sense of ethnic identity. Thus, in the third phase the immigrant is 'thrown back' upon his ancestry. Group distinctions are highlighted and the customs of heritage and ancestry become symbols of group affiliation and differentiation. In the fourth phase, therefore, Kallen describes a process that is the very antithesis of assimilation (Kallen 1925, p. 114):

Then a process of dissimilation begins. The arts life and ideals of the nationality become central and paramount; ethnic and national differences change in status from disadvantages to distinctions.

Ethnic diversity is endemic in a land of immigrants. Kallen likens it to a cacophony of many voices each singing a slightly different tune. Rhetorically he asks, should this cacophony be made into a unison or a harmony?

Critique

Cultural pluralism has had widespread influence both on America and now increasingly in Britain. Concerns for multi-cultural education, for example, are a measure of how important the theory is to contemporary society. However, the theory is not without its critics.

Glazer and Moynihan (1970) make several interesting observations. While they were perhaps the first to provide evidence that ethnic minority cultures were not being assimilated into a homogenous American identity, as expected by the melting-pot theory, they also point out that language and culture are very quickly lost in the first and second generations and that while the ethnic minority group maintains an identity, it is a changed identity. Italian-Americans of the third generation may still be identifiable as a group, yet they are different from Italian-Americans of the first generation, and much more different from Italians in Italy (Glazer and Moynihan 1970, p. 13).

. . . language and culture are very largely lost in the first and second generations, and this makes the dream of 'cultural pluralism' . . . as unlikely as the hope of a melting pot.

What persists is not so much the original culture but a strategy of social self-categorization (Glazer and Moynihan 1970, p. 13).

. . . as the groups were transformed by influences in American society, stripped of their original attributes, they were recreated as something new, but still identifiable as groups. Consequently persons think of themselves as members of that group, with that name; they are thought of by others as members of that group, with that name; and most significantly, they are linked to other members of that group by new attributes that the original immigrants would never have recognized as identifying their group, but which nevertheless serve to mark them off, by more than simply name and association in the third generation and even beyond.

Thus, in the equation $A \longleftrightarrow B = A + B$, by which cultural pluralism has been represented, the resultant is not so much $A + B$ (cultures peacefully coexisting within society), but AB, a new emergent culture which is different in many aspects from its original components.

Feminella (1979), too, corroborates the idea that ethnic groups have not 'melted' and that the emergent culture is radically different from its component parts (cited in Postiglione 1983, p. 163):

> As we review the recent studies of these groups we find that they have not 'melted'. These Germans, Italians, Irish, Jews, Poles, Africans, Japanese and others have in so many ways not become Anglo-American and indeed, they seem not to want to be Anglo-Americans. They are German-Americans, Italian-Americans, Irish-Americans, Jewish-Americans, Polish-Americans, African-Americans, Japanese-Americans and so on.

Thus, a hyphenated identity may well be the most constructive way of resolving what could be a sociological if not psychological identity crisis. For Feminella, the focus of interest is the collision or in Kallen's terms, 'the shock of confrontation' between ethnic groups. Rather than seeing ethnic conflict as a negative destructive phenomenon, Feminella sees it in a positive light: out of the impact between the two groups arises a synthesis of cultures which makes for integration (cited in Postiglione 1983, p. 170):

> . . . it is out of this impacting that new syntheses evolve. The conflict is resolved in a cultural integration that changes not only the persons involved, nor even also their groups, but the whole society itself.

Thus, contemporary theories of ethnicity, while coming to terms with the many problems that are inherent in multi-ethnic societies, are essentially optimistic in their outlook. Whether this optimism is justified will hinge upon the breadth of vision of those who inhabit the corridors of power.

4.

Psychological perspectives on ethnic minority identity

Psychology has been generally remiss in explaining the relationship between ethnic minority and majority groups and even more so in propounding models for explaining the psychology of ethnic minority identity. Some of the major social psychological theories that touch upon inter-group behaviour are: realistic group conflict theory; the frustration-aggression hypothesis; game theories; and research on the perception of out-group stereotypes. As these theories do not easily accommodate the concept of ethnic identity (Taylor and Simard 1979), they will not be discussed here. A detailed study of the above has been made by LeVine and Campbell (1972).

However, theories of more direct relevance to the present work on ethnic minority identity are: Erikson's theory of identity; Lewin's dynamic field theory; Tajfel's theory of inter-group relations; and Taylor and McKirnan's five-stage model of relations between advantaged and disadvantaged groups. Erikson, and to a lesser extent Lewin, are strongly influenced by the assimilationist thinking that prevailed well into the mid-1960s. Lewin and Tajfel, perhaps because both are members of ethnic minority groups, are less inclined to favour assimilation as the only means towards adequate integration. However, it would not be unfair to say that these psychologists, including Taylor and McKirnan, posit the need to assimilate as being essential to ethnic minority individuals. Tajfel and Taylor and McKirnan then go on to explore what happens to ethnic minority individuals when they encounter barriers which are often erected by the majority against complete assimilation. In doing so they, unintentionally perhaps, place themselves well within the boundaries of assimilationist philosophy. Any social psychological theory that does not question the 'need to assimilate' is found wanting by recent research observations. Thus, a new model is required for a comprehensive understanding of ethnic minority identity.

Erikson: identity versus identity diffusion

The term 'identity' owes much of its current widespread usage in psychology and other social sciences to the extensive writings of Erik Erikson

(1950, 1958, 1959, 1964, 1968, 1970). Until Erikson richly invested the term with meaning, 'identity' was somewhat baldly described as 'the condition or fact that a person is himself and not someone else' (*Oxford Illustrated Dictionary*, 2nd edn). To Erikson (1959, p. 23):

The conscious feeling of having a personal identity is based on two simultaneous observations: the immediate perception of one's selfsameness and continuity in time; and the simultaneous perception of the fact that others recognize one's sameness and continuity.

In order to achieve a healthy identity the growing child must feel that his own individual way of dealing with life is a successful variant of a group identity (Erikson 1964). In adolescence, even more so, because the individual is in the stage of identity versus identity diffusion, the formation of identity involves not only the need for inner sameness and continuity but also the need to be recognized by one's own community as 'a person whose gradual growth and transformation make sense to those who begin to make sense to him (Erikson 1964, p. 32).

This stage of identity formation calls for a re-evaluation and re-synthesis of all previous childhood identifications (Erikson 1959). Areas of previously unquestioned commitment are brought up for re-examination. Religious values, political ideology, cultural identification, and the attitudes and prejudices that arise therefrom; parental authority, sex role stereotypes, vocational and occupational choices; questions related to the meaning and purpose of life, are but a few of the vast panorama of conflicts the individual must resolve. According to Erikson (1959), an increasing sense of identity is manifest in a sense of psycho-social well-being, of being 'at home' in one's body, in one's home, in one's social world. This sense of well-being is at least partially dependent upon, and augmented by, recognition from significant others, be they friends or parents, groups or institutions. Psycho-social identity, as complementary to personal identity, develops within the context of role relationships. Its development presupposes a community of people whose values become increasingly important to the growing individual. In Erikson's words, identity thus depends upon 'a complementarity of an inner ego synthesis in the individual and of role integration in his group' (Erikson 1968). The sense of identity, then, can only develop if the efforts of the ego to find its boundaries and to integrate within the societal system are mutually reinforced by society.

The adolescent is faced with numerous choices: career; life-style; life-partners; and ideology. Should the individual find it impossible to make the necessary commitments, s/he characteristically withdraws into a *psycho-social moratorium* for protection (Erikson 1968). A psychosocial moratorium is a socially sanctioned refuge providing for a period of prolonged adolescence, of delayed adult commitments. It allows the individual a time for free role experimentation in order that s/he might find for him/herself his/her own unique niche in society. According to Erikson (1968), the period in the moratorium is a period of marking time before the march begins, a period of becoming accustomed to the rhythm of the music.

The danger of this stage is identity diffusion, which involves among other things a disintegration of the sense of time, morbid identity consciousness, work paralysis, bisexual confusion, and authority diffusion (Erikson 1964).

In order to maintain some sense of identity in this period of crisis, young people may temporarily over-identify with cliques and crowds, to the point of apparent loss of identity. They may become 'remarkably clannish, intolerant, and cruel in their exclusion of others who are "different" in skin colour or cultural background, in tastes and gifts and often in entirely petty aspects of dress and gesture arbitrarily selected as the signs of an in-grouper or out-grouper' (Erikson 1959, p. 92). Such intolerance is a necessary defence against a sense of identity diffusion.

For the ethnic minority individual the problems of identity formation are rooted in a deep-seated doubt of ethnic dignity (Erikson 1964). This doubt expresses itself in both extremes of behaviour—in the predominantly antisocial and the primarily prosocial, in the aggressive and the heroic, in the destructive and the creative. Where behaviour is prosocial, heroic, and creative, there is a demand to be seen and heard as a people marked with something beyond the colour of their skin; there is a struggle against the stereotypes that mark off the exploited minority. For the black American this constitutes a struggle against the associations well established in both groups: light-clean-clever-white, and dark-dirty-dumb-nigger (Erikson 1964). In cases where parents or other significant people have lost confidence in their ethnic identity, a premature identity crisis, manifested as a pathological denial of appropriate ethnic identification, may be precipitated in children as young as three or four years. Erikson (1964) cites the case of a four-year-old Negro girl who would stand in front of a mirror and scrub her skin with soap. When the soap was taken away from her she would begin to scrub the mirror. Finally, when encouraged to paint, she angrily painted in browns and blacks. Then she brought her teacher 'a really good picture'—a sheet of paper covered with white paint.

In adolescence, violent and sometimes psychotic incidents occur: staying out all night; dropping out of school; vandalism; drug addiction; and withdrawal into inaccessible moods. To the individual, this choice of a *negative identity* is preferable to having no identity at all. If parents and other adults of importance to the youth refuse to label these incidents, they often fail to acquire the same traumatic significance that they would in post- and pre-adolescent stages. If, however, the individual is prejudged by judicial authorities, psychiatrists, social workers, and parents as 'delinquent', 'vandal', 'drug addict', 'nigger', 'bum' he/she almost has no option but to comply with the expected social role: an identity has been created for him/her.

Although the need for distinctiveness, 'the need to be a special kind', is an important element in both personal and group identity, Erikson's Utopia consists of a transcendence of social identities, into a universal human identity (1964, p. 230):

> The utopia of our own era predicts that man will be one species in one world, with a universal identity to replace the illusory super-identities which have divided him . . .

Critique of Erikson's theory

As a psychoanalytic theory of social factors as they play upon individual development, Erikson's theory is a vast improvement on Freud's. Freud had paid only fleeting respect to 'social factors'—it was the parents' super-ego that was responsible for the transmission of cultural values from generation to generation—and although he claimed that 'from the very first individual psychology is at the same time social psychology', it was the individual-in-the-family rather than the individual-in-the-group that claimed his primary attention. Erikson hoped to establish the link between the individual and the group 'with greater specificity'. For Erikson, it is the confluence of history and personality, 'the mutual complementarity of ethos and ego, of group identity and individual identity', which is the focus of interest. It is, in fact, in his psycho-biographical study of people as they acquired and developed drives that enabled them, at the right time, and the right place, to assume leadership of the masses, that Erikson achieves his greatest excellence. Luther's role in the reformation (Erikson 1958) and Gandhi's role in the liberation of India (Erikson 1970) are prime examples of this.

Erikson's theory suggests not only that adolescence is the stage of an overall identity crisis but that it may also be a critical phase for the development of an ethnic identity crisis. However, the claim that an identity crisis in adolescence is a universal phenomenon must be approached with caution. In societies where the transition from childhood to adulthood is without the storm and stress phenomenon that is a characteristic of the West, in societies where roles are pre-arranged for the child by his/her family or community (as in rural India), adolescents may show little evidence of an identity crisis. Central to Erikson's theory is the proposition that identity is formed through a re-synthesis of previously unquestioned childhood identifications, a process involving some conflict with parents, some rebellion, some rejection. Unquestioned acceptance of parental values in this stage represents to Erikson a foreclosed identity.

This is an unfortunate cultural bias that works against those societies (such as rural India or traditional Japan) in which the family structure is based on a sense of unity and conformity to the needs of the family group, rather than on conflict and individuality. As Slugoski (1984, p. 3) points out:

By predicating the formation of an identity on the notion of a "moratorium" (i.e. a period of free role experimentation) Erikson neglects the objective conditions of a large segment of humankind for whom the evisaging of alternative possible futures would be a futile, self-delusory exercise. For a great many people, then, the notion of a 'normative crisis' and hence identity achievement in Erikson's sense may simply not apply; for such individuals there is no problem of identity.

Although ethnicity is of acknowledged importance, Erikson by his own admission is inadequate in dealing with this complex phenomenon. In 'A memorandum on identity and Negro youth (1964, p. 220), his opening words are:

A lack of familiarity with the problem of Negro youth and with the actions by which Negro youth hopes to solve these problems is a marked deficiency in my life and work which cannot be accounted for by theoretical speculation.

He then goes on to relate the development of 'a slave's identity' to the oral over-gratification prevalent in Negro childrearing practices. He assumes that the source of 'the problem' lies in the fact that a 'dangerous split' had occurred between this passive, always-ready-to-serve slave's identity and 'the Negro youth's unavoidable identification with the dominant race'. In that Erikson does not question the assumption that all minority groups must necessarily identify at some level with the majority group, Erikson's theory mirrors the early assimilationist thinking of the day. That the need to assimilate is not the only impetus underlying minority identity was more than adequately demonstrated in the Civil Rights Movement led by Martin Luther King Jr, a few years later, and taken up in the slogan 'Black is Beautiful'.

Yet, in spite of these obvious lacunae in his theory, Erikson draws admiration (if somewhat reluctant and ambivalent) from even his harshest critics. Isaacs, in his diatribe against Erikson (Isaac 1974, p. 19) is one such critic:

In Erikson (as in Freud) one finds the familiar blur, purposive sometimes, sophisticated sometimes, almost always literate, but still a blur. Erikson's deliberate imprecision . . . speaks to both the high merits and the high limitations of his style. It speaks to the complexity and elusiveness of the matters he seeks to deal with . . .

Ethnic minority identity is indeed a complex and elusive matter. Erikson's writing portrays vividly the conflicts and crises faced by those individuals only who wish to assimilate into the majority group. He cannot envisage that for some individuals, ethnicity may actually be a source of pride. Understandably so, perhaps, as Erikson chose to write mainly about blacks who, as we have seen in Chapter 2, are more accurately categorized as a racial minority than an ethnic minority group. A more comprehensive account may, perhaps be forthcoming from Lewin, who focuses upon a group that is without question, an ethnic minority group: the Jews.

Lewin's dynamic field theory

Contemporaneous with the extreme intra-individualistic emphasis of early psychoanalytic thought, Kurt Lewin's dynamic field theory was perhaps one of the first attempts to redress the balance. As Allport (1945, p. viii) points out

The unifying theme of Lewin's work is unmistakable: the group to which the individual belongs is the ground of his perceptions, his attitudes, his feelings. Most psychologists are so preoccupied with the salient features of the individual's mental life that they are prone to forget it is the ground of the social group that gives to the individual his figured character.

Deeply influenced by Gestalt psychology, Lewin uses both mathematical equations and graphical representations to describe the individual in the context of the group. A brief sketch of his concepts is fundamental to an understanding of his psychology of minority groups and of the later research that emerged from this theory.

Lewin conceives of the *person* (*P*) as existing within his psychological *environment* (*E*). The *life space* ($L = P + E$) contains the totality of possible facts that are capable of determining the behaviour of the individual. Thus, *behaviour* is a function of the life-space ($B = f(L)$) or $B = F(P + E)$ (Lewin 1936). Both the person (*P*) and the environment (*E*) undergo increasing differentiation with age. The adult person may be represented by a *perceptual–motor region* which is in direct contact with the environment, and which completely surrounds an *inner-personal region*. The inner-personal region, which may be thought of as roughly equivalent to the ego in psychoanalysis, contains *peripheral* cells and *central* cells. This notion of centrality was later to influence some important work on ethnic identity (Hofman and Rouhana 1976). The environment, too, is differentiated into regions, each containing a single 'psychological fact' (see Hall and Lindzey 1978). Regions are separated from each other by *boundaries*, which may be permeable, thereby allowing easy interaction between *facts* in the various regions, or impermeable, in which case certain *facts* are isolated (as in repression) from free communication with other *facts*. The permeability of the boundary around the person describes his/her readiness for social contact with other people or groups. In performing a *locomotion*, the person traverses a path through the environment. Locomotions may be performed at two levels: reality and irreality (Lewin 1952). *Reality* consists of an actual locomotion (in terms of ethnic identity, migrating from one country to another, changing one's name, etc.). *Irreality* refers to the level of imagined locomotion (daydreaming of one's acceptance into a particular group, etc.). Play can be understood as an action on the level of reality closely related to the irreal level. The *principle* of *contemporaneity* states that only present facts can influence present behaviour. The facts of infancy and childhood can have no bearing upon the behaviour of the adult unless they have managed to remain in the psychological environment in the intervening years (Lewin 1936). However, one's thoughts about the past or the future may have considerable influence upon present behaviour: the hopes of the future may serve to lighten the burdens of the present. A time dimension therefore is crucial to the understanding of behaviour as a function of life-space: the present contains a psychological *past* and a psychological *future* (Lewin 1952).

When an area of the inner-personal regions is in a state of *tension* a process of equalization is initiated whereby the system is restored to a state of equilibrium. An increase of tension is caused by the arousal of *need*. Needs may arise from either a physiological or a psychological base. When a need arouses tension, the psychological environment is differentiated into areas of positive or negative *valence*. A region of positive valence contains a goal object that will reduce the need when the person enters the region, as for example food for a hungry person. A locomotion occurs when a *vector* of sufficient strength acts upon a person.

A region of positive valence may create a vector of sufficient strength to propel the person in the direction of the region. A region of negative valence creates a vector that propels the persons in the opposite direction, for example, a child will run away from a growling dog. If there is only one vector acting upon a person, then there will be a locomotion in the direction of the vector. If two or more vectors are pushing the person in several directions, the resulting locomotion will be the resultant of all the vectors. If the person encounters no barriers in traversing the psychological environment, the goal is reached, the need is satiated, and equilibrium is restored. If barriers are encountered in the process of locomotion, then a cognitive restructuring of the environment occurs in order to discover new ways of overcoming the barrier.

It is now possible to investigate Lewin's thinking on minority groups. As mentioned before, the groups to which the person belongs determine to a large extent the current of the individual's life. Most members of the majority group have multiple group memberships and enjoy a space of free movement among them (Lewin 1948, p. 85). That is, they can move freely and without conflict among these various groups. For the minority group, however, the space of free movement is restricted by discrimination and prejudice. As Lewin (1948) points out, the Negro, the Jew, the Oriental often does not know whether s/he has a space of free movement or not: can they see themselves as American and will others perceive them as they see themselves? This uncertainty has several psychological consequences—restlessness, aggression, and at the very least an attitude of ambivalence towards one's own group.

Lewin distinguishes two types of vectors acting upon members of minority groups: one type drawing them into the group and keeping them inside, the other drawing them away. The origins of these vectors drawing him/her into the group, are many: a common heritage, a common 'fate', a sense of accordance with the ideology or goals of a group. Similarly, the forces away from the group itself may be the result of disagreeable features of the group itself, or the greater attractiveness of the majority group.

If the balance of forces toward and away from the group is negative, the individual will leave the group if no other factors intervene. Under 'free' conditions, therefore, a group will only contain those members for whom the positive forces are stronger than the negative. However, as Lewin (1948, p. 191) points out:

It is well to realize that every underprivileged minority group is kept together not only by the cohesive force among its members, but also by the boundary which the majority erects against the crossing of an individual from the minority group to the majority group. It is in the interest of the majority group to keep the minority in its underprivileged status.

Thus, if a minority group is kept together by the positive attitudes of its members towards the group, this group will have an organic life of its own: it will show organization and inner cohesion. If, however, a minority group is kept together merely by outside pressure (as when the majority group erects barriers against the assimilation of minority group members), this group will be unorganized and weak, comprising a mass of individuals without relationships with each other (Lewin 1948).

A fundamental tenet of Lewin's theory is that every underprivileged minority group will attempt to 'pass into' or assimilate into the more privileged high-status majority. For Lewin, it is an unequivocal fact that the relatively high status of the majority is sufficient to create a vector that will propel all minority individuals in the direction of the majority group.

At the very least, according to Lewin (1948, p. 177), minority group individuals experience ambivalence towards their own group:

There seems to exist in every underprivileged group a tendency to accept the values of the more privileged group in society. The member of the underprivileged group therefore becomes excessively sensitive to everything within his own group that does not conform to those values, because it makes him feel that he belongs to a group whose standards are lower . . . the result is a typically ambivalent attitude on the part of members of an underprivileged group toward their own group.

Individuals crossing the margin between social groups are often not only uncertain about their belonging in the new group, but also about their relationship with the old group. Assimilated American Jews, Lewin says, show a high degree of uncertainty in their relations with the Jewish group. This uncertainty in many cases, leads to a feeling of *self-hatred*: belonging to the minority group is seen as an impediment to reaching goals and fulfilling aspirations for the future. The result is a tendency to set oneself apart from the group and this often means cutting the psychological tie with the family group. The conflict so precipitated often results in self-hatred.

When assimilation is made impossible for the individual by the majority, a severe state of conflict is precipitated: the minority group individual dislikes or hates the group; it is nothing but a burden. Such an individual stands at the borderline between two groups, his own minority group and the majority group and experiences therefore a sense of being neither here nor there. Because most people belong to more than one social group (Lewin 1948, p. 148):

In different situations different feelings of belonging should be predominant. If an individual always acts as a member of the same specific group, it is usually symptomatic of the fact that he is somewhat out of balance, for he does not respond freely and naturally to the demands of the present situation. He feels *too* strongly his membership in a certain group and this indicates that his relationship to this group is not sound.

Lewin (1948) therefore advocates that parents of minority group children should not be afraid of bringing up their offspring with so-called 'double allegiances'. Belonging to and identifying with more than one group is both healthy and necessary.

Critique of Lewin's theory of minority group psychology

Lewin, like Erikson, unquestioningly builds up his theory upon the assimilationist philosophy prevalent in his day, namely that all minority group individuals want to and therefore will attempt to assimilate into the high-status majority group, and that, ideally, ethnic minority groups will eventually disappear completely into the majority. An inevitable conclusion from such assimilationist thinking is that minority group individuals will inevitably manifest self-hatred and low levels of self-esteem. Studies

investigating this phenomenon, which will be reviewed in Part 3, indicate
that although some minority group individuals do indeed manifest some
self-hatred, the phenomenon is by no means characteristic of all minority
individuals and that in recent years there is some indication of a reversed
trend, namely, that minority group individuals show no less self-esteem
than their majority group peers and that in some cases they show even
greater levels of self-esteem. Therefore, the fundamental basis of Lewin's
theory can be questioned.

Lewin, however, provides some very interesting concepts that may
prove fruitful for an empirical study of ethnic identity. Lewin's notion of
locomotion, of psychological movement towards or away from one or the
other group, indicates that there may be different strategies of ethnic
identification adopted by different minority group individuals. If we bring
together the various strains of Lewin's thought, it is possible to identify at
least two strategies of ethnic identification and to capture a hint of a third
and fourth type.

First, we have the minority group individual who has successfully
assimilated into the majority group. The majority group holds a high
positive valence for the individual and the vector created by such a valence
propels him/her in the direction of the majority. In his locomotion towards
the majority s/he has encountered no barriers to assimilation. Thus s/he
leaves the minority group behind and has little or no relationship with it.

Secondly, there is the marginal person who can find no home at all
either in the minority gorup or in the majority group. This person,
according to Lewin, experiences high levels of conflict, because s/he lives
on the very edge of society unable to identify with or be accepted by either
group.

Thirdly, in his essay on the psycho-sociological problems of a minority
group, Lewin hints at, but does not explore further, a third strategy of
ethnic identification (1948, pp. 145–58). There is a person who shows a
defensive, high level of identification with the ethnic minority group. This
person does not respond freely and naturally to the demands of the present
situation. S/he feels *too* strongly his/her membership of a certain group.
This strategy of identification indicates a certain level of dissociation from
the majority group and a high, somewhat inflexible level of identification
with the minority group.

Finally, Lewin indicates that another possible strategy of identification
is the formation of 'double allegiances'. In his chapter on Bringing up a
Jewish child (Lewin 1948), he advocates as healthy and necessary a type
of acculturation whereby the individual is able to hold within him/herself
several identity options which can be drawn upon according to the
demands of the situation. The reference to 'double allegiances' is disap-
pointingly cursory. However, it is possible to detect the beginnings of a
psychology that can embrace a philosophy of cultural pluralism.

Tajfel: the social psychology of minority groups

Henri Tajfel, himself a member of a minority group, presents a sensitive and persuasive understanding of the social psychology of these groups. Fundamental to his theory of inter-group relations are four processess: social categorization; social identity; social comparison; and psychological distinctiveness.

Every individual divides his/her social world into distinct classes or *social categories* (Tajfel 1972). Social identification refers to the process whereby the individual locates him/herself or another person within a system of social categorization (Turner 1982). The sum total of the social identifications the individual uses to define him/herself is his/her social identity (Turner 1982).

An assumption basic to Tajfel's theory is that individuals strive for a positive social identity. As social identity is derived from membership in a group, a positive social identity is the outcome of favourable social comparisons made between the in-group and other social groups. To the extent that the fact of belonging to the group contributes positively to his/her sense of social identity, an individual will remain a member of the group. If the group fails to satisfy this requirement, the individual may:

1 try to change the structure of the group (social change);
2 seek a new dimension of comparison by which to enhance a sense of positive social identity (social creativity); or
3 leave the group or distance himself from it (social mobility).

In all cases, individuals strive for psychological distinctiveness along positively valued dimensions.

For the minority individual achieving a sense of positive social identity is no mean task given that minorities almost always suffer inferior status in comparison with the majority. How do minorities respond to their position in the wider society? According to Tajfel (1978) there exists an underlying continuum which ranges from total acceptance to total rejection of that position.

An acceptance by the minority of its social and psychological inferiority is dependent on the perceived legitimacy and stability of the system of inequalities between the minority and the majority group. Perceived stability consists of an absence of cognitive alternatives to the status quo: there is no conceivable prospect of any change in the nature and future of the existing inequalities. Although some individuals of the minority may achieve the respect of some individuals of the majority, these people are seen as exceptions to the rule. This system of stable inequalities is exemplified in some feudal societies; a more specific example is the Indian caste system. Such systems were once perceived by members of both groups as legitimate and stable.

A system that is perceived as illegitimate carries within it the seeds of instability. The perception of illegitimacy and instability is a crucial factor in propelling a minority from total acceptance of its inferiority to total rejection of it. A system of relations between the two groups which is perceived as illegitimate will lead to the rejection of the status quo by the disadvantaged group. However, perceived illegitimacy and instability are not always inseparable. Some social and political orders are so strongly maintained by those in power that they appear to be stable, however widely perceived as illegitimate. South Africa is a case in point.

Among those minorities who have accepted their inferior status there is a conflict between satisfactory self-realization and the knowledge that membership in the minority group is likely to inhibit the achievement of satisfactory self-realization. According to Tajfel, such minorities exhibit high levels of self-hatred. The doll studies that will be examined in detail in a later chapter are quoted to substantiate this argument. However, Tajfel cautions that such self-hatred should not be taken as indicative of serious problems of personal identity but rather as manifestations of problems at the level of social identity.

There are two possible reactions to the acceptance by its members of the minority group's inferior position in society: at one extreme is a withdrawal from all social comparisons, a withdrawal from the wider community's norms, values, perceptions, and achievements, and the creation of groups which have their own values (Rastafarianism in Britain today may be an example of this). The creation of new and different groups makes possible the development of separate and socially powerful criteria of personal worth. At the other extreme, the group, because of its inability to create and maintain a social identity with its own norms, values, and prescriptions, begins to disintegrate. Tajfel maintains that most minorities who have accepted their inferior status fall somewhere between these two extremes.

When a minority group perceives the illegitimacy of relations between the two groups and when this system is relatively unstable, the minority group will tend towards a rejection of its inferior status. The problems of worth, dignity, and self-respect involved in being a member of a minority arise from social comparisons with the majority and a struggle against a future of 'inferiority' ensues, a struggle which embodies a defence 'of one's right to have and keep as much self-respect as has the next man or woman' (Tajfel 1978).

In developing this argument, Tajfel (1978) cites the example of three different types of minorities. The first type is the minority that expects to assimilate into the majority (as was the case of West Indian students arriving in Britain), but fails to do so because of barriers erected by the majority. The second is the minority that, because of an already extant tradition of history and social norms, exerts heavy pressures on individuals from the group who attempt to 'pass' into the majority. This is often characteristic of religious minorities and some national or ethnic minorities that are motivated by political or ideological commitments. The third type of minority is one which opts to shed some of its cultural, historical, and social differences from the majority while at the same time retaining some of their special characteristics in order to maintain some sense of psychological distinctiveness. If no barriers are erected by the majority, such a minority will eventually pass into or become indistinguishable from the majority even while periodically evoking the minority group labels to categorize themselves. Tajfel cites the case of the Scots in England, and the Catholics in Britain and the United States as such minorities.

The impetus to assimilate is fundamental to Tajfel's (1978) theory of minority group psychology. Tajfel quotes Simpson's (1968) definition of assimilation, which was discussed at the beginning of Chapter 2.

Tajfel (1978) distinguishes between four kinds of assimilation. The first is when no restrictions of social mobility are imposed by the majority on assimilating minority individuals. In this case, the minority group ceases to exist as a group. There is such a complete immersion into the majority group that even when the defining label is maintained and invoked from time to time, it has lost the negative connotations that once accompanied its minority categorization. Such 'successful' assimilation provides no psychological problems to the individual.

In the second case, the minority individual who wishes to assimilate encounters barriers raised by members of the majority group, even though partial access to the majority has been attained. The inherent paradox in such a situation lies in the fact that while the assimilating individual has achieved some respect from the majority, s/he is seen as an exception to the general rule (that members of the minority are inferior) and is simultaneously regarded as embodying in some important ways the negative characteristics associated with the minority. Such assimilation, because it arises from a configuration of factors in which the minority group is seen as inferior both by the majority group and the assimilating individual, is likely to cause a number of personal conflicts and difficulties. Individuals who attempt assimilation against such a background are known for their overriding concern to agree with the majority's derogatory views of the minority. For those who succeed in assimilating it is 'an uneasy experience': in order to succeed they must distance themselves psychologically from members of their previous group.

In the third kind of assimilation, the problems are even more acute, because assimilation in this case is 'illegitimate'. It consists of attempts by the assimilating individual to hide one's origins in order to 'pass' into the majority group. Such is the case of some light-skinned blacks in America.

When 'passing' is illegal, as in South Africa, the individual must employ a very careful strategy in hiding his/her origins, as the risks involved are great. More commonly, this type of assimilation involves changing one's name (for example, from Goldschmidt to Goldsmith) or as in the case of the Indian caste system, moving to a different village and assuming a different caste.

The fourth kind of assimilation which Tajfel (1978) mentions is more commonly known among sociologists as 'accommodation' or 'accultura-tion'. This consists of the minority's attempts to retain its own identity and distinctiveness while at the same time becoming more akin to the majority. According to Tajfel (1978), this kind of accommodation occurs: (1) when the successful assimilation of some members of the minority has not raised the overall status of the group in the eyes of the majority; and (2) when there exists within the minority a strong tradition of cultural norms and social roles which most of the members of the group are unwilling to give up.

Fundmentally, accommodation involves efforts to create or maintain a sense of positive social identity while still remaining a member of a group that does not get its fair share of respect from others. Often this involves a redefinition of identity elements such that what was once held in low esteem by both the majority and the minority group, is now invested with value by the minority group at least. Such an impetus lay behind the black power movement of the 1960s, such that all negative connotations associ-ated with 'black' (dark-dirty-dumb-nigger, Erikson 1964) were reversed in the slogan 'Black is Beautiful'. There is a realization here that the minority does not have to become exactly like the majority in order to merit equal status. This is a movement towards 'equal but different'. It involves a great investment of social creativity on the part of the minority as it attempts to achieve an acceptable form of group differentiation not by changing the group's position within the prevalent system of values but by changing the values themselves. Thus the first form of the minority's social creativity is to re-evaluate existing unfavourable connotations as favourable.

The second is to rediscover in the history of the group traditions myths, symbols, historical realities, special attributes and to re-invest these with new and positive significance. As language is a major symbol of psycho-logical distinctiveness carrying a positive self-definition, an accommodating minority will often revitalize its national language, as has been the case of the French in Quebec, and the Swedes in Finland.

The third form of a minority's social creativity, which is essentially a variation of the second form, lies in the creation of new characteristics which will lend the group psychological distinctiveness and consolidate a sense of positive social identity. This form of social creativity occurs when a minority group cannot find very much in the past in the way of symbols and traditions that will effectively distinguish it as having separate identity. The feminist movement is a case in point, where the initial concern was to create an awareness that women were equal but different, but where there were few situations in the past from which to draw upon in order to substantiate such an argument.

For Tajfel (1978) there are several major implications of the above for an understanding of the relations between minority and majority groups. The first is that the recognition of the majority group's 'inferior' status through social comparisons, will lead to genuine social creativity and the search for new, positively valued dimensions whereby the minority may achieve a sense of positive social identity. The next stage consists of the legitimization of these new dimensions of social comparison from within the group and from without. These new, or re-evaluated dimensions of social comparison will gain wide acceptance from within the minority only if the group as a whole perceives the illegitimacy and instability of the present system of relations and therefore rejects its inferior status. Achieving such a consensus of opinion may often prove difficult. Even more difficult to achieve, however, is the social legitimization of such new dimensions of social comparison by the majority group, whose interests are almost inevitably linked with efforts to maintain the status quo and whose sense of positive social identity is derived, at least in part, from comparisons with the minority: 'We are what we are because they are not what we are'.

Inevitably then, because of a conflict of interests both objective and psychological, a certain amount of conflict and inter-group competition ensues when a minority rejects its inferior status. No easy solution exists to such a situation. However, Tajfel (1978) is not totally pessimistic. In most present-day societies it is unlikely that a minority finds itself in a position of total powerlessness; neither do majorities hold absolute, unquestioned sway. It would be useful therefore, Tajfel (1978) suggests, to preserve and defend the interests vital to each group in such a way that the self-respect of the other group is in no way diminished.

Critique of Tajfel's social psychology of minority groups

Tajfel's understanding of the dynamics underlying minority–majority relations is perhaps the most detailed and incisive social psychological explanation of minority group psychology to date. However, certain cautionary remarks must be made.

The theory focuses on the status differential between the minority group and the majority group. The assumption is that because the majority group enjoys the higher status, the minority group will attempt to assimilate into the majority in order to achieve a positive social identity. The theory would therefore predict that as the minority group climbs the social ladder and approaches the status of the majority group, there should be a corresponding decrease in ethnic identity. Research does not bear out this prediction. Status relative to the majority group is a powerful motive, but not a sufficient impetus to assimilate: a minority group which is also an *ethnic* minority group does not inevitably opt for assimilation. The attempts of minorities to preserve their cultural traditions are dealt with only as a response to perceived inferiority. According to Tajfel, perceived inferiority results in social creativity, a re-evaluation of negative dimensions of social comparison, and rediscovery of a buried cultural past. Such theorizing is of course the logical outcome of seeing the majority group as the *only* really salient reference group for social comparison. This overlooks the fact that a positive social identity may well be achieved by comparisons with other members of the ethnic minority (Rosenberg 1979). Tajfel is surprisingly inexplicit when he posits a universal drive for a positive social identity: to whom must this identity be positive, whether to the majority group or perhaps the ethnic minority group? It is clear that an individual will arrive at a sense of positive social identity by reference to the group that is most salient to him/her. It is necessary, therefore, to establish the relative salience of the two groups to the individual, rather than attributing to the majority unquestioned salience.

In trying to maintain the inter-group nature of his theory, Tajfel has adopted a descriptive rather than a prescriptive mode. Thus, for example, minorities who perceive their inferior status to be illegitimate and the system of social relations unstable, will reject their inferior status. However, Tajfel never specifies the mechanisms underlying this perception.

Also, Tajfel seems to conceive of the minority as a homogeneous group. In concentrating on the interface between the two groups, Tajfel does not deal adequately with the fact that different individuals may adopt different methods of coping with their ethnic minority status and that the psychological mechanisms must necessarily be different. Thus, while Tajfel presents what is perhaps the most comprehensive of social psychologies of minority–majority relations he does not fully account for ethnic minority identity.

Taylor and McKirnan's five-stage model of inter-group relations

Taylor and McKirnan's (1984) model of inter-group relations draws heavily upon Tajfel's (1978) theory. It attempts, however, to answer an important issue which Tajfel's theory side-steps. In responding to social inequality, minority groups use different strategies of coping. The question is under what conditions will these different strategies of coping manifest themselves. According to Taylor and McKirnan (1984), few precise predictions regarding this issue have been made.

The five-stage model presented by the authors traces a sequence of socio-historical stages through which minority groups may pass in their dealings with the majority. Specific inter-group situations will differ according to the historical and social realities that underlie each situation. Also the length of time spent at any one stage by a particular minority group will differ. However, despite these important differences, the authors propose that *all* inter-group relations follow a similar sequential course and employ certain key social psychological processes in doing so. The five stages presented schematically consist of:

(1) clearly stratified inter-group relations;
(2) emergent individualistic social ideology;
(3) social mobility;
(4) consciousness raising; and
(5) competitive inter-group relations.

The two key social psychological processes are:
(a) causal attribution; and (b) social comparison.
  Before developing the five-stage model in detail it is necessary to elucidate the authors' choice of these social psychological processes. The authors point out that to date the causal attributions and social comparisons referred to in social psychology are largely those made at the individual level. Such principles may be effectively extended to the group level as they often arise out of macro-forces such as social ideologies, power structures, and institutionalized relationships. Thus, group-serving bias may be said to operate when internal in-group attributions are made for success and external attributions to the out-group are made for in-group failure. Social comparisons are important because they bear directly upon the groups' status and indirectly upon the individual's self-image. The model presented by the authors discusses causal attributions and social comparisons made at *both* the individual and the group level.

Stage 1: clearly stratified inter-group relations

The first stage consists of rigidly stratified relations between an all-powerful majority group and a powerless minority. This stage represents the pre-industrial feudal and caste structures, where inter-group relations were 'paternalistic' and where stratification between the groups was so pronounced that there was no perceived legitimate basis for questioning the system of relations between the groups. The authors cite the case of black slaves in America, where stratification was based entirely on race and was so entrenched that even intimate contacts between members of the groups was not perceived as threatening by the dominant group. The authors point out that black slave women were given major responsibility for the rearing of white children.

In such a situation, it is not difficult to understand why the majority is interested in maintaining the status quo. The problem lies in trying to explain the acceptance by the minority group of the status quo. The majority group defines the stratification between the groups on the basis of ascribed characteristics such as race; the minority group is led to believe that they are in some way responsible for their low status. Because the status gradient is so steep, no serious social comparisons are made by members of either group. Because minority group members are led to attribute their low status to their own responsibility, rather than to discrimination by the majority group, 'self-hate', where the individual downgrades his/her own group and him/herself as a member of that group, is a common phenomenon.

Stage 2: emerging individualistic social ideology

In the second stage, which usually occurs concurrently with increasing industrialization, an increasing value is placed on individual characteristics, such as technical skills, rather than ascribed characteristics such as race. There is a growing awareness among members of both groups that the system of stratification operative in Stage 1 is illegitimate. Rather, stratification is based on individual achievement or worth. This stage embodies an ideological shift towards equal opportunity. In spite of this, however, there is still a strong correlation between status and ascribed characteristics such as race.

Stage 2 represents a shift in the basis of causal attribution and social comparisons. Characteristics of the individual, his/her ability and effort (rather than group membership *per se*) are used as the yardstick of social comparison. Group-based discrimination is seen as illegitimate while individual-based discrimination is seen as legitimate, even when many of those who are individually unable to compete are from the minority group.

The privileged few who are able to achieve some status in this 'merito-cracy' attribute this again to factors for which they are personally respons-ible—their own ability and effort. Because stratification is individual rather than group-based, the correlation between status and membership in the disadvantaged group is seen by the majority as spurious. Thus the majority is exempted from assuming any responsibility for the causing or changing of social inequality. In so far as this ideology is internalized by the minority group, it decreases the possibility of inter-group conflict.

Stage 3: social mobility

In this stage, members of the minority group, usually relatively high-status, highly skilled, or educated individuals, attempt to pass into the majority group. Taylor and McKirnan (1984) suggest that attempts at individual mobility represent the first overt response to social stratification. Individual strategies always precede collective action. However, the length of time that a particular minority group engages in such an individualistic strategy may vary according to the inter-group situation.

Upward mobility may take two forms: the first is complete assimilation, whereby members of the minority group change their personal characteristics (proper names, place of residence, socio-linguistic reference groups) to become indistinguishable from other members of the majority. Such a strategy is characteristic of groups based on linguistic, cultural, or other modifiable dimensions. The second strategy involves members of the minority adopting some of the characteristics of the dominant group so as to gain acceptance into the group while still remaining recognizable as members of the original group. This is the case of groups formed along unmodifiable dimensions such as race or sex.

The dynamic underlying social mobility is that individuals tend to affiliate with those groups that contribute positively to their social identity. Members of minority groups are therefore motivated to leave their groups and 'pass' into the high-status advantaged group. Again, social mobility is attempted by high-status minority group members and the locus of causal attribution is individualistic: those who succeed at passing attribute their entry into the majority group to their individual effort and ability. These individuals are viewed by the majority group with special interest: first they constitute 'evidence' to the majority group that individual-based comparisons are a valid and legitimate basis for social stratification. In other words, they serve to break the covariance between group membership and social status. Secondly, these individuals are usually among those with the highest potential for leadership. Thus, the majority group profits from the inclusion of these assimilating individuals while the minority group is in a position of further disadvantage.

Stage 4: consciousness raising

Not all minority group members who attempt social mobility succeed in gaining entry into the majority group. Those who do, assimilate in the extreme; those who are not permitted access into the majority have little choice but to return to the minority group. They recognize that the only route to a positive social identity consists in attempting to persuade all members of the minority that their low status is illegitimate and that collective action is required to equalize the system of relations between the two groups. This results in efforts to raise the consciousness of the minority group. For a minority group to be propelled into the stage of consciousness-raising it is only necessary that some (not all) members of the group fail in their attempts to assimilate. Information gleaned from such individuals is often sufficient for the whole group to come to a belief in the illegitimacy of individualistic change strategies.

Although some individuals may attribute their failure to a personal lack of ability and effort, this is unlikely, as such individuals, like anyone else, are subject to self-serving biases in attribution. Thus their failure is more likely to be attributed to external factors: they will perceive the majority group as unjustly preventing access. Rather than accepting an individually based system of social stratification, they view their membership in the minority group as causally related to their failure to assimilate. Thus, group membership is once again seen as the basis of social stratification. However, in Stage 4 as opposed to Stage 1, responsibility for the low status of the minority group is attributed to discrimination on part of the dominant group, rather than to negative characteristics that inhere in the minority group. The perception of this injustice impels such individuals to persuade all members of the minority group to reject the prevailing system of relations and to prepare for collective action.

Stage 5: competitive inter-group relations

In the fifth stage, that of competitive inter-group relations, consciousness-raising is followed by collective action. There are direct attempts to augment the group's status relative to that of the majority group in order to achieve a more even distribution of material and social rewards. As long as the advantaged group is not totally dominant and the minority group not totally powerless, a state of healthy inter-group comparison ensues. If at any point either of the groups becomes consistently disadvantaged, a return to one of the previous stages is precipitated.

Social comparisons in this stage occur at the group level and are carefully monitored such that the outcome of such comparison processes is positive. Individual and intra-group comparisons are discouraged as the minority group focuses on the similarity of its members as a means of maintaining a common ideology. The majority, on the other hand, attempts to persuade members of its group that such social comparisons as are being made by the minority groups are illegitimate, and even attempts to deny the validity of categorizing society into ascribed groups. Meanwhile, the minority group attributes its low status in the past to discrimination by the dominant group and their hope for the future lies in the internal characteristics of the minority group exercised at the group level.

Once this stage has been reached, the relative outcomes for both majority and minority groups will determine the subsequent relationship between them. There are three possible outcomes:

1 the relative power between the group remains unchanged;
2 the minority group may emerge as dominant; or

3 the groups may become approximately equal in both power and resources, so that there is no clear-cut winner.

A key assumption of the theory is that attempts at individual upward mobility (assimilation) are the first strategy used by members of disadvantaged groups. It is only when these individual attempts are blocked that the overriding social philosophy is questioned and collective action is initiated. Wright *et al*. (1990) attempted to quantify this assumption. They found that subjects who believed that access to the high-status group was possible endorsed acceptance and individual actions. When access to the higher-status group was restricted even to the point of being closed (tokenism), subjects still preferred individual action. Disruptive forms of collective action were favoured only by subjects who were told that the high-status group was completely closed to members of that group.

Critique of Taylor and McKirnan's five-stage model of inter-group relations

Taylor and McKirnan's (1984) model has several interesting features: it is perhaps the first socio-psychological model that posits a universal sequence of historical stages through which all minority groups must pass. In giving history a place of central importance, the authors echo Erikson's (1959) claim that identity emerges from the confluence of history and personality. However, in Taylor and McKirnan's model an important social psychological focus, that of individual-in-a-group-among-other-groups, tends to be ignored in favour of an emphasis on the group-among-other-groups. At best, the model draws into the limelight those few high-status minority group individuals who attempt to assimilate and succeed or those who attempt to assimilate and fail. For these individuals an intricate system of causal attribution and social comparison is developed. For the large proportion of the minority group for whom by virtue of some ascribed characteristic such as race, sex, or skin colour, assimilation is not a viable option, few predictions are offered, apart from the fact that such people should manifest high levels of self-hatred. Recent studies, reinvestigating self-hatred or low self-esteem among blacks in America and Asians and Afro-Caribbeans in Britain, show there is little evidence to support such an argument. These studies will be reviewed in detail in the next chapter.

The model also emphasizes that the dynamic of the relationship between the majority and the minority group is affected by changes in the status gradient between the two groups. It thus draws upon Tajfel's (1978) theory of perceived legitimacy and stability as an important impetus behind social mobility. However, one of the more serious problems with such a theory (and this is a problem for Erikson's and Lewin's theories as well) is that it is postulated on the assumption that the low-status minority group must achieve a sense of positive social identity by becoming assimilated into the high-status majority group. If this cannot be achieved, the low-status minority must create new dimensions or rework old ones to provide a basis for self-respect. This assumption does not hold for *ethnic* minorities that are already rich in culture and history and therefore need not look elsewhere for the construction of a positive social identity.

Some concluding remarks

It is evident that the theorists considered in this chapter have contributed invaluable insights into an understanding of minority identity. Unlike sociological approaches which concentrate on the role of ethnicity in the social structure, these theories have focused on the meaning of minority identity for the individual (Erikson, Lewin) or for the minority group (Tajfel, Taylor and McKirnan).

Each theorist, from the philosophical ground upon which his theory originates, makes his own idiosyncratic contribution to this study of identity. For Erikson ethnic identity was an 'inner identity' at the unconscious level that manifested itself in cases of pathological denial and deep-seated doubt of ethnic dignity; in prosocial or antisocial behaviour among ethnic individuals, in an unconscious struggle against negative associations. For Lewin, ethnic minority identity was an overriding consciousness of being a 'people set apart'; it entailed a constant, inescapable feeling of self-hatred, rebellion against this separation, and attempts to fight this separation through assimilation. For Tajfel, the primary task of the minority group was that of coping with a negative social identity through assimilation, and positive re-evaluation of previously devalued dimensions of social comparison through the creation of new dimensions of comparison upon which a positive social identity could be built. For Taylor and McKirnan, history is seen to play a crucial role in the formation of ethnic minority identity.

The common failing of all these theories is that they are built upon the unquestioned assumption that ethnic minority individuals, because of their relatively inferior status in society, must necessarily suffer a decrement of self-esteem, and that in order to escape this intense personal suffering they have little option but to attempt to assimilate into the majority group. This failing may be attributed to a disproportionate concentration on the 'minority' aspects of identity to the almost complete exclusion of the 'ethnic' aspects, and to the undifferentiated use of the terms 'ethnic' and 'racial' when speaking of such groups. If, indeed, one's identity is defined solely in terms of one's membership in a minority group which is indistinct from the majority in every way but that of status, then perhaps the need to escape from low self-esteem will propel the individual in the direction of the majority group. However, when one comes from a minority which is endowed with a culture, tradition, and structure of its own, in other words an ethnic minority, it is not impossible to develop a sense of self-respect or even a positive social identity through social comparisons with other members of the group, even if this group is of lower status in the social pecking order. The theorists considered here have all vastly under-estimated the powerful forces that serve to keep the individual within the group and afford him/her a sense of ethnic dignity. They have addressed the issue as if the minority groups they were describing were racial minorities without an ethnic base and have in consequence concentrated on some of the more deleterious effects of minority group membership. It is clear that a new perspective on ethnic minority identity is called for.

In order to arrive at such a perspective it will first be necessary to look into the research that relates to ethnic minority identity.

Part 3 reviews patterns of ethnic identification preference and relates these to the ethnic minority individual's level of self-esteem. Thus, the doll studies and similar work will be first considered (Chapter 6). Studies investigating the salience of ethnicity are then investigated. Most of this research focuses on the situational determinants of salience, while a small portion deals with the centrality and valence of ethnicity (Chapter 7). Chapter 8 turns to the issue of the cultural adaptation of ethnic minority individuals in the countries of their adoption. Finally, the labels individuals use to place themselves in the system of social relations are discussed. Chapter 9 thus deals with strategies of self-categorization and social stereotypes. In Chapter 10, having sifted through both the theory and research related to ethnic minority identity, we will be equipped to search for a new perspective on ethnic minority identity.

III

Research Issues

5.

Trends in current research

It is the aim of contemporary social science to validate its theories by means of empirical observations. A deepening interest in ethnic minority identity, produced perhaps by increasing racial tensions in multi-racial societies alongside ideological concerns for human rights and ethnic dignity, has led to a burgeoning of research into the area. In reviewing the vast body of data that has accumulated since the late 1930s, an emphasis will be placed on how ethnic minority individuals think and feel about themselves rather than how majority group individuals think and feel about their ethnic minority counterparts.

Sue *et al.* (1982) have outlined three major historical trends in ethnic minority research:

1 the inferiority model;
2 the deficit model; and
3 the bi-cultural or multi-cultural model.

Early research saw ethnic minority individuals as socially and culturally inferior to the majority group. Society was exonerated from blame or the need for corrective action because this social and cultural inferiority was attributed to inherited racial inferiority, biologically determined and therefore beyond hope of change. The prevalent ideology of Social Darwinism served to bolster such research and bias its conclusions. In the deficit model, the deficiencies in ethnic minority identity and achievement are attributed not to genetically determined factors, but to historical, economic, political, and socio-psychological forces prevalent in society that had shaped the ethnic minority individual in certain ways. Thus, institutionalized racism was seen as responsible for the deviant, the pathological, and the underprivileged status of ethnic minority groups. Many studies underlined the fact that black Americans had high rates of drug addiction and alcoholism, exhibiting tendencies towards criminal behaviour, personality disorders, and suicide. The deficit model addressed attention to the structural defects in the organization of society which served to keep ethnic minorities in a position devoid of power, status, and voice. The model proved invaluable in stimulating debate about human rights and ethnic dignity. However, an undesirable by-product of the deficit model was an over-emphasis on the inferiorities of the ethnic minority group and a constant underlining or highlighting of the problems of being a member of such a group. The bi-cultural or multi-cultural model, therefore, emphasizes the importance of focusing on the strengths and the cultural riches inherent in ethnic groups rather than the deficiencies. Bi-cultural research attempts to study both the majority group culture and the ethnic minority culture as they interact and influence the development of ethnic minority identity. It stresses that a knowledge of the histories of these groups and the policies that have been instituted by the majority group in relation to these histories is vital to an adequate understanding of the ethnic minority individual.

No attempt will be made here to investigate the extent of racism. It is assumed that racism is prevalent in our multi-ethnic societies and manifests itself subtly in prejudice and blatantly in discrimination. Several major research areas, such as educational achievement, unemployment, segregation, etc., are beyond the scope of this book. Other areas of research interest, such as how prejudice is acquired by the majority group, will be dealt with only indirectly as they affect ethnic minority identity. More pertinent to this book are questions about ethnic identification, ethnic preference, and self-esteem; the salience, centrality, valence, and context of ethnicity; styles of adaptation to the prevalent culture/s; strategies of self-categorization; and social stereotyping. Do ethnic minority individuals identify (or align) themselves with the ethnic minority group? Do they prefer their group to the majority group? Do they suffer lower self-esteem by virtue of the fact that they belong to a group that is relegated to an 'inferior' status in society? Is their ethnicity a salient part of their self-description? How central is it to their identity, does it carry a negative or a positive valence? In what contexts do they become more aware of their ethnicity? How do ethnic minority individuals adapt to the different and sometimes conflicting demands of living within two or more cultures at once? How do they categorize themselves—with single identity labels, with multiple identity labels? What are their social stereotypes about their their own group and the majority group?

In sifting through some of the research that has attempted to answer these questions, considerable attention will be given to the methodologies that have been used to collect such data. It is hoped therefore that the student of ethnic minority identity may become familiar with the many instruments and techniques that are currently available for further research into the topic.

6.

Ethnic identification, ethnic preference, and self-esteem

One of the most fundamental facets of social identity is the individual's identification with and preference for his/her ethnic group. For most people the development of this identification and preference is a simple process: there is little conflict in seeing oneself as French, Swedish, or British if one belongs to the majority group in each of these countries. However, for the ethnic minority individual the process of developing identification and preference for one's own group is complicated by the fact that the group suffers inferior status relative to the majority group. Not all black and coloured children, for instance, identify with or prefer their own group. Rather, some of them seem to internalize white values about their group, namely, that their group is in some way inferior and they identify with and prefer the white group rather than their own. Observations of this unusual pattern of identification and preference led psychologists to believe that it must result in deleterious consequences for the individual's level of self-esteem.

One of the most import early statements of this position was made by Lewin (1948) on the theme of self-hatred among Jews and has strongly influenced social psychological thought on minority group membership. Lewin pointed out that in the period of the German ghetto the Jews were confined to special sections of the city, were restricted in their freedom of occupational choice, and were easily recognized by their yellow badge, distinctive clothes, and other overt signs. With the Emancipation, however, Jews were more able to assimilate into the larger society and were no longer so easily distinguished by their clothes, etc., from the wider population. Seeking to achieve acceptance into the high-status majority group, the Jew's religious ties were weakened. However, barriers erected by the majority group prevented complete assimilation. Socially identified as a Jew, the individual experienced ambivalent self-identification and self-hatred. Lewin then argued that self-hatred was a phenomenon not exclusive to Jews alone but was characteristic of other underprivileged groups such as the American Negroes, second generation Greeks, Italians, Poles, and other immigrants.

Most writers have subsequently assumed that, because one's group is an important part of one's self, contempt for one's group by the majority must necessarily result in lower self-esteem, and that rejection or hatred of one's group must necessarily reflect rejection of oneself. According to Kenneth Clark (1965), who did some seminal work on ethnic identification and preference:

> Human beings who are forced to live under ghetto conditions and whose daily experience tells them that almost nowhere in society are they respected and granted the ordinary dignity and courtesy accorded to others, will as a matter of course, begin to doubt their own worth. Since every human being depends on his cumulative experiences with others for clues as to how he should view and value himself, children who are consistently rejected understandably begin to question and doubt whether they, their family and their group really deserve no more respect from the larger society than they receive. These doubts become the seeds of a pernicious self- and group-hatred, the Negro's complex and debilitating prejudice against himself . . . Negroes have come to believe in their own inferiority.

Others followed the same trend of thought. In 1969, Proshansky and Newton wrote:

> The Negro who feels disdain or hatred for his own racial group is expressing—at some level of awareness—disdain or hatred for himself.

Erikson, too, spoke of ethnic self-doubt and a pathological denial of one's roots as being seminal to Negro identity (see Chapter 4). Tajfel's theory was also built upon the assumption that the achievement of a positive social identity is a prime motivating factor in inter-group behaviour and that there is almost a one-to-one correspondence between positive social identity and high self-esteem.

What empirical evidence is there for the theory that ethnic minority individuals identify with and prefer the majority group to their own? Does a majority group preference signify a low level of self-esteem? We shall first review the research on patterns of ethnic identification and preference and then investigate the issue of a damaged self-esteem among ethnic minority individuals.

Ethnic identification and preference

Most of the research on ethnic identification and preference has used dolls as stimulus materials. Clark and Clark (1940) showed 250 two- to seven-year-old black children two sets of dolls identical but for skin and hair colour. Each child was asked to select one out of the pair of dolls when asked to give the experimenter: 'the doll that you like to play with'; 'the doll that is a nice doll'; 'the doll that looks bad'; 'the doll that is a nice colour'; 'the doll that looks like a white child'; 'the doll that looks like a Negro child'; and 'the doll that looks like you'. The majority of preference selections of 'playmate' and 'nice colour' were made by black children in favour of the 'white' doll. Some 33 per cent of black children chose the white doll in response to the question: 'Give me the doll that looks like you'. This, in spite of the fact that 94 per cent of the children had correctly labelled the black and white dolls in response to the two previous questions. This misidentification of the self with the white doll stimulated a wide body of research (Adelson 1953; Goodman 1952; Landreth and Johnson 1953; Morland 1962; Radke and Trager 1950; Radke-Yarrow and Lande 1953; Sarnoff 1951; Stevenson and Stewart 1958). After reviewing the literature, Brand *et al.* (1974, p. 883) state that:

The most consistent finding in this ethnic research is preference by both white and black children for white experimental stimuli.

In a review of the research that had occurred in the ten years since the Brand *et al.* review, Tyson (1985) quotes numerous additional studies that have found a white stimulus preference amongst *both* white and black children in the United States. This preference for a white stimulus is not merely typical of the situation in the United States but has been found in both white and black children in South Africa, white and Maori children in New Zealand, white and Indian children in Canada, white, West Indian, and Asian children in Britain, white children in France and Italy, and amongst Japanese children. Such a preference has also been found among other minority groups in the United States, namely, the Chicanos and the Chinese (again, see Tyson 1985).

To expand upon just one study carried out in Britain, Milner (1975) studied 100 West Indians, 100 Indians and Pakistanis, and 100 white English children aged between five and eight, attending multi-racial infant and junior schools in Brixton and Southall in London. Milner used adaptations of the classic doll and picture techniques developed by Clark and Clark (1940) and Morland (1958). The main areas investigated were, 'identity', 'preferences', 'stereotypes', and 'aspirations'. The questions on 'identity' were intended to tap the child's *actual* ethnic identification ('Which doll looks most like you?') and his/her *ideal* identification ('If you could be one of these two dolls, which one would you rather be?'). In addition to these, the children were also required to identify which doll looked most like their mother, sister, or brother.

In order to elicit ethnic preferences the children were first asked which of the two dolls they liked best. Then they were asked to indicate who they preferred to 'play with in the playground'; 'to sit next to in class'; 'to share your sweets with'. Finally, they were asked to indicate which doll looked most like their best friend. In the *stereotypes* section, the children were asked to indicate the 'bad' doll, the 'nicest' doll, and the 'ugly' doll.

In order to assess social aspirations the children were asked to imagine they were grown up and had a house and family. They then were asked which of two families of dolls they would like to live next door to, which doll would be their best friend, which they would go to work with or go shopping with.

All the white children chose the white doll in response to the question 'Which doll looks most like you?' but only 52 per cent of the black children and 76 per cent of the Indian and Pakistani children made the correct choice. A similar pattern emerged in the family identification tests—35 per cent of the black children and 20 per cent of the Asian children misidentified the black figures. All the white children would 'rather be' white, but so would 82 per cent of the black children and 65 per cent of the Asians. In response to questions about preferences for different ethnic group figures, 6 per cent of white children made out-group choices, while 74 per cent of Asian and 72 per cent of black children made out-group choices. None of the white children held negative stereotypes of their own group, but 65 per cent of Asian children and 72 per cent of black children had negative stereotypes of their own group.

The results were quite clear: black and Asian children in Britain showed a preference for the white majority group and a tendency to devalue their own group.

It is dramatically obvious from Milner's (1975) study that Asian and West Indian children show significant preferences for and aspirations to the white majority group. In addition, they hold positive stereotypes about whites (the nicest doll) and negative stereotypes about their own group. A considerable proportion actually misidentify and show an ideal identification with whites, although the proportion is far less for the Asian group than for the West Indian group.

These and other findings have almost always been interpreted as indicative of embryonic prejudice in the white subjects and of self-rejection, psychic damage, and low self-esteem in minority subjects. The fact that a number of studies (Clark and Clark 1947; Fox and Jordan 1973; Gitter *et al.* 1972; Gregor and McPherson 1966*a*; Morland 1962; Vaughan 1964) reveal not only a preference for white stimuli but also a misidentification of racial category when asked the question: 'Which doll looks most like you?' was taken as further evidence of self-hatred in minority group children.

Several important studies, however, have contradicted the above findings. With a sample of seven- and eight-year-old children in Texas (Gregor and McPherson 1966*b*) and four- to eight-year-olds in Omaha, Nebraska (Hraba and Grant 1970), black children preferred black dolls significantly more than white dolls. Banks and Rompf (1973) asked their subjects to evaluate the performance of two players, one black and one white, in a ball-tossing game. They found that although black children showed preference for the white player in rewarding him with more candy, these same subjects when asked to choose an overall winner, chose the black player more often. They conclude that 'no consistent white preference in blacks was found to support an interpretation of global "self-rejection"'.

Kline (1970) asked 15 black and 15 white children to judge whether black and white dolls would achieve their standards and excel in attainments. Prospects for dolls of both colours were highly positive. However, as Banks and Rompf (1973) and Kline (1970) asked different questions from those of Clark and Clark (1947) it is impossible to determine whether these samples were genuinely uncontaminated by racial influences.

Greenwald and Oppenheim (1968) were concerned to use basically the same methodology as in the Clark and Clark (1947) study with a few modifications. They pointed out that the relatively high proportion of self-misidentification among Negro children observed in previous studies (13 per cent in the Clark and Clark 1947 study; 52 per cent in Horowitz 1939, which dropped to 17 per cent when a more reliable test was used; 60 per cent in Goodman 1946; 32 per cent in Morland 1958, and 54 per cent in Morland 1963) may be an artefact created by the stimulus material used in these studies. They presented their subjects with three rather than two skin colours with which to identify—black, white, and mulatto—and found that misidentifications fell to 13 per cent. That is, only 13 per cent of the Negro children chose the white doll in response to the question: 'Which doll looks most like you?' The inclusion of an intermediate (mulatto) alternative reduced Negro children's misidentifications significantly. Furthermore, there did not appear to be any significant difference between white and Negro children's misidentifications. The authors conclude that 'there is nothing unusual about Negro children's misidentification'. Several other studies both in the United States and in Britain confirm these conclusions.

Banks (1976) states that 20 per cent of the 21 studies he considered demonstrated black preference, 10 per cent demonstrated white preference, and 70 per cent showed no preference. Aboud and Skerry (1984) reviewed an additional 16 studies and brought the totals up to date as follows: 27 per cent reported black own-group preference, 16 per cent demonstrated white preference, and 57 per cent showed no consensus on preference. Thus the pattern of identification and preference among ethnic minority children is not as clear-cut as was once assumed. Since the late 1960s a number of studies have failed to find any consistent white preference and/or misidentification.

A number of arguments have been put forward to explain this discrepancy. Banks (1976), for example, states that the responses of black children should not be compared with those of whites but against chance. A re-analysis of the data (see above) showed that when frequencies of doll choices are assessed against chance, 70 per cent of the studies which had been earlier interpreted as demonstrating white preference could now be categorized as falling into the 'non-preference category', non-preference indicating 'no consistent preference' for whites among ethnic minority children.

Other researchers have suggested that the discrepant results may be due to methodological artefacts such as the race of the experimenter (Porter 1971), or contaminating cues, such as gender (Katz and Zalk 1974), or physiognomy of the stimulus material (Gitter and Satow 1969), or even the greater familiarity that both black and white children have with white dolls (Tyson 1985).

Thus, a variety of instruments have been devised in order to tap ethnic attitudes more accurately. Photographs are seen to be better than dolls (Aboud and Skerry 1984) because:

(1) they are more appropriate with children over six years; (2) they allow for variation in the features commonly found in a group of people, whereas dolls do not; and (3) it is easier to include stimulus persons other than blacks and whites and this is very necessary, as shown by the study in which mulatto dolls were included in the stimulus material (Greenwald and Oppenheim 1968).

The Katz–Zalk projective technique (1978) is a more structured adaptation of the Thematic Apperception Test (TAT) in which the subject is provided with a positive or negative behavioural description and then asked which character enacted it. The major limitation of this technique is that the nature of the task is perhaps not disguised enough and may elicit socially acceptable responses rather than personal ethnic attitudes. For example, a child of left-wing parents may have been taught that it is unacceptable to see blacks in a negative light and may therefore choose the white person as enacting the negative behavioural description. It is moot whether this choice is indicative of his/her own personal attitudes. Sociometric choices too have been used, in which children are asked to name their best friends. A problem with this measure, however, is that friendships are influenced not merely by ethnic attitudes but by other factors, such as actual proportions of a particular ethnic group in the classroom or neighbourhood. In order to overcome the forced-choice nature of the dolls tests, Likert-type continuous rating-scale procedures have been used in which like or dislike of each ethnic group was assessed separately (Aboud and Mitchell 1977; Verna 1982). Continuous rating-scale procedures suggest that the discrepancy is one of intensity (Verna 1982), and that own-group choices may be less intensely positive and other-group non-choices may be less intensely negative than forced choices would indicate.

Self-esteem

A popular explanation of the observation that ethnic minority children are no longer showing such a strong preference for the majority group is that the new trend is due to changes in the socio-political climate surrounding ethnic minority groups. The Black Liberation Movement of the 1960s, for example, brought about a gradual but widespread re-evaluation of Negroid physical attributes. Black is indeed beautiful. Proponents of this view (Davey and Mullin 1980, Epstein *et al.* 1976; Hraba and Grant 1970; Milner 1983; Rice *et al.* 1974; Ward and Braun 1972) point out that this reversal is relatively recent and that the development of black consciousness has brought about an increase in self-esteem, which in turn leads to an own-group preference.

What exactly then is the research evidence regarding self-esteem and membership in a minority group? Do ethnic minority individuals suffer lower levels of self-esteem than their majority group counterparts or have recent historical changes actually resulted in higher levels of self-esteem?

Ward and Braun (1972) found that black children who chose the black doll had higher self-concept scores than those who chose the white doll. Young and Bagley (1979) too found that higher levels of self-esteem tend to be associated with more pro-black responses in British West Indian children. Gordon (1963) found blacks to have the highest self-esteem of five groups. McDonald and Gynther's (1965) investigation of 261 black and 211 white high school seniors showed blacks to have higher self-esteem. Large sample studies by Hunt and Hardt (1969), Hunt and Hunt (1975), Powell and Fuller (1973), and Bachman (1970) all showed blacks with higher self-esteem. Studies investigating the proverbial Jewish self-hatred indicate that Jews, too, have somewhat higher self-esteem (Gordon 1963; Anisfield *et al.* 1962; Bachman 1970).

However, several studies do not support the improved self-esteem hypothesis. Branch and Newcombe (1980) found that children of black activist parents made more white doll preferences than children of less activist parents—a finding contrary to the improved self-esteem hypothesis and in line with the damaged self-esteem hypothesis.

Most studies of black self-esteem using well-established scales indicate, however, that there is no difference in self-esteem between blacks and whites (Gaskell and Smith 1981; Louden 1978*a, b*; Porter and Washington 1979; Rosenberg 1965; Williams-Burns 1980). Rosenberg (1965), for example, found 39 per cent of blacks to have high self-esteem compared to 45 per cent of whites: a difference that is not large. Wylie (1978) reviewed 53 publications dealing with the relationship between racial or ethnic status and global or specific self-esteem. Viewing all these studies together, she concluded that there is little research evidence for those who have contended that the derogated, disadvantaged social position of blacks in the United States has resulted in a seriously damaged self-esteem.

Rosenberg (1979), in an inquiry into the assumptions underlying self-esteem and minority status, suggests that most theoretical formulations assuming a relationship between the two rest largely on two concepts:

reflected appraisals and social comparisons. The principle of reflected appraisals assumes that the self-concept is largely built up by adopting the attitudes of others towards the self, and it follows therefore that if others look down on the minority group, it will come to see itself more or less as they do. While accepting that principle, Rosenberg (1979) points out that the conversion of society's attitude towards one's group into the individual's attitude towards the self is possible only if certain assumptions are made. The first is that the individual knows how the majority feels about his/her group (the assumption of awareness); the second is that s/he accepts the societal view of the group (the assumption of agreement); the third is that s/he accepts these views as being applicable to her/himself (the assumption of personal relevance); and fourth is that s/he is critically concerned with majority attitudes (the assumption of significance). Rosenberg presents convincing empirical evidence to show that these conditions must be met if the principle of reflected appraisals is to hold. In other words in those instances in which minority individuals are aware of society's derogatory attitudes towards their group, are in agreement with these views, apply these views personally to themselves, and are critically concerned with the majority attitudes, self-esteem will indeed be low. The fact that self-esteem is not always or even often low in minority individuals indicates that one or more of these criteria have not been met.

The principle of social comparison used by Tajfel in particular holds that minority group members have lower self-esteem because they compare unfavourably with the majority group both in terms of their group membership and in other ways. These unfavourable comparisons, such as low social class position, poor academic performance, or devalued skin colour—themselves often the consequences of prejudice and discrimination—are used by the minority individual as bases for comparison and can only be damaging to the self-esteem. Again, accepting the principle of social comparison as fundamentally sound, Rosenberg (1979) suggests the fact that there is no evidence of a damaged self-esteem among minority group individuals is due to the assumption that blacks are using whites as their comparison group. Rosenberg (1979) believes that black children compare themselves with other blacks, *not* with whites, and that they do so on the basis of the structure of the environment in which they live. Blacks are surrounded predominantly by blacks and hence will be comparing themselves with, and receiving feedback from, other blacks, and thus there is no reason to suppose that their self-esteem should be any different from that of whites. In contextually dissonant situations, i.e. in situations in which the individual's ethnicity or race is different to that of most others in their immediate environment, blacks should indeed suffer a decrement in self-esteem. Rosenberg (1977) verifies this in a study in which he found black pupils in white schools, who, while earning better marks than black pupils in black schools, have a lower level of self-esteem. The reason offered is that blacks in white schools are using whites as their reference group and thereby suffer by comparison.

Appealing though this argument is, viz. that blacks typically use blacks and not whites as their comparison group, it is not entirely convincing. First, a study by Hofman *et al.* (1982) found no differences in self-esteem for young minority Arabs in Israel, when in a contextually consonant situation or in a contextually dissonant situation. Secondly, studies of social comparison processes suggest that the outcome of a deleterious comparison does not always result in a damaged self-esteem. Mann (1963) found, for instance, that although Indians in South Africa suffered by comparison with whites on almost every socio-economic, political dimension, they prided themselves on their superior spirituality.

These studies suggest that low esteem is not an inevitable outcome of social comparison with the majority group, if other dimensions exist or can be created whereby a sense of psychological distinctiveness may be achieved or maintained within the minority.

During childhood, social comparisons *may* be made exclusively with members of one's own racial/ethnic group as Rosenberg (1979) suggests. It would seem, however, that social comparisons with the privileged majority are inescapable in adolescence and adulthood, when occupational choices must be made, political ideologies formed, and sex roles sorted out (Erikson 1959). However, the fact that the minority group is also a significant comparison group, as Rosenberg argues, must be seriously considered. It becomes increasingly obvious that it is the *balance* of the individual's identification with *both* the majority group *and* the minority group that must be measured, in order to understand the different ways of coping with ethnic minority identity.

This review of the literature on self-esteem as related to ethnic identification and preference seems to indicate that psychologists have been searching somewhat in vain for a logical and empirically verifiable connection between minority group membership and its consequences for self-esteem. This may be due to a widespread misreading of Lewin's (1948) original statement on self-hatred. It is possible that Lewin's primary interest was not in *individual* self-hatred or low self-esteem but in the individual's hatred or rejection of the *group* to which s/he belongs. If this is true, then one need not assume an inevitable connection between personal self-esteem and the individual's acceptance or rejection of the minority group to which s/he belongs.

If it is the individual's acceptance or rejection of his/her minority group membership that should be the focus of social psychological attention, then very little research to date has been carried out in this area. A study by Majeed and Ghosh (1982) found that the scheduled caste in India, the lowest in the caste hierarchy, displayed a markedly negative in-group evaluation compared to high caste Hindu and Muslim subjects. However, their personal identity as measured by the same adjective scales did not show a corresponding decrement. Rosenberg (1979) calculated a racial group rejection or attachment score and found virtually no relationship between the black child's rejection of his/her race and global self-esteem. The global self-esteem of those whose attachment to the minority group was relatively weak differs little from that of those with strong attachment to the group. Instead, global self-esteem was much more closely related to pride or shame in certain personal traits (intelligence, appearance) and achievement (school marks) than in aspects of social identity such as race or religion.

Examining closely the concept of group rejection, Rosenberg (1979) suggests there may be three aspects which may be variously related to each other. One of these aspects refers to *lack of pride* in one's group. This dimension was tapped by asking respondents: 'How proud are you of being Negro?' A second aspect of group rejection deals with *introjection*, which refers to the extent to which the group is experienced as an integral and inseparable part of self. This dimension was indexed by the question: 'If someone said something bad about the Negro or coloured race, would you feel almost as if they had said something bad about you?' A third dimension is *importance*, which refers to the rank of ethnicity relative to the individual's hierarchy of values. This was measured by asking respondents: 'Is being Negro very important to you, pretty important, or not very important to you?' Presumably, 'group self-hatred' is a phenomenon which occurs in those individuals who lack pride in their group but who introject strongly, i.e. who experience an attack on the group as an attack on the self. Such individuals should also manifest low levels of self-esteem. On the other hand, the person who lacks group pride *and* introjection, should suffer no injury to self-esteem. Rosenberg (1979) suggests that this is indeed the case: among those who have low group pride, if racial introjection is strong, then 46 per cent have low self-esteem. However, these differences are not statistically significant, as very few children in the sample actually manifested low group pride. Only 33 children out of a sample of more than 1000 black children manifested low group pride and only 11 of these showed high introjection as well as low self-esteem. Hence, little that is conclusive can be said about 'group self-hatred', except that even when the concept is reformulated and refined it does not seem to be as widespread as predicted by theoretical speculations. However, high group pride is almost invariably associated with high introjections: 82 per cent of those who were very proud of their group membership also said they would feel bad if their race was insulted.

Dreidger (1976), in a study on ethnic affirmation and ethnic denial, found little evidence of self-hatred among seven different ethnic groups in Canada. However, as predicted, those who identify strongly with the ethnic group also show the highest ethnic affirmation, while those who are attempting assimilation show the least ethnic affirmation. From an experimental perspective, Wills (1981) hypothesized that people low in self-esteem should engage in self-enhancement strategies by derogating the out-group. This hypothesis is known as downward comparison theory. In testing this theory, Crocker *et al.* (1987) used the minimal group paradigm (see Chapter 8), and found that people who are low in self-esteem

(1) showed the same degree of favouritism of the in-group over the out-group as did people with high self-esteem; and
(2) tend to rate both the in-group *and* the out-group generally more negatively than people who are high in self-esteem.

This is contrary to Will's (1981) theory. Crocker and Luhtanen (1990) then suggested that there are two types of self-esteem, personal self-esteem and collective self-esteem. Collective self-esteem was operationalized as the extent to which individuals 'generally evaluate their social groups positively' (Crocker and Luhtanen 1990, p. 60). They hypothesized that people who are high in collective self-esteem respond to threats to collective self-esteem by derogating out-groups and enhancing the in-group. In their study, both personal and collective self-esteem were measured. They found that subjects high in collective self-esteem used an in-group enhancing strategy when their collective self-esteem was threatened, whereas subjects low in collective self-esteem did not. Analyses based on personal self-esteem did not show this interaction. Thus, according to these authors, the predictions of social identity theory which suggest that people strive to maintain a positive social identity through in-group favouritism may apply only to people high in collective self-esteem, and not to those low in collective self-esteem.

Conclusion

All the theories that have been put forward to explain the psychology of minority group individuals have in some way invoked the concept of self-hate and low self-esteem. In fact, Tajfel (1982, p. 12) unequivocally states that:

There is a good deal of evidence that members of groups which have found themselves for centuries at the bottom of the social pyramid sometimes display the phenomenon of 'self-hate' or self-depreciation. It was one of the merits of the studies on in-group devaluation in children to have provided an accumulation of clear and explicit data on the subject.

This review challenges the unquestioned acceptance of statements such as this. It shows that out-group selection (selection of white stimuli in the doll studies) is not necessarily indicative of in-group devaluation but may be due to artefacts of the experimental situation (gender, physiognomy, familiarity of the stimulus material). It also indicates that when self-esteem is measured more directly, there is little evidence of significantly lower levels of personal self-esteem among minority group members, as would be predicted by these theories. The lack of a relationship between self-esteem and membership of an 'inferior' group cautions against assuming a one-to-one relationship between social identity and self-esteem. The little evidence that exists of minority group individuals who lack pride in their group, indicates that even 'group self-hatred' is not a common phenomenon among minority groups. The paucity of empirical work on minority individuals' acceptance or rejection of their group calls for further research in this area. This review on self-esteem in ethnic minority individuals highlights several important lacunae in the field of ethnic identity research. Most of the work on ethnic identification and preference has been carried out on very young or pre-adolescent children. Little is known about ethnic identity in mid-adolescence when, in multi-racial Western societies at least, peer group influences are greatest and therefore likely to pull the individual in several directions at once. It is therefore important to establish patterns of ethnic identification and preference in adolescents.

For the study of adolescent ethnic identification and preference, it is obvious that the doll choice techniques would be inappropriate. It is necessary to select areas of personal and social identities (for example, preference for ethnic media, or the wearing of ethnic clothes) within which to investigate styles of cultural adaptation.

The above techniques used in studies of ethnic identification and preference suffer one major limitation. The instruments *force* the individual to make a choice between a black or a white doll. However, it is unlikely that ethnic identification and even ethnic preference is a simple either/or matter. The one study (Morland and Hwang 1981) in which children were allowed to respond that they looked like 'neither' doll, indicates that the response of 'neither' with regard to ethnic self-perception turned out to be highly important in relating ethnic identity to its societal setting. For the present research it would be important that any instrument that may be devised to measure styles of cultural adaptation should allow for responses that indicate identification with neither or both groups. Finally, this review indicates that personal self-esteem is not fruitful for the study of ethnic minority identity. However, the individual's evaluation of and emotional contentment with the fact of belonging to an ethnic minority group may bear some investigation.

7.

The salience, centrality, and valence of ethnicity

The salience of ethnicity

In discussing the psychological consequences of ethnic minority group membership, Kurt Lewin (1935) pointed out that the characteristics of a social situation might cause some aspects of the person to become so salient as to determine the individual's responses to the situation. Later, researchers have explicitly manipulated group membership salience and measured the effect on various social behaviours. Festinger (1950a) found that Catholics and Jews tended to vote for the person identified as a member of their group in a situation where the religious affiliation of the candidates was made known to them and they were required to elect a club officer. Lambert et al. (1960) demonstrated an increase in tolerance for pain when membership feelings of Christians versus Jews were made salient. Subsequently, social psychologists have developed an interest in implicitly manipulated group salience.

Shomer and Centers (1970) implicitly manipulated the sex composition of their groups and found that there was a significant difference in male attitudes towards feminism depending on the number of females in the experimental situation. Taylor et al. (1977) found that a black in an otherwise white group, a male in an otherwise female group, or a female in an otherwise male group drew off a disproportionate amount of attention as against a comparable individual in a racially or sexually mixed group.

To describe one of a series of studies (Taylor 1981), subjects listened to a tape-recorded discussion among six men. As each of them spoke, a slide of the person speaking was shown to the subjects. In this way, it was possible to alter the race of the person belonging to each voice on the tape. Thus the racial composition of the group was varied across two conditions. In one condition (the integrated condition), three white and three black males were portrayed as being in discussion with each other. In the second condition (the solo condition), the group consisted of one black and five whites. The one black in the second condition was in fact one of the three blacks of the integrated condition, but the hypothesis was that this context-based distinctiveness would make him much more salient in the solo condition and would therefore influence subjects' perceptions of him. Compared to the integrated condition, the same person in the solo condition was perceived as more active and talkative, as having had more influence on the group discussion, and was rated more extremely on personal characteristics. Also, subjects remembered more of what the black said in the solo condition than when he was part of the integrated group. Thus, the same person was rated differently when his group membership was made salient.

Interest in the salience of various aspects of the self stem from theoretical contributions regarding figure–ground relationships. The perception of a 'figure' is related to the ground upon which it is thrown, and upon the momentary needs within the individual—for a thirsty man a glass of water becomes a salient 'figure' on his ground. After his thirst is quenched, this figure may lose its salience.

Salience has been variously defined. *The Shorter Oxford English Dictionary* (1980, p. 1877) states that salience is

The quality of leaping or springing up, the fact, quality, or condition of projecting beyond the general outline.

Extrapolating from the work on object perception, psychologists have applied the principles governing perceptual salience (brightness, movement, complexity, and novelty) to problems of social psychological concern. For example, Taylor *et al.* (1979) assume that people (stimuli) who are distinctive (novel) in the immediate social environment have an automatic capacity to attract attention, as described earlier. McGuire *et al.* (1978), applying the same principles to self-perception spawned a tradition of research (which we will return to later in this chapter) known as distinctiveness theory, which postulated that the salience of any aspect of the spontaneous self-concept is determined by its relative distinctiveness in the immediate social milieu. Thus, being male in a household where females are in the majority will make one's maleness salient (McGuire *et al.* 1979) or being black in an otherwise white environment will make one's ethnicity salient (McGuire *et al.* 1978). The special failure of this school of research, which has produced results that are at best equivocal, is the lack of attention addressed to the distinction between 'minority group' in the numerical sense and 'minority group' in the socio-cultural sense (Oakes 1987). Minority groups in society are linked by common experiences of social disadvantage. Under conditions of prejudice and discrimination, it is likely that group membership will become more (rather than less) salient as the group becomes numerically preponderant in the immediate social milieu (Krishna 1990; Sapru 1989). As Moscovici and Paicheler (1978) point out, nomic (positive self-image) minorities will assert their particularity and self-definition. This assertiveness distinctiveness is qualitatively different from the numerical distinctiveness that governs perceptual salience.

For an understanding of a salient *group membership* we can draw upon the work of Oakes (1987, p. 118). She says,

By a salient group membership we refer to one which is functioning psychologically, to increase the influence of one's membership in that group on perception and behaviour, and/or the influence of another person's identity as a group member on one's impression of and hence behaviour towards that person.

According to Oakes's (1987) analysis, the salience of group membership is governed by an interaction between the 'accessibility' of a particular social categorization and its 'fit' in the immediate social environment. 'Accessibility' refers to the relative 'readiness' of a social category to become activated, and 'fit' refers to the actual match between the characteristics of the social environment and the category specifications. Thus, I am in a hurry to get to college, my tasks, goals, and purposes make my 'taxi' category particularly 'accessible', and it becomes 'salient' as a taxi rounds the corner ('fits' the needs of the moment). Of all the social categorizations available to me at any given moment (female, lecturer, Indian) only that which is accessible and which fits the perceptual field will become salient.

How salient is ethnicity to the ethnic minority individual? Are ethnic minority individuals always aware of their ethnicity? Or is this awareness dependent upon the 'ground' upon which their ethnicity occurs?

The measurement of the salience of ethnicity has typically involved one of two types of comparison. Some authors have interpreted salience as the importance of a particular category to the individual (Gordon 1968; Kuhn and McPartland 1954). Studies using such an interpretation have, therefore, indexed salience by means of *intra-individual* comparisons of category content. Other authors (Bochner 1976; McGuire *et al.* 1978) emphasize the importance of an *inter-group* interpretation of the meaning of salience. Authors using this type of comparison argue that when ethnic *minority* identity is under investigation, then the salience of ethnicity must surely be studied in reference to other *groups* in society. Using an *inter-group* interpretation of the meaning of salience, these authors have attempted to investigate whether ethnicity is significantly *more* salient to ethnic minority individuals than to their majority group peers. Both these approaches to the salience of ethnicity will be investigated in some detail.

Study 1

Intra-individual comparisons

For the most part, intra-individual comparisons have been concerned with the place occupied by various self-descriptive categories within the individual's total configuration of the self, and not with ethnicity *per se*.

However, data for the present study conducted by the author were collected with the specific purpose of investigating the frequency with which ethnicity is mentioned relative to other categories and attributes of the self. The concern of the study was to create profiles of identity components produced by some open-ended instrument which would afford the individual the freedom to describe him/herself in whatever terms were most appropriate. A modification of the Twenty Statements Test (TST) was used to capture this configuration for three groups, namely, South Asians and Afro-Caribeans, who constitute two important ethnic minority groups in Britain, and a third group, the English, who are the dominant majority group. The term 'South Asian' denotes people who originate from the Indian subcontinent, namely, India, Pakistan, and Bangladesh. It also includes those Indians who have been ousted from countries in East Africa by dictatorial regimes. 'Afro-Caribbean' refers to people of African origin who prior to their entry into Britain have lived for many generations in the West Indies. The term English does not generally include people of Welsh, Scots, or Irish origin. Thus the three terms, South Asian, Afro-Caribbean, and English, are merely terms of convenience used to distinguish the various ethnic groups from each other, and are not necessarily the terms used by people from these groups to describe themselves. In the TST (Kuhn and McPartland 1954), the subject is given 12 minutes to respond to the question 'Who am I?' on a sheet containing 20 numbered blanks. Each subject was given a sheet containing the following instructions:

Please tell us who/what you are by filling the blanks with ten short statements about yourself.

Underneath this statement were 10 numbered spaces each beginning with 'I am . . .'

After the subjects had read this instruction they were then given an example:

For example, one girl said
'I am Catholic;
I am a believer in equality for all people;
I am an SDP supporter;' and so on . . .

Following this, there were 10 numbered spaces, each beginning with 'I am not . . .' This modification of the TST was introduced because there is a growing interest in the formation of a sense of identity in terms of the development of the capacity to think in negative terms. Wallman (1983, p. 5) makes the following statement:

The question 'Who am I?' necessarily requires me to consider who I am not. Like all identity questions, it is a prelude to differentiation which in turn requires the drawing of some kind of line between things like and unlike.

Kitwood (1983, p. 143), referring in particular to South Asian Muslim adolescents in Bradford and Manchester, says:

Through an understanding of who they are not, they have a more assured understanding of who they are.

Following this trend, Apter (1983, p. 80) argues strongly that the development of a sense of identity and the maintenance of this sense of identity in the face of threat is dependent on the capacity to think in a negative way:

We understand what we are to some extent in terms of our rejections, be they rejections of parents, school political party, religious belief or whatever. Knowing oneself is saying 'No' to what one is not.

It was considered worth while, therefore, to explore the negative aspects of identity by asking the subjects to describe themselves in a further 10 statements, beginning with 'I am not . . .' Again, examples of 'I am not' statements were read out by the author to the subjects. These were:

I am not National Front . . .
I am not Irish . . .
I am not always kind to people . . .

After all the instructions were given to the subjects, they were asked to ensure that they had completed all the blanks.

Biographical information concerning the following was collected after the subjects had completed the 'Who am I?' test.

(a) The country of origin—'Which country did your family originally come from?'
(b) Place of birth—'Where were you born?'
(c) Age of entry into Britain (if not born here)—'If you were not born in Britain, how old were you when you came into this country?'
(d) Religion—'What religion does your family observe?'

The participants were adolescents with an average age of 14.6 years. They were of South Asian origin, Afro-Caribbean origin, and English parentage. They were drawn from two schools in Oxford and two schools in Birmingham. Of the total sample only 18 were born outside Britain.

As much of the data generated by this study was used in the studies in the next section on inter-group comparisons the biographical information obtained from the subjects is presented in detail in Appendix 1.

Three sample protocols, one from each ethnic group, are presented below:

A 15-year-old South Asian boy wrote:

I am . . . a student
I am . . . a Hindu
I am . . . a vegetarian
I am . . . envious
I am . . . helpful (but not all that helpful at home)
I am . . . kind
I am . . . smart (in dress)
I am . . . good in science
I am . . . shy
I am . . . ambishious (*sic*)

I am not . . . a Christian though I believe in one God
I am not . . . jelious (*sic*)
I am not . . . good around people
I am not . . . good at present in maths
I am not . . . rich
I am not . . . that interested in books
I am not . . . a child
I am not . . . violent
I am not . . . greedy

A 15½-year-old Afro-Caribbean girl wrote:

I am . . . an Anglican
I am . . . 5 ft 2½ inches tall
I am . . . black
I am . . . Jamaican
I am . . . in the 4th at St Alban's School
I am . . . on a diet
I am . . . short
I am . . . quite pleasant
I am . . . fairly kind

I am not . . . an only child
I am not . . . fat
I am not . . . skinny
I am not . . . unpleasant
I am not . . . tall
I am not . . . short
I am not . . . racialist
I am not . . . very talkative
I am not . . . very good at maths
I am not . . . Asian

A 14-year-old English boy described himself as follows:

I am . . . well looked after
I am . . . healthy
I am . . . English
I am . . . Roger Dawkins
I am . . . averagely behaved
I am . . . one in every friend (*sic*)
I am . . . a supporter of Birmingham City FC
I am . . . a schoolboy
I am . . . stupid sometimes
I am . . . a believer of Mediumism

I am not . . . bad behaved
I am not . . . some stranger, I don't know (*sic*)
I am not . . . rich
I am not . . . poor
I am not . . . a thief
I am not . . . a murderer
I am not . . . tall
I am not . . . small
I am not . . . black
I am not . . . any colour, but white

The richness of such data calls for an extensive coding system to do it justice. Kuhn and McPartland (1954), using a five category scoring system, were able to classify the behaviour of psychiatric patients by coding the respondents' most frequently used types of responses. However, the Kuhn and McPartland system would do irreparable damage to the data through excessive reduction. Gordon (1968) developed a 30 category system, which, although far from ideal for the content analysis at hand, will suffice for the structuring of profiles of identity. Montemayor and Eissen (1977) used Gordon's (1968) categories effectively with five different age-groups in order to trace the development of self-concept from childhood to adolescence. Bond and Cheung (1983) used a combination of Gordon's categories with Kuhn and McPartland's original coding scheme to index the spontaneous self-concept among respondents in Hong Kong, Japan, and the United States. These studies suggest that Gordon's coding scheme is appropriate not only for a wide range of subjects, but also across different cultural backgrounds. Descriptions of these categories, together with examples from both the 'I am not . . .' and 'I am . . .' sections of the data, appear in Appendix 2.

A simple tally was kept for the frequency with which each of the categories was used. This frequency was then converted into a percentage.

Thus, Inter-personal style (category 27) was mentioned 25 times by the 44 South Asians in the sample, thus rendering a value of 56.8 per cent. The Afro-Caribbeans mention Inter-personal style 37 times. As the number of Afro-Caribbeans in the sample was 32, this means that a number of individuals have used this category more than once, yielding a percentage of 115.6 per cent. Inter-personal style was recorded 33 times for the sample of 34 English adolescents, giving rise to a value of 97 per cent. Figures 7.1 and 7.2 represent graphically the data obtained. Figure 7.1 refers to the data obtained in the 'I am . . .' section and Figure 7.2 represents data elicited in the 'I am not . . .' section.

The main self-descriptive categories for Asians in the 'I am . . .' section (Fig. 7.1) were Psychic style (90.9 per cent) and Ideological and belief references (90.9 per cent). This was then followed by Religious categorization (70.6 per cent). The next most frequently used categories were Inter-personal style (56.8 per cent), Competence (54.6 per cent), and Moral worth (52.3 per cent). Age (49.9 per cent) and Sex groups (40.9 per cent) were reasonably prominent. It is interesting that the Race (36.4 per cent) and Nationality (31.8 per cent) categories were not of overriding importance to these South Asian adolescents. In the 'I am not . . .' section (Fig. 7.2), Psychic style (79.5 per cent), Competence (70.5 per cent), and Inter-personal style were the most frequently used categories. Nationality is of considerable importance (47.7 per cent) but Race was hardly mentioned at all (11.4 per cent).

In reviewing the data from the Afro-Caribbean subjects (Fig. 7.1) Physical self (121.9 per cent), Inter-personal style (115.6 per cent), and Psychic style (112.5 per cent) were overwhelmingly significant descriptions of the self, whereas Race (59.4 per cent) and Nationality, (31.3 per cent) were moderately used as a category of self-identity. The 'I am not . . .' data (Fig. 7.2) showed approximately similar trends with Inter-personal style (140.6 per cent), Psychic style (84.4 per cent), Physical self (78.1 per cent), Competence (62.5 per cent), and Moral worth (62.5 per cent) claiming the top five ranks: Race was used only very moderately (34.4 per cent).

In Fig. 7.1, for English adolescents the most frequently used categories were Judgements and tastes (108.8 per cent), Inter-personal style (97 per cent), Competence (70.6 per cent), and Physical self (61.7 per cent). Nationality (38.2 per cent) and Race (26.5 per cent) were also reasonably important to these individuals. In the 'I am not . . .' section (Fig. 7.2), Inter-personal style (126.4 per cent) and Ideological and belief references (76.4 per cent) were the main categories of self-description. Differentiation in terms of Race (20.6 per cent) and Nationality (11.8 per cent) were infrequently used by English adolescents.

Looking across the ethnic groups, it appears that there are many similarities in the way adolescents describe themselves. Like adolescents

Percentage referring to the particular category

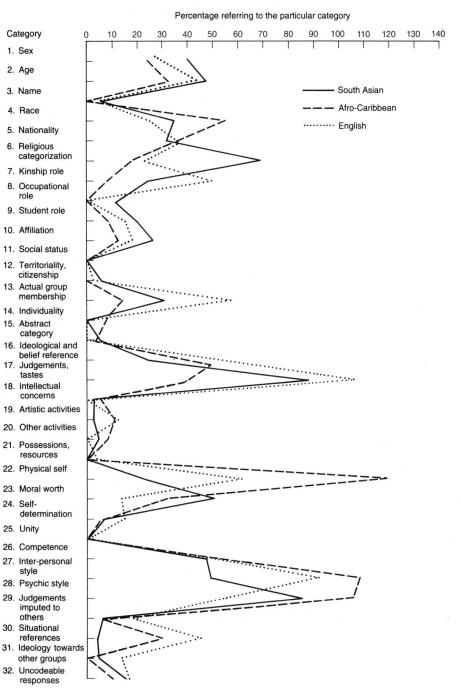

Fig. 7.1.   Study 1: profiles of identity, 'I am . . .'.

Ethnic minority identity

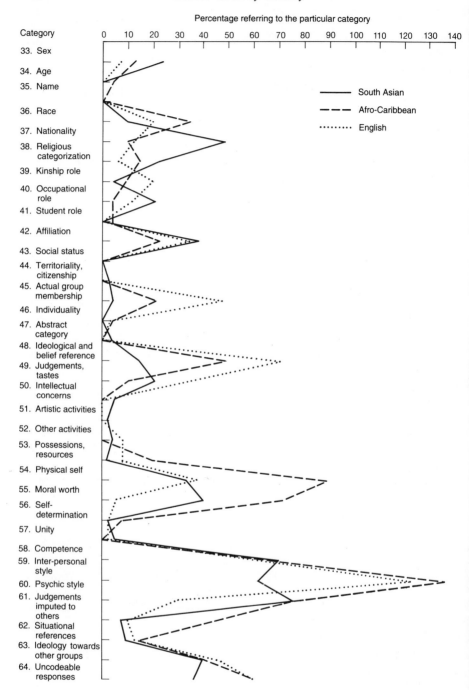

Percentage referring to the particular category

Fig. 7.2. Study 1: profiles of identity, 'I am not . . .'.

all over the world, the issues that claim self-attention are those of how they relate to others, (Inter-personal style), who they are as people (Psychic style), how competent they are to meet the demands of life (Competence), and how good-looking (or bad-looking) they are (Physical self) in relation to others.

These identity profiles seem to suggest two important points:

(1) that there is no 'racial' or particularly 'ethnic' personality profile that is typical of any of the three ethnic groups studied here; and
(2) that although nationality and race are mentioned by some South Asians and some Afro-Caribbeans, ethnicity as measured on these dimensions is by no means of overriding concern to the *whole* South Asian or the *whole* Afro-Caribbean group.

Ethnicity does not seem to be a focal point in the self-conception of these ethnic minority adolescents. What role does ethnicity play, then, in the identity of ethnic minority adolescents? Is it at least more salient to ethnic minority individuals than to majority group individuals? An answer to this question will be sought in the section on inter-group comparisons. It is likely that these various self-descriptions serve different social functions for each of the three groups. It is of importance to establish exactly what functions religion, race, and nationality represent to South Asian and Afro-Caribbean adolescents.

Inter-group comparisons

A number of studies were concerned to investigate the relative salience of ethnicity across various groups in a given society. Trew, (1982*a*) surveyed five independent research studies (Gamble 1982; Mullan 1981; Trew 1981*a, b*, 1982*b*). She expected that in a highly dichotomized society, such as Northern Ireland, where these studies were conducted, religion would be highly salient in the spontaneous self-description of subjects. However, only a small minority of subjects in all these studies referred to their religious denomination. Trew (1982*a*) suggests that two interpretations of these results are possible. First, that in the everyday life of these subjects there are few occasions when they are required to see themselves in terms of the polarized 'Catholic' and 'Protestant' identity, and that religion, therefore, is not really a salient dimension of comparison in Northern Ireland. A second interpretation is that religion may be so salient in Northern Ireland as to be supressed by the majority of subjects. Dove (1974) presented 98 English adolescents with a photograph showing an everyday scene in English schools or streets. In most of the photographs, children or adults of various races and ethnic groups were shown but there were, deliberately, other points of interest apart from their racial content.

The subjects were required to spend five minutes jotting down anything they found of interest in the photographs, and their answers were analysed for mention of race, ethnicity, or nationality (REN), Dove found that Afro-Caribbeans (67 per cent) and Asians (62 per cent) were far more likely to mention REN than were Cypriots (33 per cent) or white English adolescents (45 per cent). Dove (1974) then experimented with a paper-and-pencil technique where 45 subjects were told that he (Dove) would like to remember them should he come back to their school again, and would they write down a few things about themselves that would help him to identify them next time. With this procedure 66 per cent of the Afro-Caribbeans mentioned REN compared to 49 per cent of Asians, 30 per cent of Cypriots, and 8 per cent of white English adolescents.

The observation that ethnicity (whether measured in terms of race, religion, or nationality) is far more salient to ethnic minority groups rather than to majority groups is evident even from a number of doll studies. Greenwald and Oppenheim (1968), for example, found that black (minority) four-year-olds were more accurate than whites in indicating which dolls were black and which were white; also that blacks were more likely to identify themselves as black, than white children were to judge themselves as white. Crooks (1970) found that black pre-school children were more accurate than whites in identifying the ethnicity of dolls. Among adolescents in the United States, Hoetker and Siegel (1970) reported that black high-school children in inter-racial settings were more conscious of race than were the whites. In another US study, McGuire *et al.* (1978) found that 17 per cent of the black and 14 per cent of the Hispanic minorities spontaneously mentioned their ethnicity compared with only 1 per cent of the white majority group.

Study 2

A study carried out in the United Kingdom by the present author replicates these findings (see also Hutnik 1985*b*).

In this study, the subjects were 43 South Asians, 33 Afro-Caribbeans, and 29 English adolescents resident in Britain ($n = 105$): the sample characteristics are described in Appendix 1. It was discovered that the English sample contained five second-generation adolescents of Irish descent. These individuals were left out of this and subsequent studies in order to obtain more homogeneous groups. All the South Asian and Afro-Caribbean participants were included in this study and the ethnic and religious distribution of these subjects is given in Tables 2–5 of Appendix 1.

A problem concerning this study was to decide what constitutes ethnicity. Most studies measure ethnicity in terms of race, nationality, or religion. The previous study (see Figs. 7.1 and 7.2) seems to indicate that race is an important component in the total identity profile for Afro-Caribbeans, religious categorization is important for South Asians, and (although this may be an artefact of the fact that the English sample in Study 1 contained some subjects of Irish descent) nationality for the English. This holds strongly for the 'I am . . .' section and, to a lesser degree, also for the 'I am not . . .' section. This study suggests that the dimensions of ethnicity may be different for different ethnic minority groups. As the protocols obtained by the TST techniques are amenable to the scoring of all three dimensions of ethnicity, any mention of race, nationality, or religion was coded for each individual. Thus, for the 'I am . . .' section each statement was scored for the presence of some reference to:

1. Nationality, for example, 'I am Indian', 'I am English . . .'
2. Religion, for example, 'I am a Hindu', 'I am a Muslim . . .'
3. Race, for example, 'I am black', 'I am white'

For the 'I am not . . .' section, each statement was scored for some indication of psychological differentiation from other groups according to the same three categories:

4. Differentiation from other groups on the basis of nationality, for example, 'I am not English', 'I am not a Paki . . .'
5. Differentiation from other religious groups, for example, 'I am not a Muslim . . .'
6. Differentiation from other groups made on the basis of race, for example, 'I am not white', 'I am not coloured . . .'

Finally, a seventh category was included:

7. Ideological frame of reference to other groups, for example, 'I am not prejudiced', 'I am not racist . . .'

Although this category was not directly relevant to the study of the salience of ethnicity, its implicit reference to other social groups was considered to be of interest.

For each of the above dimensions, subjects from all three ethnic backgrounds were assigned to one of two mutually exclusive groups: those who did refer to that dimension and those who made no mention of that dimension.

The chi-squared (χ^2) test for independent samples was used to analyse the data. This test is a statistic that is used when the data consist of frequencies in discrete categories and the significance of differences

Table 7.1 Study 2: results of the chi-squared (χ^2) contingency text

Variable	Examples	χ^2	Level of significance (p)	South Asians using variable (%)	Afro-Caribbean using variable (%)	English using variable (%)
Nationality	I am Asian, I am English, etc.	6.28	0.05	55.3	28.1	37.9
Religion	I am a Hindu, I am a Catholic, etc.	5.88	0.05	61.7	39.4	37.9
Race	I am black, I am white, etc.	21.01	0.0001	8.5	53.1	20.6
Differentiation from national groups	I am not English, I am not a Paki, etc.	8.68	0.01	36.2	9.4	17.1
Differentiation from religious groups	I am not a Muslim, I am not a Christian, etc.	3.44	n.s	14.9	25.0	8.6
Differentiation from racial groups	I am not white, I am not black, etc.	18.15	0.0001	6.4	30.3	2.8
Ideology towards other groups	I am not prejudiced, I am not racist	0.39	n.s	40.4	46.9	45.7

p, probability; n.s., not significant.

between groups is to be tested. The results of the chi-squared test for independent samples are shown in Table 7.1.

Table 7.1 shows significant chi-squareds for nationality and race in both the 'I am . . .' and the 'I am not . . .' sections. For both ethnic minority groups ethnicity is salient, on different dimensions, however. For the South Asian group nationality and religion are the salient dimensions. Fifty-five per cent of the South Asians mention some aspect of their national identity in the 'I am . . .' section and 36 per cent differentiate themselves from other national groups in the 'I am not . . .' section. In contrast, only 28 per cent of Afro-Caribbeans mention their national origins and only 9 per cent express any psychological differentiation from other groups in terms of nationality. In fact, the majority group, the English participants, show higher national self-consciousness than their Afro-Caribbean counterparts. It is evident that a sense of national identity is not strong among the Afro-Caribbean group. Religion is a second major ethnic marker for the South Asian group. Some 62 per cent of the South Asians assert their ethnic distinctiveness by mentioning their religious affiliation, compared with only 39 per cent of Afro-Caribbeans and 38 per cent of English participants. However, the religious dimension is not significant in the 'I am not . . .' section.

For the Afro-Caribbean group, the race dimension proves extremely significant, with 53 per cent asserting their black identity and 30 per cent dissociating from being white. For the South Asian group, the race dimension is mentioned by only 9 per cent in the 'I am . . .' section (compared with 21 per cent of the English participants), and 6 per cent in the 'I am not . . .' section. One can only speculate on the reasons for this. Perhaps there is some suppression of the 'coloured' identity, either because of negative consequences of being coloured in a white man's country, or because of an unwillingness to associate with other 'coloureds', or both. Whatever the reason, South Asians do not use the 'black' or 'coloured identity to define themselves. Finally, it is interesting that the non-significant chi-squared result on ideology towards other groups points to the fact that all three groups see it as important to be free from prejudice.

From the results it is evident that ethnic consciousness is significantly more salient in each minority group than in the English group, although on different dimensions.

The question now arises: Why are ethnic minority individuals so much more aware of their ethnicity than their majority group counterparts?

One possible explanation is that it is their very membership in an ethnic *minority* group that makes them more conscious of their ethnicity. They suffer the undesirable consequences of being unlike the majority. They share a common culture, a common history, and a common tradition. They are victims of a 'common fate' in that they are recipients of prejudice and discrimination, however subtle. This does not necessarily or always serve to bind them together as a group, but it might serve to make ethnicity more salient to them.

Study 3

It is, of course, possible that South Asians and Afro-Caribbeans are intrinsically more conscious of their ethnicity, whether or not they are in a minority. Study 2 lacked an adequate counterbalancing manipulation in order to prove conclusively that ethnicity is salient *because* of one's ethnic minority group membership. A third study was therefore undertaken to measure the salience of ethnicity in Indian adolescents on the Indian subcontinent where, of course, they are a majority group, and to compare their responses with those of their minority group counterparts in Britain. The hypothesis underlying this study is that ethnicity is more salient in the self-description of individuals when the ethnic group is an ethnic *minority* group than when it is a majority group.

In Study 3 the focus of investigation was narrowed to adolescents of Indian origin. (Afro-Caribbeans are not included in this study because it was not possible to go to the West Indies in order to obtain the necessary data.) Study 2 had revealed that nationality and religion are two salient dimensions of ethnic self-categorization for South Asian adolescents in Britain. Only the nationality dimension of ethnicity is considered in Study 3. It was hypothesized that assertions of national identity will occur more frequently in the self-description of the South Asian adolescents than in those of Indian adolescents, that is, for Indians in Britain nationality is a more salient dimension of the self than for Indians in India because the former belong to an ethnic minority group, with all the disadvantages this entails.

As the TST is an open-ended technique, it is particularly amenable for use in cross-cultural situations. The test and the instructions were therefore translated into Hindi. The protocols of the South Asian adolescents of Study 2 were used to represent the ethnic minority group in Britain.

The choice of subjects on the Indian subcontinent proved difficult. It was decided that it would not be feasible to collect data from each of the countries represented in the South Asian sample, namely, India, Pakistan, Bangladesh, and East Africa. Participants were therefore selected from one country, India, with the expectation that they would be reasonably representative of the other countries as well.

However, having chosen a country, it was then necessary to decide upon the subjects themselves. This was complicated by the fact that the South Asian subjects resident in Britain, although predominantly from the working class, are exposed to the influence of a highly technological society which may significantly alter their self-conceptions. In this dimension, it is likely that they are more comparable with upper or upper middle class Indian adolescents than with those of the Indian working class. However, membership in a particular class category *per se* is also known to affect one's self-description significantly, and it was necessary to compare the South Asian ethnic minority sample with their working class counterparts in India. In order to resolve this paradox, it was decided that two schools would be approached, one a state-run school where the students were predominantly working class and Hindi-speaking (School G), and the second a convent school where the students were predominantly upper middle class and English-speaking (School C).

Data were collected from 32 subjects in School G and 33 subjects in School C. However, 14 protocols had to be eliminated from this sample as they came from Christian and Sikh students. Christians and Sikhs are minority groups in India and are therefore liable to confound the major purpose of this study, namely, to study the salience of ethnicity when the ethnic group is a majority compared to when it is a minority. All the remaining subjects were Hindu. This therefore left 51 subjects from the Indian subcontinent: 26 from School G and 25 from School C, and together with 43 South Asian adolescents, the total number of participants in this study was 94.

A chi-squared analysis was used on the data in a step-wise fashion. First, the South Asian minority subjects were compared with their peers of approximately the same social class (students from School G). They were then compared with their more Westernized, English-speaking peers in School C. Finally, School C and School G were collapsed into a single category and chi-squared comparisons were again made.

The first chi-squared analysis, comparing South Asians in Britain with Indians on the Indian subcontinent who were of similar social class background (School G), was significant at the $p < 0.05$ level ($\chi^2 = 4.08$) on the nationality dimension. Fifty-five per cent of South Asians mention their nationality compared with only 30 per cent of Indians in School G. Results on the 'I am not . . .' section were not significant.

The second chi-squared analysis compared South Asians with English-speaking, more Westernized, middle class adolescents in School C. Here, the chi-squared analysis were significant at the $p < 0.05$ level ($\chi^2 = 6.49$) both in the 'I am . . .' and the 'I am not . . .' sections. Fifty-five per cent of South Asians mentioned their nationality compared to 24 per cent of Indians. In the 'I am not . . .' section 36 per cent of South Asians differentiated themselves from other national groups compared to only 8 per cent of Indians, again a significant difference ($\chi^2 = 5.93$, $p < 0.05$).

The results indicated that there is a significant difference in the frequency with which nationality is mentioned in the 'I am . . .' section, with South Asians using this dimension more frequently than their Indian counterparts. Little explanation is forthcoming for the unexpected non-significant difference found in the first chi-squared analysis in the frequency of differentiation from other national groups. It was observed that working class Indian adolescents tended to say 'I am not American', 'I am not British', 'I am not Japanese' more frequently than they referred to other national groups. A tentative explanation for this might be that the Americans, British, and Japanese symbolize an affluent life-style which these adolescents do not have, but may aspire to have, or may want to reject. This explanation lies very much in the realm of speculation and must not therefore be unequivocally accepted.

The results also appeared to indicate that the frequency with which nationality group is mentioned does not seem to be affected by the class background of the Indian adolescents. Except in the category of differentiation from other national groups, the pattern of the chi-squared is similar in both cases.

As the overall pattern of the chi-squared analysis was so similar, the students in School G and School C were collapsed into a single category in order to increase the power of the analysis by increasing the number in the sample. Again, the pattern was similar. The chi-squared analyses on both the 'I am . . .' and the 'I am not . . .' sections were significant, the first at the $p < 0.01$ level ($\chi^2 = 7.79$) and the latter at the $p < 0.05$ level ($\chi^2 = 4.57$). Fifty-five per cent of South Asians mentioned their nationality as compared to only 28 per cent of Indians in the 'I am . . .' section. Their 'I am not . . .' protocols showed that 36 per cent of South Asians differentiated themselves from other groups compared to only 18 per cent of Indians.

Next, it was necessary to compare these Indian adolescents (resident in India) with their English peers to check for differences. According to the argument presented earlier, there should have been no significant differences in the frequency with which nationality is mentioned by Indian and English adolescents because in the context in which they were tested they were both majority groups. This chi-squared analysis yielded non-significant results in both the 'I am . . .' and the 'I am not . . .' sections. Twenty-eight per cent of Indians ($n = 51$) resident in India mentioned their nationality compared with 38 per cent of English adolescents ($n = 29$). In the 'I am not . . .' section, 17 per cent of Indians and 17 per cent of English participants differentiated themselves from other national groups.

These results provide confirmation of the hypothesis. Nationality shows trends in the expected direction: a greater proportion of South Asians use nationality in their descriptions of themselves than do Indian adolescents. Also, Indian adolescents, when they are a majority, do not mention nationality any more frequently than do English adolescents. From Study 2, a significantly greater proportion of South Asian adolescents use nationality in their self-description than do Afro-Caribbean or English adolescents. This seems to indicate that nationality is salient to South Asian adolescents in Britain *because* of their ethnic minority group membership. That is, nationality is more salient in the self-description of individuals when the ethnic group is an ethnic *minority* group than when it is a majority group.

Although this study attempted to find a counterbalanced situation where the ethnic group is in one case a minority group and in the second a majority group, this is a more complicated matter than it first appears. In order to achieve a better counterbalance, it is necessary, ideally, to compare Hindus in Britain, where they are *both* a religious and a national minority, with Hindus in India, where they are a majority in both dimensions.

The South Asian sample contained seven Hindus, two of whom were from East Africa, whereas the remaining five originated from India. Thus, only the data for the five Hindus of Indian origin could be used. It was, therefore, not feasible to make such a counterbalancing check. There was no a priori reason to believe that the results of such a check would run contrary to expectations.

We have seen that South Asian adolescents in Britain are more aware of their ethnicity than are English or Indian adolescents, and this is probably because they constitute an ethnic minority group within the wider British society.

Study 4

When investigating the psychological mechanism underlying the salience of ethnicity among ethnic minority individuals McGuire *et al.* (1978, 1979) suggested that salience is operationalized in terms of one's distinctiveness in the immediate social environment.

Thus, as mentioned earlier, according to the distinctiveness hypothesis, boys who come from households where females are in the majority will spontaneously refer to their maleness more often than boys who come from households with male majorities. The hypothesis implies that aspects of the self become salient in so far as those aspects are different from distinctive features of the social milieu. By altering the social milieu, so that a different characteristic becomes distinctive, it is possible to alter the individual's self-concept in predictable ways. Thus, a black woman in a group of white women will think of herself as black; should she move into a group of black men her blackness will lose salience and she will become more conscious of being a woman.

The distinctiveness hypothesis is not unlike the theory of contextual dissonance put forward by Rosenberg (1979, p. 99):

That the social similarity or dissimilarity of the individual to those around him may affect his experience and in consequence his self-concept is obvious. For example, the experience of being black when mostly surrounded by blacks is plainly different from being a black in a white environment. Similarly, the meaning of being Jewish in a gentile neighbourhood is not the same as being Jewish in Jewish neighbourhood. The difference reflects the consonance or dissonance of the environment for the individual.

Rosenberg's consonance/dissonance (ethnically homogeneous/ethnically heterogeneous) hypothesis suggests that self-esteem is higher in consonant situations than in dissonant situations.

There is evidence that the distinctiveness hypothesis holds for certain dimensions of self-conception (although (Oakes 1987) suggests that alternative explanations are available to account for the observed effects). For gender, for example, there are data to support the hypothesis that one's sex becomes salient as a function of one's distinctiveness in the environment (McGuire *et al.* 1979): even for transient *ad hoc* groups this holds true (Cota and Dion 1986). Gerard and Hoyt (1974) experimentally manipulated the distinctiveness of social categorization and measured attitudes towards in-group members. They found that the smaller the in-group, the more favourable were evaluations of in-group members relative to out-group members.

However, with regard to ethnicity, there is some important disconforming evidence. Rosenberg (1979) studied the effects of a consonant (ethnically homogeneous) or a dissonant (ethnically heterogeneous) situation on the self-esteem of blacks. Although he concluded that self-esteem is lower for blacks in a dissonant situation, the evidence he presented is somewhat at variance with his conclusion (see Rosenberg 1979, pp. 102–3). Although the percentage of blacks with *low* self-esteem (25 per cent) is consistently higher in the dissonant situation compared with the consonant situation (19 per cent), and the percentage of blacks with *high* self-esteem (37 per cent) is consistently lower in the dissonant situation compared with the consonant situation (43 per cent), it is not clear whether these differences are significant—it would seem unlikely that they are. Also, and perhaps more importantly, Rosenberg is unable to explain why more than 75 per cent of his black sample in the dissonant situation have high or medium self-esteem compared with only 23 per cent who have low self-esteem in the same situation. It would seem that the conclusion that 'the results show that self-esteem is lower in the dissonant context' (Rosenberg 1979, p. 102) needs several major qualifications.

McGuire's own study (McGuire *et al.* 1978) disconfirms the hypothesis, that is, when blacks comprised less than 10 per cent of the students in their school (and were therefore more 'distinctive') only 5 per cent mentioned their ethnicity, but when they constituted 10 per cent of the student population, 26 per cent mentioned their ethnicity. A study conducted by the author showed results in a similar vein (Hutnik 1985a). Two schools in Birmingham, England, were selected. In School S the South Asians were a 12 per cent minority at fifth-form level. In School H, the South Asians constituted 66 per cent of the student population at fifth-form level. The sample characteristics of the adolescents who participated in this study are given in Appendix 3. Again, the TST was used and contextual variations in the salience of ethnicity were investigated.

A chi-squared analysis was computed between South Asian students of School H, where they were a numerical majority, and South Asian students of School S, where they constituted a numerical minority in the immediate social milieu. The chi-squared analysis was found to be significant at the $p < 0.01$ level ($\chi^2 = 6.79$). Sixty per cent of the South Asians in School H mention their national origins compared with only 30 per cent of South Asians in School S. That is, as the ethnic group becomes numerically dominant in the immediate social setting, ethnicity becomes more rather than less salient in the spontaneous self-concept. The South Asian students in School S were few and far between and were unlikely, therefore, to be able to or even to want to create a feeling of ethnic distinctiveness, that is, they lacked the 'critical mass' that makes ethnicity salient. One alternative explanation could be that for the students of School S, ethnicity is so extremely distinctive as to be suppressed. We have no current evidence to substantiate this explanation. It appears reasonable to conclude that when South Asians are in a numerical majority in the immediate social setting, ethnicity is more salient than when they are in a numerical minority. This finding is a direct contradiction to the distinctiveness hypothesis: it would seem that as the ethnic minority group becomes less distinctive in the immediate social setting, ethnicity becomes a *more* salient component of identity.

McGuire *et al.* (1978) explain their contradictory finding as being due to superseding sociological factors, such as the 'black consciousness' movement. This must have resulted in consciousness-raising interventions among black students which have made ethnicity salient but only if there is a 'critical mass' in excess of 10 per cent of black students in the school environment.

It is the tendency to overlook important sociological factors that has caused some social psychologists to make some considerable errors. One failing common to many studies on minority groups is the implicit assumption that minority groups are defined merely as numerical minorities. Thus, Moscovici and Paicheler (1978) divided their group of subjects into a majority group and a minority group (ostensibly according to their preference for one of two artists) but actually on the basis of an arbitrary numerical manipulation and expected the minority to assert its particularity and its distinctiveness simply because it was in the minority (Moscovici and Paicheler 1978, experiment 1). That this does not occur to any substantial degree should not be surprising, as the minority group in question was not bound together by anything but the fact that their preference for a particular artist was not a widespread preference.

The Lemaine *et al.* (1978) experiment possibly indicates a more accurate understanding of the salience of minority group membership even though this was not the original purpose of their experiment. Here, the subjects were engaged in a hut-building competition. One group of boys was deliberately put at a disadvantage by Lemaine *et al.* by being given inadequate tools and materials for the task. (In this respect, they can be considered to be a minority group in that while they were not numerically inferior they were put under conditions of social disadvantage.) The disadvantaged group concentrated on creating a beautiful garden around their badly built hut and later asserted to the judges that the garden around the hut was at least as important as the hut itself. Being disadvantaged in one dimension, they asserted their equality with the more advantaged group by creating a dimension where they could achieve psychological distinctiveness.

When dealing with the salience of ethnicity in ethnic minority groups in society at large, it should not be forgotten that minorities are held together at least as much by experiences of common disadvantage as by the fact that they may constitute a numerical minority, and that it is this experience of disadvantage that will make ethnicity salient in the self-concept. It is therefore necessary to modify McGuire's distinctiveness postulate, although its essence still remains: ethnicity is salient to the extent that one's group is distinctive in the social environment, but distinctiveness cannot be reduced to a ratio of the number of ethnic minority individuals to majority group individuals in the immediate social setting. The relationship is probably much more complex.

It is now suggested that a sense of ethnic distinctiveness is not a function of mere numerical scarcity in the immediate social milieu. When considering ethnic groups, a sense of distinctiveness is defined in apposition to the majority group within the larger society, and is defined by a culture, history, or tradition that is held in common with other members of the ethnic minority group. This in effect means that it is more rather than less likely that ethnicity will be salient when the ethnic minority group exists as a substantial proportion in the immediate social situation. Should members of the ethnic minority group become too few, opportunities for experiencing a sense of solidarity with like individuals also become fewer, and ethnicity will be less salient unless one's ethnicity is the target of constant prejudice and discrimination.

The centrality and valence of ethnicity

Notions of the centrality and valence of ethnicity originate from Lewin's (1948) conceptualizations. According to Lewin, the person can be conceptualized as comprising a perceptual–motor region and an inner-personal region. The inner-personal region is further differentiated into central cells and peripheral cells.

If ethnic minority identity is a sub-identity of the total configuration of identity components, then centrality refers to the importance of the sub-identity for the person and valence has to do with the attractiveness of that sub-identity for the person. Individuals will invest cognitive effort to make the more central sub-identity appear more attractive. According to Lewin's theory, one exception to this is the self-hatred of the Jews, where high centrality should be combined with negative valence. However, a study conducted in Israel indicates that the national and civic sub-identities of most Jewish Israelis, for example, have positive valence, much central-ity, and considerable consonance (Hofman 1983), whereas those of Arabs tend to differ in valence and centrality and are therefore often quite dissonant (Hofman and Rouhana 1976). It seems that there is little evidence for Lewin's expectation of self-hatred among Jews. However, one possible explanation for Hofman's (1983) findings is that his study tapped a situation in which Jews are in the majority; the Arab minority in his sample manifest differences in centrality, valence, and consonance. The fact of being an ethnic minority group within a dominant majority may be crucial for the manifestation of self-hatred.

Apart from the above study, very little work has been done to assess the centrality and valence of ethnic minority identity to the individual. A further study was therefore undertaken by the author.

Study 5

The purpose of this study was twofold. First, it sought to establish how central or 'close to the core' of identity ethnicity is to ethnic minority individuals. Secondly, it attempted to establish whether ethnicity carries a positive or a negative valence to ethnic minority individuals, thereby exploring whether the concept of self-hatred has credence.

Some authors (Bochner 1976; Kuhn and McPartland 1954) equate salience with centrality, and expect, therefore, that the hierarchial order in which a response is given to the TST reflects its relative importance (or centrality) to the individual. Using this criterion, the first response to emerge is interpreted to be the most important self-description category for that individual. The stance taken in Study 5 was that salience is *not* equivalent to centrality; that social identity elements may be important to the individual even though s/he may give them little conscious thought and that often the most 'central' aspects of the self are precisely those which lie deeper and therefore occur later rather than earlier in the individual's self-descriptions.

Thus, the primary concern of Study 5 was to establish the relative centrality of ethnicity in the total configuration of identity components. It was therefore necessary to find an adequate index of centrality. Hierarchial order of occurrence, although used by previous researchers, was seen to be somewhat ambiguous for reasons just mentioned. It is possible, nevertheless, to ask the subjects to choose, from their 10 self-descriptions, five statements that best describe who they are as a person in order to tap the five most central components and then to get them to rank these five central components in order of importance. This procedure should then facilitate the creation of a profile of the most central components of personal and social identity. By comparing the self-assigned rank of each central component with its corresponding position in the hierarchy of responses, it will be possible to shed some light on the debate as to whether the most central components occur later rather than earlier in the order of the individual's self-descriptions.

The concept of valence as used in this study originated with Lewin (1948) and is pivotal to the understanding of ethnic minority identity. According to Lewin, a region of positive valence can create a vector of sufficient strength to propel the individual in the direction of that region. A region of negative valence will propel the individual in the opposite direction. Self-hatred in the light of this discussion can then be operation-alized as a region of high centrality and negative valence: for example, an adolescent who sees herself as fat and rates this as negative may be said to have a certain level of self-hatred for her physical self. The ethnic minority individual whose ethnicity is both highly salient and central but also carries a strong negative evaluation to him/her can be said to manifest self-hatred. Conversely, the individual who manifests high centrality *and* positive valence with regard to his/her ethnic background may be said to manifest a high level of identification of self with the ethnic minority group. Thus, a 'crude' measure of valence may be obtained by requesting subjects to rate the five most central components of their identity as positive or negative qualities of the self.

As Study 4 has shown that the salience of ethnicity is influenced by the context, whether consonant or dissonant, in which it occurs, it is necessary to also check for this effect on centrality. Presumably, ethnicity will be central due to factors that lie deeper than those found in the immediate situation, and therefore the context is not expected to exert any apprecia-ble effect on this concept.

This study was therefore geared towards establishing the relative cen-trality of ethnicity to ethnic minority individuals: the hypothesis was that although ethnicity may be salient to a relatively large proportion of ethnic minority individuals, it is *not* always central. Secondly, it aimed to establish the valence of ethnicity to ethnic minority individuals and thereby to investigate how widespread the phenomenon of self-hatred, as defined above, is. In the process of these investigations, it also sought to discover whether the most central components of identity occur early or late in the TST protocol. Finally, it explored the effects of consonant and dissonant contexts on the centrality of ethnicity.

In order to measure the centrality and valence of ethnicity, a few further modifications were made to the TST. The following instructions were added to the end of each sheet.

Now go back to the 'I am . . .' statements and put a tick (√) against the 5 statements which best describe who you are as a person. Now rank these in order of importance with the most important getting a rank of 1 and the least important getting a rank of 5. Do you see these aspects of yourself as good qualities that add to who you are, or bad qualities that detract from who you are? If they are good qualities put a + sign, and if they are bad qualities put a − sign in the given column. Then do the same for the 'I am not . . .' statements.

Three columns were drawn along the left-hand side of each sheet. The first was headed by a tick mark (√), the second by 'Rank', and the third by a positive and a negative sign(+/−).

The protocols obtained for Study 4 were used for this study. The sample characteristics of the 70 subjects obtained are given in Appendix 3. Initially, the data from Schools S and H were collapsed into a single sample. When investigating the effects of consonance and dissonance on centrality, data from the two schools were separated.

The scoring procedure was as follows. The 'I am . . .' section was dealt with first. The five components rated by the subjects as being most central to their identity were coded according to the 32 categories described in Study 1 (Gordon 1968). The rank assigned by the subjects to each of these components was then noted. Next, the rank assessed by the hierarchical order of occurrence in the protocol was noted. For example, the statement 'I am friendly' may have been given a rank of 2 by the subject but might have occurred seventh on the list of 10 'I am . . .' statements. This statement would first be categorized under Inter-personal style; it would have an assigned rank of 2 and a hierarchical rank of 7. The same scoring procedure was used for the statements in the 'I am not . . .' section. The statistical procedures used in this study were straightforward.

A. Centrality was assessed by computing the mean assigned and the mean hierarchical rank for each content category (see Fig. 7.3 and Fig. 7.4). The association between assigned and hierarchical ranks was investigated by means of Pearson's Product Moment Correlation.
B. Frequency counts were kept to assess salience versus centrality and valence.
C. Chi-squared analyses were computed to explore possible effects of consonant and dissonant contexts.

A. *The relative centrality of ethnicity*

Centrality was assessed by calculating the mean assigned rank and the mean hierarchical rank of each content category (see Figs. 7.3 and 7.4).

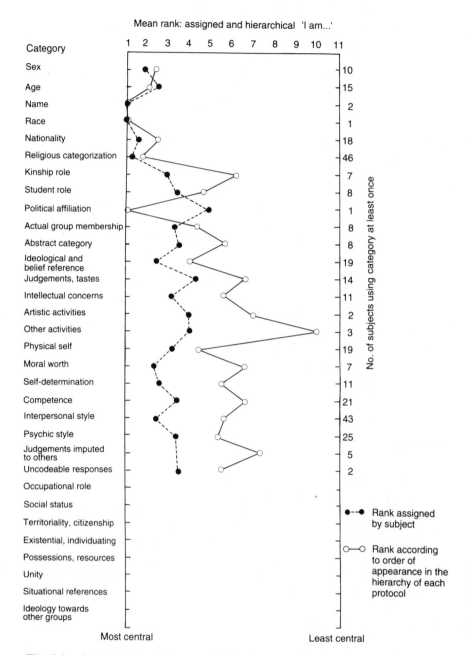

Fig. 7.3. Study 5: the relative centrality of personal and social identity components, 'I am . . .'.

Mean rank: assigned and hierarchical 'I am not...'

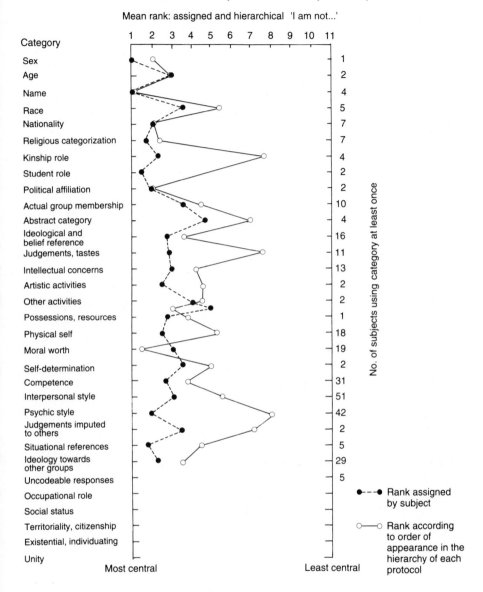

Fig. 7.4. Study 5: the relative centrality of personal and social identity components, 'I am not . . .'.

As the subjects were required to select the five most central identity components, the number of subjects using each category differed widely. In the 'I am . . .' section, the most frequently chosen categories were, in descending order, Religious categorization (46), Inter-personal style (43),

Psychic style (25), Competence (21), Abstract category (19), Other activities (19), Nationality (18), Age (15), Ideological and belief references (14). In the 'I am not . . .' section, they were: Inter-personal style (51), Psychic style (42), Competence (31), Ideology towards other groups (29), Moral worth (19), Physical self (18), Ideological belief reference (16). Several categories in both the 'I am . . .' and the 'I am not . . .' sections were not chosen by any of the subjects and these too were of interest. Although they differed slightly in each of the sections the categories were: Occupational role, Social status, Territoriality, Existential individuating, and Unity.

However, the frequency with which each category was used was not a sufficient indication of the degree of centrality; it simply described the most common categories chosen as being central. The degree of centrality is more readily apparent in Figs. 7.3 and 7.4. It is obvious that Nationality and Religion both had a very high degree of centrality to those who had chosen to use these categories. In the 'I am . . .' section, Fig. 7.3, the mean assigned rank for Nationality was 1.89 and the mean hierarchical rank was 2.55. In the 'I am not . . .' section, it was 2.0 for both the assigned and hierarchical rank. The data indicated that, for the 18 subjects who chose to use this category, Nationality was a very central self-defining concept. So too Religion, with an assigned rank of 1.37 and a hierarchical rank of 1.91 in the 'I am . . .' section. It is difficult to draw any definitive conclusions about the Race variable. To the one subject who used this category in the 'I am . . .' section it was *the* most central category, receiving an assigned rank *and* a hierarchical rank of 1.0. In the 'I am not . . .' section again only a very few subjects used the Race category ($n = 5$), and both the mean assigned rank (3.6) and the mean hierarchical rank (5.6) were relatively less central than other categories. Other categories of high centrality and relatively high frequency of use in the 'I am . . .' section were Moral worth, Inter-personal style, Ideological and belief references, and Age (mean assigned ranks ranged from 2.29 to 2.58), but these were substantially less central than Nationality and Religion. In the 'I am not . . .' section, categories of high centrality and high frequency of use were Ideology towards other groups (I am not prejudiced, I am not racist, etc.), Moral worth, Physical self, Ideological belief reference (mean assigned ranks ranged from 1.97 to 2.81), and again these were generally less central than Nationality and Religion. Thus, it would be valid to conclude that the two major dimensions of ethnicity, namely, Nationality and Religion, were highly central to those who used these categories.

Figures 7.3 and 7.4 show consistent differences between the assigned ranks and the hierarchical ranks: the statements that are assigned greater centrality consistently appear later rather than earlier in the hierarchical order of the responses. For example, the kinship role is assigned a rank of

3.0 but appears at a mean hierarchical position of 6.29 in the order of occurrence on the protocol. It is well documented (Khan 1979*a,b*; Kitwood 1983) that the family occupies a central role in the identities of people of South Asian origin. It would therefore be more valid to see the assigned rank rather than the hierarchical rank as a more accurate index of centrality. The difference, namely that the hierarchical rank is greater than the assigned rank, is shown not merely in the kinship category, but in 20 out of the 24 categories that are used by the subjects in the 'I am . . .' section.

The direction is reversed for Age ($n = 15$) where the mean hierarchical rank is less than the mean assigned rank, and Political affiliation ($n = 1$). For the Name ($n = 2$) and Race ($n = 1$) categories both the assigned and hierarchical ranks are the same. In the 'I am not . . .' section, 21 out of the 27 categories are in the expected direction, with the assigned ranks being assessed by the subjects as being more central than their corresponding position on the hierarchy of responses would indicate. This finding is in contradiction to Kuhn and McPartland's (1954) assertion that the earlier a reference comes in the 'Who am I?' protocol, the greater its importance (or centrality). Figures 7.3 and 7.4 in conjunction suggest that the most central aspects of the self are less immediately available and will therefore occur later rather than earlier in the protocol. Although this is true for most of the data, it should be noted, however, that the difference between the assigned rank and the hierarchical rank is not appreciable for the Nationality dimension and the Religious categorization, although it is in the expected direction.

Pearson's Product Moment Correlations were computed for the Nationality and Religious dimensions of ethnicity to investigate the apparent association between assigned and hierarchical ranks in these two dimensions. The correlations in the 'I am . . .' section showed only very moderate levels of association between assigned and hierarchical ranks. In the Nationality dimension, $r = 0.21$ ($n = 33$, $p < 0.23$), and in the dimension of Religion, $r = 0.22$ ($n = 56$, $p < 0.11$). The 'I am not . . .' protocols showed similar correlational trends. Therefore, these also disconfirm Kuhn and McPartland's suggestion that the hierarchical position of a response is an accurate index of how important that response is to the subject.

B. The relationship between the salience and centrality of ethnicity

If salience is defined in terms of the appearance (or non-appearance) of a particular content category in each protocol, and centrality as the five most important identity components chosen by the individual as most descriptive of him/herself, then nationality is both salient and central for

18 individuals in the 'I am . . .' section and for 7 individuals in the 'I am not . . .' section.

However, this group of 18 individuals for whom nationality is both salient *and* central constitutes only a small proportion (a) of the total sample, and (b) of those for whom ethnicity is salient but *not* necessarily central. Thus, of the total of 70 individuals in Study 5, only 25.7 per cent mentioned their ethnicity (nationality) *and* chose it as a central component of their identity. For a considerably greater number ethnicity was salient but *not* central, that is, national origins were mentioned in the 'I am . . .' protocol far more often than they were chosen as central. With reference to the results of Study 4, 30 per cent (9 individuals) of School S and 60 per cent (24 individuals) of School H mention their nationality. As this study combined the data of both schools, a total of 33 individuals indicated that their ethnicity was salient to them. This means that of the sample for whom ethnicity was salient ($n = 33$), for only 54.5 per cent ($n = 18$) was ethnicity also central to their identity. For 45.5 per cent ($n = (33 - 18) = 15$) ethnicity was salient but not central. The proportion was roughly similar for the nationality dimension in the 'I am not . . .' section: for only 7 out of a total of 13 individuals (53.84 per cent) was ethnicity both salient and central. For the remaining proportion (46.15 per cent), ethnicity was salient but not central. Thus, it would be too hasty a conclusion to assume the direct equivalence of salience and centrality to the nationality dimension of ethnicity.

In the religious dimension, however, there does appear to be greater concordance. In the 'I am . . .' section, a total of 56 individuals mentioned their religious affiliation and 46 of these (82.14 per cent) also chose this component as being central to their identity. The picture was not as clear in the 'I am not . . .' section: for only 35 per cent (7/20) is religion both salient and central.

It was also seen as being important to explore the valence (or value) of ethnicity in order to investigate whether the theories that expect minority individuals to manifest substantial levels of self-hatred have any basis in empirical data. Self-hatred was operationalized as an evaluation of the ethnic group as being highly salient and central, but carrying a negative valence to the ethnic minority individual. The data were unambiguous: not a single individual who mentioned ethnicity in his/her self-description and then chose it as one of the central five components of identity, evaluated it as negative, either on the Nationality dimension or the Religious categorization in the 'I am . . .' section. That is, there was no evidence of self-hatred among ethnic minority individuals as was expected, by all the theorists reviewed in Part 1. All the individuals (100 per cent) who saw their ethnicity as central to their identity also rated it as being positive. In the 'I am not . . .' section, there was only one exception to this otherwise clear pattern. One subject described herself as being 'not

English' and rated this as negative. This may be seen as a desire to belong to the English majority. It may also be a mistake in the use of the double negative. The others who also saw themselves as being 'not English' either did not see this as central to who they were not ($n = 5$) and therefore were not required to rate this component, or if they did see it as central, they rated this as positive ($n = 2$). Thus, the results of Study 5 do not support the idea that ethnic minority individuals are burdened with feelings of self-hatred. It may be, however, that the instructions given to the subjects did not adequately tap this dimension. It will be recalled that the subjects had to choose from their five most central identity components 'bad qualities that detract from who you are'. However, a review of the data (not presented here) indicates that these instructions were effective for many other dimensions, such as physical self, inter-personal style, and psychic style.

This study has operationalized self-hatred as an ethnicity that is salient with high centrality but carrying a negative valence. If, however, self-hatred were merely operationalized as a salient ethnicity which is also evaluated negatively (rather than a salient *and* central ethnicity which is evaluated negatively, as in the present study), the picture *might* have been somewhat different.

Unfortunately, the instructions required the subjects first to choose and then to evaluate the five most central components of their identity. It was, therefore, regrettably not feasible to check the latter possibility from the obtained data set. This issue may be investigated in future simply by asking the subjects first to evaluate all 10 statements in each section as positive or negative and only then to choose the five most central components.

C. Possible effects of consonant and dissonant contexts

Finally the question arises as to whether a consonant context affects the centrality of ethnicity in the way that it seems to affect its salience. The data were therefore separated out again into samples: School S, where South Asians were a numerical minority, and School H, where they were a numerical majority. A chi-squared analysis was computed by calculating the number of individuals in each context who rated ethnicity not only as salient but as one of the five most central components of their identity and comparing these individuals with the remainder of the total sample in each context. The chi-squared analysis was not significant: 23 per cent of South Asians in School S compared to 30 per cent of South Asians in School H, mentioned their nationality. Thus it seems that although the immediate social situation has an effect on the salience of ethnicity (Study 4) the consonance or dissonance of the context does not affect the centrality of ethnicity for ethnic minority individuals.

Study 5: Summary

Ethnicity (nationality) was seen as being a salient and central identity
component by about a quarter of the total sample. Of the sample for
whom ethnicity is salient, in that it is mentioned in the self-description of
these individuals, 46 did not rate ethnicity as a central component of their
identity. The hypothesis that although ethnicity may be salient to a
relatively large proportion of the sample, it is not always central, has been
confirmed.

With regard to valence, there was no evidence of self-hatred as
operationalized in this study among these second generation South Asian
adolescents. On the contrary, those individuals who rated ethnicity as
central to their sense of identity also rated this as positive.

It was also established that the most central identity components occur
later rather than earlier in the hierarchy of responses. This finding
disconfirms Kuhn and McPartland's (1954) hypothesis that there is a direct
association between centrality and hierarchical position, and also casts
some doubt on Bochner's (1976) studies. In fact, the correlation of
coefficients showed very little association at all. And finally, it was seen
that context has little effect on the centrality of ethnicity to ethnic minority
individuals.

Conclusion

What then can be deduced from this review of the research regarding the
salience, centrality, and valence of ethnicity?

Studies on intra-individual comparisons suggest that ethnicity is not a
very salient component relative to other components of identity, such as
Psychic style and Inter-personal style. It must be remembered, however,
that the subjects used in these studies were in adolescence, when the
personal identity crisis (Erikson 1958) is at the forefront of the individual's
concern. It may well be that ethnicity becomes more salient on the intra-
individual dimension in young adulthood, when the individual is required
to make choices regarding his/her political affiliations, or is confronted
with serious discrimination when making occupational choices.

On the inter-group dimension, it would seem that ethnicity is significantly more salient to ethnic minority individuals than to their majority
group counterparts. This is true *because* of their membership in an ethnic
minority group: when the ethnic group is a majority group, for example
Indians resident in India, ethnicity is not particularly salient to its
members. Nor is the salience of ethnicity a function of one's numerical
distinctiveness in the environment. In fact, it would seem that the group
must exist in sufficient numbers in the immediate social setting for ethnicity

to become a salient component of the self-concept. Further research is required to determine when ethnicity crosses the threshold of salience.

Finally, ethnicity, while being salient to a considerable proportion of the ethnic minority group, is salient *and* central to only a small proportion of the group as a whole. It would seem that one may be aware of one's ethnicity without its becoming an all-consuming preoccupation, or even a focal point of one's identity. There is also little or no evidence for self-hatred, if self-hatred is defined as a salient and central ethnicity that carries a negative valence. It may be that an instrument sensitive enough to pick up feelings of shame or denial is yet to be devised. However, from the studies reported here, it would seem that the proverbial self-hatred, which forms the launching-pad of so many theories of ethnic minority identity, is slow to surface in empirical research.

8.

Styles of cultural adaptation

Although inter-cultural exchanges are by no means a new phenomenon, the increasing ease with which people are able to travel across cultural boundaries has made cross-cultural contact the subject of much debate. Early models describing the experience of travelling, or sojourning, concentrated on the more unpleasant aspects of cross-cultural contact. A major early influence was Stonequist (1937) who, drawing upon the work of Park (1928), published a book, *The marginal man*, in which he envisaged immigrants as people caught between two cultures and feeling at home in neither. In 1960, Oberg introduced the notion of culture shock, in which entrance into a new culture is seen as a confusing and disorienting experience. About the same time (i.e. the late 1950s), the notion of the U-curve of adjustment was introduced. This model suggested that cross-cultural sojourners progress through three main phases: an initial state of elation and optimism; a second stage of frustration, confusion, and depression; and a third in which there is a gradual increment in confidence and satisfaction with the new society (Coelho 1958; Deutsch and Won 1963). These early models were characterized by the notion that travelling produced a state of mental disorientation similar to that found in clinical subjects (Furnham and Bochner 1986).

More recently, theoretical models of the cross-cultural experience have eschewed the assumption of a breakdown in normal healthy functioning of the individual which was the foundation of the earlier models. The new models (Bochner 1982; Furnham and Bochner 1986) equate cross-cultural exposure to a learning experience, and therefore propose programmes for the acquisition of culturally appropriate social skills. The social skills model (Argyle and Kendon 1967) regards the behaviour of people interacting with one another as a mutually organized skilled performance. According to Bochner (1982), who draws upon this model, cross-cultural problems arise because sojourners have trouble negotiating certain social situations. They are unfamiliar with appropriate ways of expressing attitudes, feelings, and emotions, adopting appropriate postures, understanding patterns of eye contact, carrying out ritualized greetings, leave-takings, etc. Thus it is necessary to identify the specific social situations which trouble the sojourner and then train the person in those specific skills that are lacking. In addition to appropriate social skills, Bochner draws attention to the importance of the social-support system of the sojourners (such as friendship patterns) as the context in which appropriate culture-learning can take place (Bochner *et al*. 1977, 1985).

Models relating to sojourners are important in that the experience of travel and tourism is becoming increasingly common for large numbers of people as communication across national boundaries improves. However, immigration and ethnic minority identity tap the sojourning experience at a deeper level. Here, people travel to a country where they intend to spend many years, if not the rest of their lives. The experience of immigration touches the core of the self. As such, then, the acquisition of appropriate social skills may be a semi-conscious choice reflecting the individual's style of cultural adaptation. If, for example, individuals long for their home country and dislike the new country, then they may never acquire appropriate social skills. If, on the other hand, they are relieved to be away from their home country and are happy to live in the culture of their adoption, then the motivation to acquire appropriate social skills will be high. Thus, the phenomenon of immigration is in a category separate but akin to that of sojourning.

The body of research on immigrants and their adaptation to the culture of their adoption is very great. Much of the work has concentrated on crime rates, juvenile delinquency, drug addiction, educational achievement, unemployment, housing, etc. Although this constitutes a fascinating study it is not of direct relevance to this book.

Several studies, investigating the mental health of ethnic minority individuals (Cope 1989; Harrison *et al*. 1988; Ineichen 1987, 1989; McGovern and Cope 1987), report a higher incidence of schizophrenia among Asians and Afro-Caribbean immigrants to Britain than among the white population (see Littlewood and Lipsedge 1982; London 1986, for reviews). Not only do more Afro-Caribbeans than expected enter the psychiatric in-patient system, but they are more likely to be detained under the Mental Health Act and to receive treatment in secure facilities. Furthermore, the admission rates for schizophrenia among second generation Afro-Caribbeans are even higher than those of their parents (Cope 1989). This finding contradicts the early models that predicted, because the mental disorientation associated with travelling and immigration was a problem pertinent to the first generation, that psychiatric morbidity levels of the second generation would be similar to those of the white population.

A number of arguments have been put forward to account for the higher admission and detention rates of ethnic minority individuals into psychiatric institutions. Cope (1989) suggests that the stress experienced by Afro-Caribbeans of living in a discriminatory society together with the effects of socio-economic disadvantage contributes to their relatively poor levels of mental health. Together with this, Fernando (1988) mentions institutionalized racism in the form of Western diagnostic research criteria used by the white psychiatric establishment, which fails to take into account racial differences and the culture of the ethnic groups investigated. More pertinently, some work has studied the mental health of immigrants (Bianchi *et al.* 1973; Cochrane and Stopes-Roe 1980) or their personality adjustment (Aellen and Lambert 1969) with relation to their ethnic identification. For example, Bianchi *et al.* found that of the four scales they used to measure cultural identity and its relation to mental illness, the Retention of Traditional Beliefs scale was found to have correlations with reported medical symptom levels. The fundamental assumption underlying much of the recent work in this area is that persons and groups undergoing social or cultural change will experience a certain amount of psychological discomfort. Coelho (1972) has subjected this assumption to detailed scrutiny and has concluded that an association exists between socio-cultural change and mental health. However, a large-scale empirical survey in six countries casts serious doubts on their proposition (Inkeles and Smith 1970). A study conducted by Ginsberg and Gioelli (1979) pointed to an absence of acculturative stress in the descendants of Japanese born in Brazil when compared with Japanese in Tokyo and other Brazilians, again contradicting the clinical model of migration. Community surveys (Cochrane and Stopes-Roe 1981*a,b*; Cochrane 1983) found Asian-born immigrants generally better adjusted psychologically than comparative English samples on measures such as psychological symptoms.

Other studies have investigated the personality correlates of the ability to adapt to a new culture. For example, Berry and Annis (1974) provide evidence that acculturative stress is lower for individuals who exhibit high psychological differentiation (or field independence). Seelye and Brewer (1970), in a study of North Americans in Guatemala, suggest that factors such as the length and extent of contact with the foreign culture, especially as it is associated with an increased sense of security within the culture and reduced commitment to the original in-group, have greater impact on adaptation than personality disposition.

If personality factors are a somewhat non-productive line of research into styles of cultural adaptation, then perhaps the contact situation provides a better launching-pad for research. Bochner and his students (Bochner 1982) have developed the 'best friends' technique as a measure of integration. In a study conducted together with Novakovic (1977) it was hypothesized that as the peer group is second only to the family in serving as a reference group for growing children, the ethnic composition of the peer group would reflect whether the child retained his/her culture or adopted a new one. Novakovic (1977) asked a large sample of second generation Yugoslav children in Australia to name or state the ethnic identity of their three best friends. From this group of respondents, three groups emerged: one group whose three best friends were all Australian; a second group whose three best friends were all second generation

Yugoslavs; and a third group who had a mix of Australian and Yugoslav friends. A test was next devised which measured acceptance or rejection of Yugoslav customs and traditions, such as food, language preferences, national identification, rules for social interaction, etc. The prediction that subjects with all Australian friends would have the highest rejection rate, subjects with all Yugoslav friends would have the lowest rejection rate, and subjects with friends from both groups would be intermediate in their rejection of the parent culture was borne out by the data.

Crowley (1978) similarly used the best friends technique with a group of third generation Australians from British–Irish stock, and found that the level of world-mindedness versus ethnocentrism was related in the predicted direction as to whether the individual had an ethnically homogeneous or heterogeneous set of friends.

One of the major drawbacks of the best friends technique is that it does not control for the level of contact between the two cultures. If the individual lives in an ethnic enclave or goes to a school which is predominantly Yugoslav, then it is unlikely that the best friends technique will uncover self-made choices related to ethnic identification. Rather, it is an index of predetermined sociological conditions that have resulted in the ethnic minority group's banding together. Also, the actual choice of best friends is heavily weighted by similarity in attitudes and values, complementarity of needs, physical proximity, attractiveness, etc. Although these factors may be related with the ethnicity of the individual's best friends, a causal relationship cannot be assumed.

Research on ethnic minority identity arising out of the Eriksonian tradition has stimulated some interest in recent years. Hauser (1971) conducted a longitudinal study over three years with a small sample of white and black male high-school students from lower socio-economic backgrounds, using a combination of interview and Q-sort procedures. He found that white adolescents show a pattern of 'progressive identity formation' characterized by frequent changes in self-concept during the early high-school years followed by increasing consistency and stability as the person approaches high-school graduation. In contrast, the black adolescents showed a general stability in their identity elements over the entire period, a pattern which Hauser termed 'identity foreclosure'. He interpreted this lack of change as reflecting a problem in development in that important developmental issues had been dodged rather than resolved. Many of the stable identity elements were defined in the negative, that is, the adolescent knew what he did not want to become rather than what alternative he actively wanted to pursue. The result, according to Hauser, was a rigid and impoverished self-definition, due to greater discrimination directed toward poor blacks than towards whites from the same background. Although Hauser's conclusion is commendable, namely, that it is necessary to eliminate racial discrimination, several criticisms may be levelled at a study such as this. Firstly, Hauser's interpretation of his findings is somewhat questionable. The black adolescents in his study are in a 'no-win' situation: stability of identity elements is reinterpreted as identity foreclosure and that these stable elements are defined in the negative, for example, 'I am *not* going to be a university student', is interpreted to indicate an impoverished identity. Recent work questions the implicit assumption that self-definition in negative terms is an index of a 'lesser' identity. Apter (1983) has argued that the development of a sense of personal identity, and its maintenance in the face of threat, is fundamentally dependent on the capacity to feel, think, and act in a negativistic way. Kitwood (1983) has shown that it is through an understanding of who they are *not* that ethnic minority adolescents achieve a more assured understanding of who they are. More importantly, however, this study (Hauser 1971) does little to highlight the specific role of ethnicity in the development of the black adolescent's sense of identity.

Rae Sherwood (1980) considerably extends Erikson's concept of identity in her study of the psychodynamics of race. Social groups (class, religious, racial groups) serve as ways of differentiating between people and enable the individual to identify and locate him/herself in relation to others. Groups may also be used as repositories for aspects of the self which are too painful to face. Thus, groups may suffer *racial misuse*. One example of racial misuse is prejudice which serves to protect the prejudiced individual's identity and to bolster a psychological equilibrium which is felt to be precarious. Racial misuse thus often stems from feelings of inadequacy and low self-esteem.

Some individuals, when hurt or angered, respond in ways which serve to inflame and exacerbate racial tensions, so becoming caught up in and perpetuating *vicious spirals* of behaviour, characterized by mounting intolerance and escalating hostility; whereas others manage to deal with their hurt and anger by setting in motion constructive behaviour constituting *benign spirals*. Vicious spirals are of two types which are distinguished by the relative intensity of the forces playing upon the individual. There are those spirals which arise from urgent inner pressures, from acute unresolved identity conflicts, such as a low level of self-esteem. And there are those spirals that spring from incessantly aggravated and extreme forms of environmental provocation, such as periods of widespread unemployment, which constitute a threat to identity and which therefore serve to increase the incidence of vicious spirals.

Sherwood's in-depth case history analysis of three families, Afro-Caribbean, South Asian, and English, is rich in the understanding of the dynamics underlying ethnic minority identity. The concepts of racial misuse, benign, and vicious spirals are beguiling because they are equally applicable to both minority and majority groups. However, the psychodynamic technique of unstructured case histories is expensive, not just in terms of cost, but in time and effort, and the generalizability of the findings gleaned from such a methodology is limited.

Weinreich (1980, 1982, 1983*a,b*) follows the Eriksonian tradition closely, but borrows from personal construct theory in his attempts to operationalize concepts, such as identity diffusion, foreclosure, identification, etc. In order to evaluate Weinreich's success in the measurement of ethnic identity, it is necessary first to examine in some detail his theoretical extensions of Erikson's theory.

Weinreich's Identity Structure Analysis (ISA) is a theoretical framework which claims not only to embrace individual psychological problems but also societal problems that arise from identity development within the context of specific historical and cultural circumstances. Thus, according to Weinreich, the ISA is particularly sensitive to the measurement of ethnic identity.

Much of the work on ethnic identity hinges upon group identification. Weinreich (1983*b*) points out that most definitions of ethnic group identification embrace only those individuals with a *positive* orientation to the ethnic group; he makes a distinction between *empathetic identification* and *reference group identification*. The former denotes that the individual recognizes a commonality of experience and culture between the self and other members of the group. The latter refers to the individual's wish to emulate a positive reference group and aspire to the life-style and values it stands for. Thus, the individual may be empathetically identified with one group, while wishing to emulate another group.

Weinreich also makes a distinction between a person's social identity as *externally designated* by others and as *internally recognized* by the self. Thus, an *alter-ascribed social identity* is a categorization of ego as a member of a social group or category by an alter. An *ego-recognized social identity* is the ego's recognition of a categorization of self as a member of a social group or category. Mismatches between an alter-ascribed and an ego-recognized social identity may occur, as when an English-speaking Dutch visitor to Britain is designated as being British by an Irish person. In other situations, the individual may wish to deny an alter-ascribed social identity because it is not an ego-recognized one (as is perhaps the case of assimilating individuals who attempt to hide their ethnic origins). Underpinning an individual's identity is a system of constructs (Kelly 1955), or cognitive categories which the individual uses to differentiate between self and others. Thus, as a first step in ISA methodology it is necessary to generate a 'grid' of bi-polar constructs with which the individual construes his/her personal and social world and to elicit a list of 'significant others' consisting of people who are of primary importance to the individual. Identity, then, is the totality of the individual's self-construal, past, present, and future. Identity diffusion is operationalized as a dispersal of conflicted identifications across significant others, i.e. a person is said to have a diffused identity if the number of his/her conflicted identifications exceeds an optimal limit. A foreclosed identity is defined as those states in which individuals manifest minimal levels of conflicted identifications. A foreclosed identity with a high self-evaluation is termed 'defensive high self-regard'. That is, a person with too few identification conflicts with significant others (such as parents, teachers, etc.), and high self-esteem as measured by the ISA, is seen as protecting a threatened identity.

Weinreich's system of theoretical concepts and operationalizations is of limited use in the study of ethnic identity. In his study of 94 adolescents (English, $n = 38$; Asians, $n = 15$; Afro-Caribbean, $n = 41$) Weinreich (1983b) reports that both Asians and Afro-Caribbeans have high identification conflicts with representatives of their own ethnic group, whereas English adolescents manifest optimal levels of conflict. Also, immigrant girls show significantly higher levels of identity diffusion than English girls, although this trend was not found for boys. Immigrant boys, however, show a substantial degree of 'defensive high self-regard', which is another term for identity foreclosure. Foster-Carter (1986) points out a 'glaring double standard' in Weinreich's system: the black child with positive self-esteem is displaying an 'inflated' or 'defensively high self-esteem', whereas the black child who wishes to identify with his white friends is categorized as confused and in need of seeing a black psychiatrist. However, the same assertions are not made about the mental health of a tomboy who identifies with males at an early age, or the working class child who has middle class friends or who aspires, ideally, to be middle class in a rigidly stratified society. Also, the assumption underlying the construction of the instrument, namely, that an optimal level of conflicted identifications with significant others together with high self-esteem is what constitutes a confident identity, must be seriously questioned as being biased in favour of the Western family structure. If this in-built cultural bias is acknowledged, it is not at all remarkable that immigrant adolescents either fall into the foreclosed or diffused identity status, whereas their English counterparts manifest optimal levels of conflicted identifications. Thus, although Weinreich is concerned to take into account the historical and societal contexts from which these different identities emerge, he is unable to control for the consistent differences in the way each ethnic group uses its reference models. For example, Stopes-Roe and Cochrane (1990) found that obedience is very highly valued both by Asian parents and Asian young people and that Asians value conformity more and self-direction less than the English.

However, Weinreich's conceptualizations have yielded a number of valuable insights. His study of national and religious allegiance in Protestant and Catholic adolescents in Belfast (Weinreich 1983b) is particularly revealing. For the dimension of nationality, subjects were required to rate themselves on two scales: 'British—Not at all British' and 'Irish—Not at all Irish'. For the religious dimensions, two further bi-polar constructs were used: 'Protestant—Not at all Protestant' and 'Catholic—Not at all Catholic'. In presenting his subjects with these scales it would be possible for the individual to describe him/herself as being *both* Irish and British or as being neither Irish nor British, thus indicating a configuration of identification with more than one group at once.

Liebkind (1983, 1989), using a similar technique to that of Weinreich but borrowing more from the Tajfelian tradition, arrives at a more productive framework for understanding ethnic minority identity: it is the second generation who are creating new identities, identities which do not exactly reproduce either those of their parents or those of their peers born to indigeneous parents. Aidan Kelly (in Liebkind 1989) points to a wide variation of identities within ethnic groups. He notes the differences of identity creation between traditional and progressive young Pakistani Muslims in Britain and concludes that it is too simple to talk of an ethnic identity as if it were a unitary concept. In her study of the Swedish-speaking minority in Finland, Liebkind underlines the importance of social self-categorization as a cornerstone of ethnic identity. She points out that bilingual language *proficiency* and bilingual language *identification* are two separate phenomena: knowledge of the two languages (Swedish and Finnish) is not correlated with the wish or the capacity to identify with the two language groups. A small number (19 per cent) of Swedes in Finland do not speak Finnish at all. Most speak both languages. However, most of the Swedes in Helsinki identify themselves with the Swedish-speaking group only. Leibkind (1983) finds that the strategy which the individual chooses to identify him/herself with the two language groups (Swedish only, Finnish only, bilingual) is correlated with the number of identification conflicts as measured by Weinreich's ISA. There is a heightened level of identity problems amongst those who see themselves as only Swedish-speaking as well as those who identify themselves as being bilingual. The bilinguals had the greatest identification conflicts with members of the Finnish-speaking majority. The core construct system (as measured by the percentage of variance across the grid) is fairly tight, indicating a relatively rigid and inflexible identity structure, whereas the Swedish speakers have a somewhat more flexible structure. These tight structural features and high levels of identification conflicts among the bilinguals all create, according to Liebkind, a picture of a somewhat defensive accentuation of bilingual identity. As their identification conflicts are primarily with Finns, and as most of them have developed their bilingualism from pure 'Swedishness', they seem to experience pressure toward further reconstruction of their linguistic identity towards increased 'Finnishness'. In order to avoid complete assimilation they therefore defend their bilingual identity.

Liebkind's use of repertory grid technology to measure conflicts in identification is perhaps more justified in a society that is relatively homogeneous in its family structure and similar to that of the English in Britain, where Weinreich's ISA technique was developed. However, a further limitation of this technique comes to light. An initial stage in the preparation of the ISA is the eliciting of a list of significant others in the individual's life. Thus, elements in the grid may consist of parents and siblings, who are often representatives of the ethnic minority group and teachers, friends, and people the individual admires or dislikes, who may be representatives of the majority group. Identification conflicts are then measured against these significant others, and conclusions are then drawn regarding the individual's ethnic minority identity. The implicit assumption underlying this procedure must be questioned: measuring identification conflicts against a few representatives of each group does not validate the generalization that conflicts are therefore experienced with the group as a whole. According to this approach, conflicts in ethnic identity are represented in the number of significant others of the ethnic minority group. Is it not possible to come from a family situation in which marital discord is rife (and therefore identification conflicts with parents are presumably high) and yet appreciate and affirm one's ethnic background? Identification conflicts need not be *ethnic* identification conflicts.

Leo Dreidger (1976) has tested Lewin's (1948) thesis that individuals need a firm, clear sense of identification with an ethnic or majority culture in order to find a secure basis for a sense of well-being, and that insufficient in-group security results in self-hatred and in-group denial. Following Rothman's (1960) summary of Lewin's theory, Dreidger studied ethnic self-affirmation, ethnic denial, and marginality among seven major ethnic groups in Canada. In expanding Lewin's concept of ethnic self-hatred, Dreidger (1976) describes ethnic affirmation as 'the extent to which members identify with the ethnic support provided by their in-group'. Ethnic self-affirmation has to do with pride in belonging to the ethnic group and participation in ethnic group activities. Ethnic denial, on the other hand, includes 'feelings of inferiority, of being restricted by and annoyed with the in-group, or a necessity to hide cultural identity'. Dreidger (1976) defines marginality as the 'discrepancy between in-group members' real and ideal identification'. A low level of discrepancy suggests that ethnic individuals are consistently successful in meeting their needs according to their level of expectancy, whereas a high degree of discrepancy indicates an inability to achieve expectancy levels. Of the seven ethnic groups, Dreidger classifies the English and Scandinavians as majority assimilators, the French and Jews as ethnic identifiers, and the Germans, Ukrainians, and Poles as cultural marginals. Cultural marginals represent the mid-point between the English and the Scandinavian groups, on the one hand, who neither strongly affirm their ethnic identity nor have much reason to deny it, and the French and the Jews, on the other hand, who have a strongly developed sense of ethnicity and who also have little reason to deny it.

Fourteen Worchel-type questions (Worchel 1957), each beginning with 'I am a person who . . .', measured ethnic self-identity. As was expected, the ethnic identifiers scored highest on ethnic affirmation, the majority assimilators scored least, and the cultural marginals scored intermediately. On ethnic denial, contrary to Lewin's assumption of widespread self-hatred among minority group individuals, none of the ethnic groups (with the exception of the Germans who showed high *ideal* denial) wished to deny their ethnicity. All the means (even for Germans) fell *below* the mid-point of the five-point scale. However, between the groups there were significant differences. The significantly higher German ideal denial was explained in terms of the role played by Germany in two world wars. Jews showed the highest *real* denial of all groups. As predicted, the English and French were significantly lower in real denial than the cultural marginals. Also, as predicted, the cultural marginals showed the highest discrepancies between real and ideal ethnic affirmation, and with the exception of the Jews, the highest discrepancies between real and ideal ethnic denial.

Dreidger's attempt to operationalize ethnic self-hatred must be commended. The concepts of ethnic affirmation and ethnic denial are invaluable to the study of ethnic identity. However, as will be discussed later, any study of ethnic identification must also measure the ethnic individual's identification with the majority group. This configuration of two continua is necessary in order to capture the variations in style of cultural adaptations within any ethnic minority group. Thus, ethnic minority individuals may choose to identify exclusively with their own group and dissociate themselves from the majority group (the dissociative style), or they may identify exclusively with majority group and deny their ethnic origins group (the assimilative style). A third option would be to affirm both the minority and the majority (the acculturative style), and finally, there are those individuals who choose not to or somehow cannot identify with either group (the marginal style). According to this model, which will be discussed in detail in Chapter 10, both acculturative and dissociative individuals should show high levels of ethnic affirmation and low levels of ethnic denial. The crucial difference between these two groups of people lies in their affirmation of the majority groups: acculturative individuals should show high affirmation of the majority group, whereas dissociative individuals should manifest a low level of affirmation of the majority. Thus, to measure ethnic affirmation without *also* measuring majority group affirmation is to describe only a small part of the total configuration.

Dreidger (1976) classifies the seven ethnic groups into the three categories: majority assimilators; ethnic identifiers; and cultural marginals, on the basis of the degree of institutional completeness. Institutional completeness (Breton 1964) refers to the degree of social organization of ethnic minorities in terms of the number of established 'ethnic' institutions—schools, religious institutions, etc.—which are credited with the ability to hold members within the ethnic group. Although his data confirm that there is some justification to this classification, it might be more desirable to construct an objective measure of ethnic identity in terms of behavioural and attitudinal measures and thereby to determine the predominant identification strategy of each ethnic group.

Also, Dreidger's concept of marginality as the discrepancy between real and ideal ethnic affirmation and denial perhaps needs refinement. Is marginality really the difference between what the individual actually feels about his/her ethnic group and what s/he would like to feel? ('I feel proud to belong to the ———— group' versus 'I would like to feel proud about belonging to the ———— group'). It might be better conceived as the experience of living within two cultures and being able to identify with neither. Because Dreidger (1976) has made no attempt to measure the ethnic individual's level of identification with the majority group, an adequate operationalization of marginality was not achieved in this study.

Several other sociological studies on ethnocentrism, acculturation, assimilation, and marginality have supported the idea that there exist various styles of cultural adaptation *within*—not just between—ethnic groups. Himmelfarb (1979), in a study of patterns of assimilation in American Jews, found that a 'polarization' of the community is occurring, i.e. there is a loss of ethnic identity at one end and greater ethnic identity at the other. Pienkos (1974), too, found two distinct sub-cultures coexisting within the Polish minority in Milwaukee: although most Poles are increasingly becoming assimilated to American societal norms, a smaller number, although already fully adapted to life in America, retain strong ethnic feelings. (For expositions of sociological work on ethnicity see Glazer and Moynihan 1975; McCready 1983; Postiglione 1983.)

A number of studies have attempted to measure ethnic identification in terms of behavioural and attitudinal measures. In a study mentioned previously, Seelye and Brewer (1970) measured acculturation and ethnocentrism using a combination of social psychological measures. It was predicted that high involvement in the new culture, non-authoritarian attitudes, a positive attitude towards deviants from established social norms, high feelings of security and comfort, reduced commitment to the original nation, and high frequency of social intercourse with people of the new culture would all be positively related to acculturation and inversely related to ethnocentrism. As predicted, all these variables were positively related to ethnocentrism (although not all significantly so). A multiple regression analysis revealed involvement in the new culture to be the single best predictor of acculturation. This was measured in terms of an index of intermarriage, group membership, social activities, consumer habits, familiarity with the language, and attention to mass media.

Masuda *et al.* (1970, 1973) developed the Ethnic Identity Questionnaire (EIQ) as a means of measuring the magnitude of ethnic identification in Japanese-Americans. It incorporated 50 items measuring preferences for Japanese things (food, films, etc.), personality characteristics, childrearing customs, family kinship items, social relationships, racial discrimination, cultural heritage, sex roles, inter-racial attitudes, etc. Respondents were required to rate on a five-point scale his/her degree of agreement or disagreement with the items. The total ethnic identification score is the sum of the scores on the 50 items, with high scores indicating high ethnicity. Ethnic identity scores by this method were higher with high income and increasing age, and lower with educational achievement. Females tended to have higher EIQ scores, as did Buddhists when compared with non-Buddhists.

Danziger (1974) studied the acculturation of Italian immigrant girls in Canada, in terms of sex-role specialization, autonomy in decision-making, and responsibilities within the home. He found a higher level of role specialization and a lower level of autonomy in immigrant versus non-immigrant girls.

Another study by Dreidger (1975) sought to investigate ways in which ethnic groups seek to maintain separate identities in the face of pressures to assimilate. A search for the cultural identity factors revealed ethnic identity to be a multi-dimensional concept clustering around factors such as language use, religion, endogamy, parochial education, choice of in-group friends, and ethnic organizations (including ethnic media). A correlation was found between attitudinal and behavioural factors. This study is significant for the present research because it suggests variables that may be incorporated into a study of various styles of cultural adaptation.

In Britain, a number of studies are beginning to look at the second generation South Asian adolescent minority. Thompson (1974) asked the question: 'The second generation—Punjabi or English?' Thompson concluded that there are two types of adolescent reaction to ethnicity: the in-group reaction where the option is to behave, speak, and *be* entirely Punjabi; and the rebel reaction in which the option is to behave as an English person. According to this study, the majority of the second generation do not want to give up their Punjabi identity and wholly adopt English norms of behaviour; instead they want to liberalize the traditional village and family regime of Punjab.

In the second generation among South Asians the celebration of marriage remains among the strongest assertions of ethnic identity. According to Brah (1978, 1979), who has perhaps made the most extensive social psychological analysis to date of South Asian teenagers, the overwhelming majority of her respondents (n = above 300) wished they had the freedom to go out with the opposite sex. None disapproved of courtship in principle, but most were cautious about actual involvement. It is generally thought that as the second generation is consistently exposed to the Western model of marriage based on individual choice of partners, adolescents who have been born and brought up in Britain will be likely to reject the system of arranged marriage for themselves. This hypothesis received only partial support: it was found that the influence of the Western model was apparent at the level of ideology rather than envisaged practice.

This discrepancy between ideology and practice has been interpreted by a number of writers to signify a clash of cultures. In essence, the argument is that second generation adolescents are caught 'between two cultures', that of their parents and that of the larger society. This argument is reminiscent of Weinreich's (1980) premiss that ethnic adolescents, because they are required to move within and between two sometimes opposed cultural frameworks, should show high levels of identity diffusion.

Kitwood (1983, p. 132) summarizes the position (which he rejects) well:

As adolescents, the theory suggests, they would be likely to find it extremely hard to develop a consistent style of life and a unity in their ordering of experience. They are required to act within two very contrary cultural frameworks. They might be supposed to have a particularly strong tendency to reject identifications with parents and others in the Asian community, while perhaps having insufficient contact with the kind of people with whom they could realistically identify elsewhere. Such roles as are objectively available in the host society may be unfamiliar or unacceptable. Personal experimentation is severely restricted because of the traditions of the Asian family. There is a common tendency, for the girls especially, for the period of adolescence to be curtailed by withdrawal from school at the first opportunity, or by early marriage. Thus, if any group could be held, prima facie, to exemplify Erikson's theory in its negative aspect—the probability of failure to complete the 'task' of adolescence—it is this. And Muslim adolescents because of the radical incompatability of their parents' outlook with Western ways might be expected to show 'identity-confusion' to a marked degree.

Kitwood's (1983) study of self-conception among young British Asian Muslims convincingly refutes this argument. According to this study, details of which are reported in Kitwood and Borrill (1980), Muslim children from the very first have a strong sense of being part of a wide net of relationships, mainly that of the extended family but also that of the Muslim 'community' as a whole. Rather than contributing to a sense of identity confusion, their unique position in the social group as son, brother, sister-in-law's nephew, or whatever, accentuates a sense of unique identity, although not in a Western or Eriksonian sense. From the first point of entry into the life of the majority group, they are likely to face racist attacks or insinuations: 'Paki', 'Wog', etc. This experience does not, according to Kitwood (1983), undermine the sense of who they are; rather, it tends to enhance it. By the time they reach their teens, their sense of identity, far from being 'diffused', is far more secure than that of their English counterparts. The system of social feedback both from the home community and the host society constantly delineates the parameters of their identity. Social comparisons are made with other Muslim adolescents: thus, there are those who are relatively traditional or modern, those who are devout or irreligious, and those who are aware of Asian culture versus those who are not. It is doubtful whether the peer group friendships formed with people of different ethnic backgrounds constitute a major force towards assimilation—far less towards identity diffusion. Racism simply becomes an accepted part of the world in which they live, something to be handled with skill. From the very first, they learn to interact acceptably with people from different cultures, adopting different roles and different accents according to the demands of the situation, without suffering feelings of personal inconsistency. Kitwood argues that it is an essentially Western conception that a sense of identity must be based on personal consistency of behaviour. He concludes (1983, p. 145):

> The striking thing is that generally 'young Muslims' do not find the fact of existing 'between two cultures', and of being a 'halfway generation' intrinsically problematic.

Ballard (1979), too, comes to essentially the same conclusion. She argues that although many of the second generation Asians in Britain may rebel against their parents' social and cultural values during their early teens, by their late teens and early twenties the majority of them largely conform to Asian norms. She suggests that the early rebellion may focus on the relevance of elaborate social and religious rituals, the segregation of the sexes, dietary restrictions, restrictions on the wearing of fashionable clothes, arranged marriages, etc., but that, by and large, Asian families succeed in maintaining good relations between the generations. This is corroborated in Brah's (1978) study, where only four of more than 300 respondents expressed resentment against their parents. Thus the predication of a theory of ethnic minority identity on the assumption of greater identity diffusion finds little basis in empirical observation.

Study 6

The survey of Asian studies has pointed out, in addition to variables such as ethnic media, language use, choice of in-group friends, etc. (Dreidger 1975; Novakovic 1977; Masuda *et al.* 1970), the issues of courtship, arranged marriages, religious observance, and the wearing of ethnic clothes pertinent to South Asian ethnicity in Britain. These, together with variables tapping preferences in music, food, and overall culture preferences, were incorporated into a study of styles of cultural adaptation in second generation South Asian adolescents. In this study the term 'adaptation' will be defined in Taft's words as 'the changes made by the immigrant in order to fit in better with the environment' and 'includes changes in attitudes as well as behaviour' (Taft 1973, p. 227).

In this study, it is first hypothesized that ethnic minority individuals will adopt one of four (not two) cultural adaptation styles:

1. *The assimilative style*: those who adapt themselves exclusively to the majority group and not to the ethnic minority group.
2. *The dissociative style*: those who adapt themselves exclusively to the ethnic minority group and not to the majority group.
3. *The acculturative style*: those who identify with both the ethnic minority group culture and the majority group culture.
4. *The marginal style*: those who identify with neither group.

For every area of cultural adaptation (ten in all) a *pair* of questions was constructed: of the two questions one made reference to the ethnic minority group and the other to the majority group. For example:

> I am a person who enjoys watching Indian films.
> I really like British films.

These statements were then rated on two Likert scales ranging from Strongly Agree to Strongly Disagree.

The subjects were requested to read the statements in pairs. Affirmation of both groups (in terms of agreement with both statements) constituted an *acculturative* score, negation of both groups constituted a *marginal* score, affirmation of the ethnic minority group and negation of the majority group constituted a *dissociative* score, and negation of the ethnic minority group and affirmation of the majority group constituted an *assimilative* score. Thus, the individual's overall style of cultural adaptation may be assessed by calculating his/her total score on the Indian items of the questionnaire *and* his/her total score on the British items relating to the same variables. A high Indian score and a low British score would then constitute evidence for dissociation, a high British score and a low Indian score would indicate assimilation, high scores on both Indian and British items can be interpreted as acculturation, and low scores on both Indian and British items may then be seen as indicating a degree of marginality.

Data were collected initially from 118 adolescents, but the inability of Wishart's Clustan Program (1982) to deal with protocols containing missing data meant that only 103 protocols could be used. All subjects were girls from the fourth, fifth, and sixth forms of a school in Birmingham, with a mean age of 16.2 years. Of the total sample, 91.3 per cent were of Indian extraction, 3.9 per cent came from mixed backgrounds, 2.9 per cent were East African Indians, and one girl came from Pakistan. The sample contained a mixture of Hindus and Sikhs but the majority were Sikh (60.2 per cent Sikh, 26.2 per cent Hindu, 1.9 per cent Muslim, and 11.6 per cent did not fill in this question). Most of the adolescents came from nuclear families (85 per cent), 5.8 per cent were from extended families, and 6.8 per cent from single-parent families. Sixty per cent of the fathers of these girls were employed, and 36 per cent of them were not. The large majority of those who were employed came from Classes 5–7 of the Hall–Jones Scale of Occupational Prestige (this distribution is given in Appendix 4).

A cluster analysis was performed on the ten pairs of cultural adaptation variables using Wishart's (1982) Clustan program and Ward's method of hierarchical agglomeration. The dendrogram of this analysis is presented in Figs. 8.1 and 8.2 and the graph suggesting the best cluster solution is given in Fig. 8.2.

Figures 8.1 and 8.2 in conjunction suggest that a four-cluster solution is most appropriate for the data on cultural adaptation. The dissimilarity coefficients along the vertical axis of the dendrogram range from 0.84 to 13.06, with the lower coefficients indicating greater similarity of the subjects who are arranged along the horizontal axis. According to Wishart (1982) one method for establishing the significant number of clusters is to choose a division that makes a significant 'jump' in the similarity value of the clusters. Figure 8.2 indicates the elbow of the curve occurs between four and three clusters. Hence, a four-cluster solution seems most appropriate for these data.

Next, the item-total reliability for the Indian scale was calculated and found to be 0.50 and for the British scale 0.40. Therefore, it was considered reasonable to use the individual's total score on the Indian scale and his total score on the British scale in the next calculation.

An ANOVA with repeated measures was performed using four levels of cluster membership obtained from the above cluster analysis and two repeated measures which comprised: (1) the sum of the Indian scores; and (2) the sum of the British scores for each individual. This was done in order to determine whether there was a significant difference between the clusters and thus to confirm or reject the cluster solution chosen. The results of this are reported in Table 8.1. Figure 8.3 shows the cell means for each cluster over the total of the Indian scores and the British scores.

Table 8.1 indicates that the clusters are significantly different at the 0.01 level. The nature of this difference is readily evident in Fig. 8.3, Cluster 1 ($n = 18$) manifests a very low mean for the Indian items (0.78), and the highest mean for the British items (10.06). Clearly, this is an assimilative cluster—it affirms the British items to a much greater extent than the Indian. Cluster 4, on the other hand ($n = 52$), is highly affirmative of both

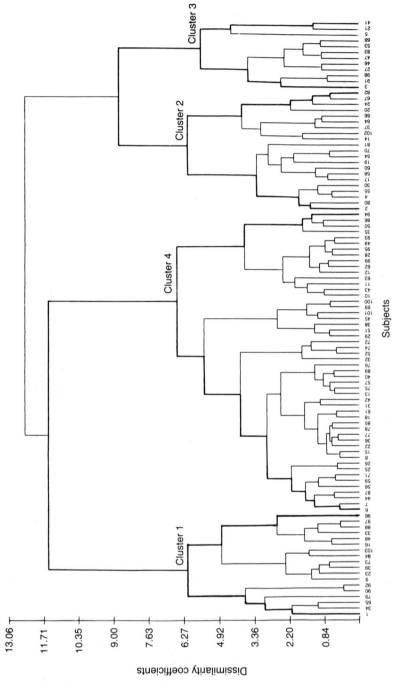

Fig. 8.1. Dendrogram analysis of social adaptation variables.

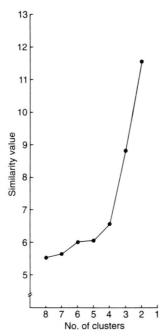

Fig. 8.2. Significance of the number of clusters calculated by using the similarity value associated with the clusters.

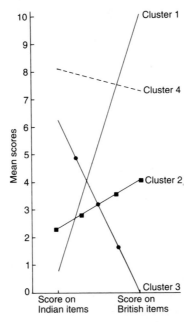

Fig. 8.3. Mean score for each cluster over the Indian and British items.

Ethnic minority identity

Table 8.1 Summary of repeated measures ANOVA for clusters by scores

Source	Sum of squares	d.f.	MS	F
Cluster	831.27	3	277.09	30.83[b]
Error	902.84	99	9.11	
Scores	51.91	1	51.91	3.23
Scores × cluster	854.87	3	284.96	17.75[a]
Error	1589.74	99	16.05	

[a] $p < 0.05$; [b] $p < 0.01$.

the ethnic group and the majority group. This will be termed the acculturative cluster. Cluster 2 ($n = 25$) scores low on both the ethnic group and the majority group items. This will therefore be called the marginal cluster. Cluster 3 ($n = 8$) scores high on the Indian items and very low on the British items. It is therefore dissociative in nature. Several points of interest emerge. The highly acculturative group ($n = 52$) claims 50.5 per cent of the individuals in the sample. It would seem that the majority of second generation Indian adolescents have learned to affirm effectively both the ethnic minority group and the majority group in this sample of cultural adaptation variables. Only 17.5 per cent of the sample prefer the majority group culture over the minority group culture. It is also worth while noting the very small size of the dissociative cluster. As four significantly different clusters emerge from the data of cultural adaptation, it is confirmed that a quadri-polar (rather than a bi-polar) model is vital to an understanding of ethnic minority adaptation.

Conclusion

There seems to be clear evidence that ethnic minority identity must be conceptualized along at least two main dimensions: one relating to the degree of identification with the ethnic minority group; and the second relating to the degree of identification with the majority group.

Second generation ethnic minority individuals will make cultural adaptations according to one of four styles. Most of the earlier research has measured degrees of assimilation and/or degrees of dissociation by placing these concepts at the opposite ends of a single continuum. This study has shown that it is necessary to introduce a second continuum. A person adopting a dissociative style finds great enjoyment in using the ethnic language, wearing ethnic clothes, viewing ethnic films, listening to ethnic music—but so too does a person adopting an acculturative style. The crucial difference is their level of enjoyment of aspects of the majority group culture. The acculturative individual is high on this continuum, whereas a dissociative person scores low. Similarly, assimilative and acculturative individuals look remarkably alike if one measures merely their appreciation of the majority group culture. The critical difference between these two styles of cultural adaptation lies in their appreciation of the ethnic minority culture, with the assimilative person wanting to deny, forget, break ties with the culture of his origin, whereas the acculturative person is happy to be immersed in the ethnic culture.

It is therefore necessary to treat ethnic minority individuals' identification with the ethnic minority group and their identification with the majority group as two separate (although not necessarily independent) continua, in order to arrive at an accurate portrayal of their style of cultural adaptation.

9.

Self-categorization and social stereotypes

Another major area of interest to students of ethnic minority identity is the research related to self-categorization and social stereotypes. Most of the recent work on these topics is ensconced in the domain of social cognition, which has sought to investigate the role of cognitive structures and processes in our understanding of social groups. The foundation was laid in the early 1970s with the work of Henri Tajfel and his colleagues and has since developed into an impressive body of research.

Historically, the main features of psychological group formation were conceived in terms of identity (that group members define themselves as being part of a distinct social category), inter-dependence (that people form themselves into groups for the mutual satisfaction of their needs), and structure (that groups stabilize over time into a set of structured relations and develop a system of social norms and role differentiations regarding matters relevant to the group) (see Turner 1985). Research was thus directed at issues such as: problem-solving in groups (Shaw 1932); leadership styles (Lewin *et al.* 1939); communication networks (Leavitt 1951); group cohesiveness (Lott and Lott 1961); inter-personal attraction (Cartwright and Zander 1968); and inter-group co-operation, competition, and conflict (Sheriff 1966).

The Tajfel *et al.* studies were not so much interested in the processes of group formation as in the minimal conditions under which inter-group discrimination would manifest itself. The original idea was to strip bare the number of variables in the experimental situation so that no inter-group discrimination would occur and then to add variables cumulatively so as to pinpoint the precise moment at which in-group favouritism occurred. What they found changed the direction of research into group processes.

In the original experiment, Tajfel *et al.* (1971) divided their subjects (schoolboys) into two groups ostensibly on the basis of a trivial criterion, but in fact randomly. In later experiments they made this division in an explicitly random manner (the toss of a coin). This division of subjects into groups was unconfounded by the variables that were thought to determine intra- and inter-group attitudes. There was no social interaction or contact between or within groups, no history of hostility, no current conflict of interest, nor any other form of inter-dependence. In addition, individuals did not know which group their classmates belonged to, they knew only of their own·group membership. The subjects' task was to award money to others who were identified merely by a code number and their group membership. Under such 'minimal' conditions, no inter-group discrimination was expected. The unexpected finding was that subjects discriminated in favour of their own group and against out-group members even under these minimal conditions. It appears that the very act of categorizing people into social groups, even on a random basis, is sufficient to produce discriminatory inter-group behaviour. This finding has been replicated in many studies (for a review, see Tajfel 1982) and the data are well established, reliable, and robust.

The mere act of social categorization leads to a number of effects. First and foremost there is an increase in perceived intra-group similarity and an accentuation of inter-group differences (Tajfel *et al.* 1964; Tajfel and Wilkes 1963). That is, group members tend to assume that other in-group members are similar to themselves (even on issues unrelated to the criterion of social categorization) and that out-group members are dissimilar to in-group members. Out-group members are rated in more homogeneous terms (Park and Rothbart 1982) and are evaluated more extremely on various psychological characteristics than members of the in-group (Linville 1982). Studies have also shown that there is significantly better memory for negative out-group behaviours (Howard and Rothbart 1980) and that perceivers make differing causal attributions, with more favourable attributions being made to the in-group members (Taylor and Jaggi 1974). Thus, the mere act of categorizing people into groups produces discrimination in favour of the in-group and has many other far-reaching implications.

Self-categorization and ethnic minority identity

The fact that people very quickly develop biased attitudes towards the groups they belong to, was first interpreted by Tajfel to be an exemplification of Sumner's (1906) theory of ethnocentrism, which postulated a 'generic norm' that all people learn in order to favour the in-group and discriminate against out-groups. Tajfel later modified this interpretation considerably when it was pointed out (Moscovici and Paicheler 1978) that research on the ethnic preferences of minority group children revealed a substantial out-group (rather than in-group) bias. Rather than being a generic norm, the effect of social categorization was then interpreted to produce a sense of psychological distinctiveness which then resulted in in-group favouritism.

For ethnic minority individuals, the mere categorization effect is complicated by the fact that they belong simultaneously to two categories:

by birth and by cultural tradition they belong to the ethnic minority group; by nationality and citizenship they belong to the majority group. What happens, then, when categories are crossed such that some subjects become members of groups they once perceived as out-groups?

Deschamps and Doise (1978) investigated the effects of crossing age and sex categories. In the simple categorization condition, subjects were asked to characterize, on a list of adjectives, people of the female sex, people of the male sex, young people, and adults. In the crossed categorization condition, subjects were asked to characterize on the same adjective list, *young* people of female sex, *young* people of male sex, female adults, and male adults. The results showed that when the subjects were requested to characterize groups of people assigned into opposite categories according to one criterion and belonging to the same category according to another criterion, the perceived differences between these groups were smaller than between groups assigned to strictly dichotomous categories. These results were replicated when a pre-existing categorization (sex) was crossed with one which was experimentally induced (an arbitrary division of the group into 'reds' and 'blues').

Commins and Lockwood (1978), in a similar experiment in Northern Ireland, investigated the effects of crossing a highly salient categorization (Catholic–Protestant) with a minimal categorization based on a dot-estimating task. The hypothesis was that, when compared with single religion groups, discrimination against the out-group and favouritism for the in-group would be significantly *reduced* in the criss-cross (mixed religion) groups. The basis for the hypothesis was that in the mixed condition subjects would reduce their discrimination against the out-group for fear of penalizing members of their own religion who might be in the out-group. Results showed a non-significant trend in the predicted direction: the mixed condition showing less discrimination against the out-group and less favouritism to the in-group than in either the Catholic or Protestant conditions. Vanbeselaere (1987) designed an experiment to correct the possible flaws that Brown and Turner (1979) had noted in the Deschamps and Doise (1978) procedures, and found similar results: subjects who were categorized on more than one dimension showed little inter-group discrimination, measured both by performance evaluations and by general attitude questions.

There is also evidence from anthropological studies (see Levine and Campbell 1972) that inter-group conflict is more controlled in some tribal societies through various methods of 'crossing' the membership of groups, so that some individuals find themselves belonging to one group on the basis of one set of criteria (say by birth) and to another group by another set of criteria (say by marriage and residence).

Wadell and Cairns (1984) working in Northern Ireland, observe that the structure of Northern Irish society is totally lacking in cross-cutting categories, i.e. it is not possible to have loyalties to both the Protestant and the Catholic group and that 'passing' from one group to another is a virtual impossibility. When social categorizations are strictly dichotomous the in-group 'we'-feeling predominates strongly over the out-group 'they'-sentiments. Wadell and Cairns (1984) cite evidence for the strength of this dichotomization: most people in Northern Ireland have 'almost violent' reactions to marriages between Protestants and Catholics. This extreme polarization of identities which is true of places riddled with a history of intense inter-group conflict (South Africa is another case in point, as is the Hindu–Muslim conflict in India) is not necessarily evident in all multi-ethnic societies. Peres and Yuval-Davis (1969) found that the national identity of Israeli Arabs embraced *both* Israeli and Arab elements. Sommerlad and Berry (1970) asked aboriginals in Australia whether they identified themselves as being Australians or aboriginals and found that a group of their subjects refused to categorize themselves in terms of a single identity label but saw themselves as 'both'.

Study 7

The question then arises as to what social categories ethnic minority individuals apply to themselves. In real life individuals acquire social categories through the processes of socialization, the persuasive influence of significant others, and the media. Self-categorizations are labels that individuals use to locate themselves within the system of social relations. As members of an ethnic minority group by birth and as members of the majority group by citizenship, ethnic minority individuals may well cat-egorize themselves along two dimensions (rather than merely one): the first is the extent to which they conceive of themselves as part of the ethnic minority group, the second is their willingness or unwillingness to categor-ize themselves with the majority group label.

The 'Who am I?' studies presented in Chapter 7 suggest that the same paradigm as was used for the study of styles of cultural adaptation may be applicable to self-categorization. Some subjects, albeit a few, mentioned that they were of Indian origin but British by nationality; others mentioned only that they were Indian; still others referred only to the fact that they were British; and for many, neither the Indian nor the British categoriza-tion was salient enough to enter their self-descriptions. It was therefore decided to formalize a measure of self-categorization by the juxtaposition of two scales: one measuring categorization in terms of the majority group; the other measuring categorization in terms of the ethnic minority group. It was with this purpose in mind that the eleventh pair of questions was included in the questionnaire used in the study presented in Chapter 8. The data referred to in Chapter 8 yielded: (1) an overall index of cultural adaptation as provided by the cluster analysis; and (2) a measure of self-categorization.

Similarly then, to their styles of cultural adaptation (see Chapter 8) ethnic minority individuals may use one of four strategies of self-categorization (see also Hutnik 1986):

1. *The dissociative strategy*: where categorization is in terms of ethnic minority group membership and not in terms of the majority group dimension of their being.
2. *The assimilative strategy*: where self-categorization primarily emphasizes the majority group dimension and denies the ethnic minority roots.
3. *The acculturative strategy*: where the self is categorized approximately equally in terms of both dimensions.
4. *The marginal strategy*: where neither dimension is important or salient to self-categorization. Here, the self may be categorized primarily in terms of other relevant social categories: student; squash player, etc.; or, there may be a conscious decision not to choose an ethnic identity or a majority group identity.

The self-categorization statements were as follows:

(a) I think of myself as British.
(b) Fundamentally, I do not think of myself as Indian.

The subjects (the same ones as in Chapter 8) were required to express their level of agreement with these two statements on a five-point scale ranging from strongly agree to strongly disagree. The five-point scale was then collapsed into a three-point scale. Those who agreed with both statements were classified as assimilative. Those who disagreed with both statements were classified as dissociative. Those who disagreed with the first statement and agreed with the second statement were put into the acculturative category. The marginal category was obtained in the following way: first, those who were neutral on both statements were put into this class; secondly, those who agreed that they did not think of themselves as Indian and also disagreed that they were British were coded as marginal. In cases where one statement of the pair was neutral and the other statement elicited agreement, the individual was classified according to the direction of affirmation. Thus, for example, if the individual was neutral on the Indian item, but agreed that s/he was British, s/he was classified as assimilative.

The frequencies and percentages relative to the four strategies of self-categorization are presented in Table 9.1 The table provides substantial evidence that self-categorization processes in ethnic minority individuals

Table 9.1 Study 8: Frequencies and percentages of the four strategies of self-categorization

Strategy of self-categorization	Frequency	Percentage
Assimilation: British only (not Indian)	37	35.9
Dissociation: Indian only (not British)	30	29.1
Acculturation: Both British and Indian	24	23.3
Marginality: Neither British nor Indian	12	11.7
Total	103	100.0

may be more accurately indexed by the use of a quadri-polar rather than a bi-polar model of ethnic minority identity (see also Fig. 10.1). That 36 per cent of the sample identify themselves as British only and not Indian indicates that a substantial amount of assimilation has occurred in terms of self-categorization structures among second generation Indian adolescents. However, 29 per cent see themselves as both Indian and British and a small proportion of the sample (12 per cent) opt for the marginal strategy, identifying themselves as being neither British nor Indian.

Self-categorization and cultural adaptation

We have seen in Chapter 8 that ethnic minority individuals use one of four styles of cultural adaptation for the purposes of everyday living, and in this chapter we have seen that they employ one of four strategies of self-categorization by which they locate themselves in the network of social relationships. What is the relationship between the individual's style of cultural adaptation and his/her strategy of self-categorization? In other words, does social behaviour correspond with the labels of self-categorization? Historically, there has been an implicit assumption that they do, i.e., if a person much prefers aspects of British culture (films, music, food, clothes, etc.) to Indian culture then that person will categorize him/herself in terms of the majority group dimension of his/her identity and will reject the ethnic minority label.

This assumption of a one-to-one correspondence of cultural adaptation and self-categorization has recently been questioned. Billig dwells upon this theme at some length in an essay on social identity and social categorization (Billig 1976). Freud, he point out, identified himself strongly as being a Jew and yet he shared no common set of attitudes, cultural traits, nor any congruence of belief with fellow Jews (Billig 1976, p. 334):

The feeling of similarity might in its starkest form be associated with the label of group membership, rather than any traits of significant social fact underlying the label. Freud considered himself a Jew and identified strongly with Jewish tradition but was greatly perplexed about the actual content of this identification.

Billig mentions a study by Moerman (Billig 1976) of ethnic identification among the Lue. This study revealed that the 30 traits mentioned by the Lue as being the essential difference between their group and other out-groups referred to cultural practices now obsolete. In other words, the mere act of social categorization was sufficient to perpetuate a sense of ethnic identity long after the cultural practices that gave rise to the original ethnic differentiations ceased to exist.

This persistence of social categorizations is also mirrored in sociological studies of the assimilation of ethnic groups into the dominant culture. Chance (1965) observes that the mere adoption of Western technology does not necessarily signify a similar change in ethnic identification. Gordon (1964), in a study of assimilation in American life, observes that 'cultural assimilation' often precedes and may occur independently of 'identificational assimilation', i.e. ethnic groups tend to be absorbed into the majority culture in terms of behaviour and attitudes long before they are willing to drop the labels of their ethnic identity.

In a study by Cairns and Mercer (1978), 900 adolescents were asked to describe themselves on a list of 18 bi-polar adjectives. Only 3 per cent of the sample failed to categorize themselves as being either Catholic or Protestant. However, whereas large proportions of the sample applied to themselves religious labels appropriate to their group membership, almost half of those labelling themelves as Protestant and one-third of those labelling themselves as Catholic did *not* consider themselves to be religious. This is further evidence that the cognitive functions of social categorization are little related to the behaviour and attitudes they may have originally represented.

In Study 8, it was hypothesized that there would be little or no relationship between styles of cultural adaptation and strategies of self-categorization. Because the same subjects were used for both studies, it was a simple task to cast one dimension against the other in a Contingency C table, i.e. for each individual his/her membership in a particular cluster (obtained from the study reported in Chapter 8), was compared against his/her own particular strategy of self-categorization (obtained in the study just described). (See Table 9.2.)

Table 9.2 reveals that the coefficient fails to reach significance at the 0.05 level. This chi-squared analysis is 12.96 with an associated probability of 0.16. This means that there is only a very moderate relationship between the individuals chosen style of cultural adaptation and his/her strategy of self-categorization. Fifty per cent of the assimilative cluster see

Table 9.2 Contingency C table investigating the relationship between strategies of self-categorization and styles of cultural adaptation

	Strategy of self-categorization			
Style of cultural adaptation	Marginal (neither Indian nor British)	Assimilative (British only, not Indian)	Acculturative (both Indian and British)	Dissociative (Indian only, not British)
Cluster 2 (25) Marginal	4 16.0 33.3	7 28.0 18.9	9 36.0 37.4	5 20.0 16.7
Cluster 1 (18) Assimilative	1 5.6 8.3	9 50.0 24.3	3 16.7 12.5	5 27.8 16.7
Cluster 4 (52) Acculturative	5 9.6 41.7	16 30.8 43.2	11 21.2 45.8	20 38.5 66.7
Cluster 3 (8) Dissociative	2 25.0 16.7	5 62.5 13.5	1 12.5 4.2	0 0.0 0.0
Total (103)	12	37	24	30

Note: The first number in each cell is the frequency, the second number is the row percentage and the third number is the column percentage.

χ^2, 12.96 (d.f., 9); p, 0.16; contingency coefficient, 0.33.

themselves as fundamentally Indian and 16.7 per cent see themselves as both Indian and British. Just over a third (38.5 per cent) of those who are highly acculturative in their behaviour see themselves as essentially Indian while 30.8 per cent of this cluster see themselves as British and less than a quarter (21.2 per cent) of this cluster see themselves as both Indian and British. In Table 9.2, 66.7 per cent of those who identify as Indian only are highly acculturative in their behaviour, but 16.7 per cent are actually assimilative. Of those who see themselves as both British and Indian, a total of only 45.8 per cent fall into the acculturative cluster. Of this group, 37.4 per cent are actually marginal in their cultural adaptation, 12.5 per cent are assimilative, and 4.2 per cent are dissociative. Of the group that sees itself as British only and not Indian, 43.2 per cent are acculturative in their cultural adaptation, and only 24.3 per cent are assimilative both in their strategy of self-categorization and their style of cultural adaptation. Of those who use the marginal strategy of self-categorization, 41.7 per cent are acculturative.

The results of this study lend little support to models assuming a simple relationship between styles of cultural adaptation and self-categorization strategies. That one may be dissociative in terms of one's social identity yet highly acculturative (or even assimilative) in terms of one's behaviour suggests that self-categorization in the second generation may in fact become independent of the individual's everyday functioning within the two cultures. That is, the individual's sense of who s/he is or is not does not necessarily have implications for how s/he will behave. In effect, the ethnic minority individual may have a strong sense of being Indian while yet being entirely British in his/her media preferences, language usage, styles of heterosexual relationship, marriage, choice of clothing, etc. or s/he may see him/herself as British only and yet positively affirm many aspects of the culture of his/her origin. In some cases there is a greater degree of correspondence between self-categorization and cultural adaptation. This is best exemplified in the words of the 15-year-old subject who wrote:

I think of myself as British and Indian because my ideas are of the Western side, but I am Indian by race.

Conclusion

In Study 8 we have seen that self-categorization may lag behind or run ahead of cultural adaptation and that there is only a very moderate relationship between the two. That is, for ethnic minority individuals the process of self-categorization does not lead directly or immediately to an unqualified affirmation (in-group favouritism in terms of cultural preferences) of the group whose label they have chosen to adopt. This is reminiscent of the cross-categorization studies mentioned earlier in the chapter, which showed a decrease in in-group favouritism. Neither is there unequivocal evidence that ethnic minority individuals prefer the out-group, as some researchers have suggested, whether it be on cultural adaptation variables or on self-categorization strategies. The finding of a general non-correspondence between these two dimensions of ethnic minority identity leaves a number of questions unanswered. Of course, it could be that the measuring instrument was not sensitive enough: the juxtaposition of the two scales, with one scale worded so that subjects were required to be proficient in the use of the double negative, may have built into the situation certain demand characteristics, which then produced results in the expected direction. Research into the relationship between self-categorization and styles of cultural adaptation is very new and further studies are required to refine the measuring instrument.

However, if indeed there is a genuine non-correspondence between cultural adaptation and self-categorization, then what is the role of self-categorization in ethnic minority identity? If ethnic minority individuals choose only the majority group label for self-categorization then the discrepancy between their perception of themselves and others' perceptions of them (by virtue of racial characteristics or other ethnic features) will produce an area of tension (in Lewinian terms) in the individual's psyche. If, on the other hand, the individual uses only the ethnic minority group label for self-categorization, then because the group suffers low status in the social hierarchy, this choice would militate against a sense of positive distinctiveness (Tajfel 1978). In this case, too, there will be an area of tension. In both the assimilative and the dissociative strategy, the tension systems produced by the choice of self-categorization strategy are likely to 'burst' when one's choice is questioned by others, or comes 'under attack'. It seems that the acculturative strategy and the marginal strategy would provide for greater flexibility and permeability of ethnic boundaries. When under attack regarding one's identity, the person who uses multiple ethnic labels for self-categorization will defend both labels equally and need not therefore adopt a defensive stance as an assimilative or dissociative person will do. For the marginal individual, the question of being 'under attack' is, of course, a non-issue.

The way in which self-categorization mediates social identity is still an unexplored field and these hypotheses are merely tentative suggestions for an area that requires much further research. See Turner (1987) for new directions in this field. Turner's theory is discussed later in this chapter.

Social stereotypes

Studies on social identity have suggested that there is an important link in the process of social categorization and the development of stereotypes. Social categories are divisions of people by people and these divisions carry a variety of cognitive and affective connotations which determine the extent to which an individual is prepared to approach or avoid members of the stereotyped out-group (Tajfel 1978).

Historically, the study of social stereotypes has been approached from one of three different prespectives (Ashmore and Del Boca 1981). One perspective, the motivational perspective, views stereotypes as functional for the intra-psychic needs of the perceiver. Thus, through the process of stereotyping, members of the minority group are made into scapegoats for the perceiver's feelings of inadequacy and low self-esteem. A second perspective, the socio-cultural approach, has focused on the role of socialization influences, such as the media through which stereotypes are developed and maintained. The third approach, of primary interest here, is the cognitive perspective. This approach to the study of stereotyping has sought to investigate the role of cognitive structures and processes in our understanding of human groups and social categories. From a cognitive perspective, then, a stereotype may be defined as (Hamilton and Trolier 1986, p. 133):

A cognitive structure that contains the perceiver's knowledge, beliefs and expectancies about some human group.

Stereotypes are developed in order to process information about people and they contribute to the way people interact with others from different social categories. Like all other categorization processes, stereotypes are developed in order to classify, encode, store, and retrieve information from a social world which is extremely rich in variety. Thus, commonalities among people are sought in order to reduce the complexity and richness of the data into more manageable units. Stereotypes are therefore formed around easily identifiable features: gender; race; age; occupation; accent; style of dressing. To the extent that these stereotypes reflect *actual* similarities and differences, they serve a useful function. However, the studies quoted in the previous section of this chapter have shown that the mere act of categorization serves to accentuate differences among people of different groups and to increase the perception of similiarity for members of one's own group. This, as well as the other consequences of stereotyping as it affects causal attributions, memory for negative out-group behaviours, and the illusion of out-group homogeneity, suggests that stereotyping can be dysfunctional in that it build barriers rather than bridges between people of different groups. Traditionally, research on stereotyping has almost always focused on ethnicity as a stimulus variable, merely investigating the effect of a target person's ethnicity on various evaluations. In other words, studies of stereotypes have sought to determine the *content* of the subject's stereotypes, rather than the processes related to stereotyping itself (Hamilton 1981).

The first study of stereotypes was carried out in 1933 by Katz and Brayly: Princeton University undergraduate students ($n = 100$) were asked to pick out, from a list of 84 adjectives, those adjectives which best described members of 10 different ethnic groups. They found extraordinary agreement on the first 10 traits chosen for each group, showing that there was a commonly agreed-upon stereotype. For instance, 84 per cent of the sample called blacks superstitious, 75 per cent saw them as lazy, and 38 per cent saw them as ignorant. This study was replicated twice, once in 1951 and again in 1967 and a number of important changes were noted (Gilbert 1951; Karlins *et al.* 1969). Specifically, there was a tendency for students to attribute more positive characteristics to most groups in later years. Hence, by 1967, blacks were most frequently called musical (47 per cent) and happy-go-lucky (27 per cent)—still not particularly flattering, but improvements on the adjectives chosen in earlier years. Secondly, the degree of agreement for the most often chosen adjectives was lower, suggesting less consensus on stereotypes. Finally, when Katz and Brayly (1933) first carried out the study, subjects readily assigned traits to the various groups. In later replications they sometimes complained about the procedures, and in some instances declined to carry out the task. Therefore, it is possible that subjects may have become more sensitive to the negative implications of stereotyping and that they have become more circumspect about expressing negative evaluations of a particular group (see Brigham 1971, for a review).

The bulk of studies investigating stereotyping processes in ethnic minority individuals indicate that ethnic minority individuals internalize self-derogatory stereotypes with regard to their own group and a favourable stereotype with regard to the majority group. For instance, Vaughan (1964) presented Maori and Pakeha (white) children with a stereotype test which consisted of six pairs of pictures, three pictures depicting males and three females. Each picture was matched as closely as possible, except that one picture represented a Maori, the other a Pakeha. Subjects were asked to choose one figure of each pair who was lazy, mean, clever, kind, clean, honest. Both Pakeha *and* Maori children between the ages of 4–12 favoured Pakeha pictures, i.e. while Pakeha children show a significant in-group bias, the ethnic minority Maori children show an out-group bias. Such findings are replicated in a number of other studies. When negro and white children were shown pictures of black and white children and asked to exemplify adjectives such as those used in Vaughan's study, children of *both* races tend to choose pictures of white children to illustrate positive attributes and pictures of black children to represent negative attributes (Banks and Rompf 1973; Cantor 1972; Cantor and Paternite 1973; Doke and Risley 1972; Spencer and Horowitz 1973; Stevenson and Stewart 1958; Williams *et al.* 1975). In one study (Sagar and Schofield 1980), children were told stories in which the central character, who was described as being either black or white performed acts that might have been aggressive (for example, bumping into someone in the hallway, or using another's pencil without asking). Children of both races rated the behaviour as more violent and threatening when the character was black than when the character was white.

Moscovici and Paicheler's (1978) study of assertive distinctiveness in minority groups suggests an explanation for these discrepant results. The authors hypothesized that those minority groups seeking social recognition will tend to stress their particularity and their self-definition so as to accentuate appropriate differences between themselves and others (assertive distinctiveness). On the other hand, negative self-image (anomic) minorities, devoid of resources or feeling threatened and uncertain, will attempt assimilation towards groups that are superior and legitimate. This hypothesis was tested within the minimal groups paradigm. Three variables were manipulated: (1) an in-group–out-group categorization based on aesthetic preferences for one or the other of two painters, Klee and Kandinsky; (2) the minority–majority representation in which subjects were told that their expressed preferences represented the preferences of either a small minority of the subjects (18.2 per cent) or a large majority of the subjects (81.8 per cent); (3) preceding the divisions mentioned above, subjects were given a creativity test and then randomly assigned to either a high- or a low-creativity group. This was done in order to induce a positive or a negative self-image in each of the groups. The results indicated that minorities with a positive self-image (nomic) did indeed show very high levels of in-group favouritism (assertive distinctiveness), whereas minorities with a negative self-image (anomic) displayed the highest percentage of out-group favouritism (17 per cent) when compared with the other groups (14–15 per cent). It is not clear from the data whether this out-group favouritism was significantly higher for the anomic minority than for the other three groups. Also, it must be noted that the predominant strategy even for minorities with a negative self-image was a balance between in-group favouritism and fairness.

Studies such as this would seem to suggest that minorities with strong cultural and social links, such as French Canadians and Indians (in Britain), may be able to resist the deleterious stereotypical images that the powerful majority group holds of the ethnic group. These minorities will show significantly more favourable evaluations of the in-group than the majority group. On the other hand, minorities without a strong social network will be more likely to accept negative images of themselves. As Tajfel (1978, p. 328) points out:

The continuous and daily interactions with the outside world, and the consequent *psychological* participation of a group in the system of values and network of stereotypes at large creates a degree of acceptance by the minority of its deleterious image; at the same time, some measure of protection is offered by the social and cultural links surviving within the group.

Milner's (1975) research on the negative self-images of Afro-Caribbean and Asian children in Britain is a good example of this: although both groups equally reproduce white values about their groups, they do not equally accept the implications for themselves; the derogatory personal image is less easily imposed on Asian children. 'It is as though the same pressure simply meets with more resistance' (p. 138). Milner explains the resistance in terms of the fact that the entirely separate cultural tradition of the Asian community provides these children with a strong sense of identity. Afro-Caribbean culture, on the other hand, is seen to have an English component; this, together with the bias towards whites in Afro-Caribbean society, would enhance a positive orientation towards whites in this country. Milner further observes that in the American studies (quoted earlier) many black children internalized the racial values that were imposed upon them by the dominant white group, so that they had difficulty in identifying with their own group and were positively disposed towards the white group. In this way, the Afro-Caribbeans in Britain and the blacks in America displayed similar tendencies towards the acceptance of a negative self-image. If stereotyping is used as a means of differentiating one's own group from other groups, as Tajfel's theory would predict, then ethnic minority individuals who come from groups with a rich cultural heritage should rate their own group significantly more favourably than the majority group. However, only a few studies indicate that ethnic minority groups show a preference for their own group, rather than the majority group.

Furnham and Kirris (1983) found that British Cypriot adolescents show a high level of in-group favouritism when rating a typical British girl, a typical British-Cypriot girl, and a typical Greek-Cypriot girl on fifteen bipolar semantic differential scales. Mann and Taylor (1974) found French Canadian subjects to be more ethnocentric than English Canadians when attributing ethnic categorizations to socially desirable and undesirable behaviour. Subjects were given a questionnaire enumerating ten common actions: five positive (socially desirable) and five negative, and asked to describe as a percentage rating, the degree to which the behaviour was caused by relatively stable personality traits of the actor. They were then asked to identify the ethnic group of the actor, the social class of the actor, and finally, the ethnic group *and* social class of the actor. French Canadians tended to emphasize ethnic differences, whereas for English Canadians social class was the important differentiating factor. This tendency towards in-group differentiation or 'ethnic distinctiveness' is also found in minority groups inside Jakarta (Jaspars and Warnaen 1982), who rated the Javanese and Sundanese (majority groups) less favourably than their own groups. Foster and Finchilescu (1986) also found that Indian nurses in South Africa rated their own group far more favourably than the white majority.

More equivocal results were obtained by Callan and Gallois (1983), however. They found that bilingual Greek Australians and Italian Australians rated their own group and Australians almost equally favourably and above other nationality groups, whereas Anglo-Australians held somewhat less favourable attitudes towards Greeks and Italians.

Study 9

A study by the present author found that Indian British adolescents rated Indians living in India (with whom they had little or no contact) very favourably. Next highest were Indians living in Britain, and least favourably rated were English people, who averaged around the neutral point of the bi-polar adjective scales presented to the subjects.

The subjects were 95 fourth- and fifth-year students at a comprehensive school for girls in Birmingham, the ethnic composition of which was predominantly Asian. Questionnaires obtained from subjects of Afro-Caribbean or English origin were not used. Of the sample, 93.5 per cent were of Indian origin. This was determined by asking the subjects to name the country in which their father was born and the country in which their mother was born. A very small percentage came from Pakistan or Bangladesh (3.2 per cent) and an equally small number were East African Indians (3.2 per cent). The great majority of the sample (91.4 per cent) were born in Britain; only 8.6 per cent were born outside Britain. However, 96.7 per cent of the sample had taken up residence in Britain before they were four years old. The sample was therefore second generation in essence, i.e. they had known only Britain as 'home'. The religious composition of the sample was as follows: Hindu 38.9 per cent; Sikh 55.6 per cent; Muslim 2.2 per cent; Christian 2.2 per cent; other 1.1 per cent. Most (80.7 per cent) of the subjects came from nuclear families, 12 per cent came from extended families, and 7.2 per cent came from single-parent families. While a few of the subjects came from Grades 2 and 3 of the Hall–Jones Occupational Prestige Scale (25 per cent), most of the fathers of these girls had occupations that fell between Grades 5 to 7 of the same scale (75 per cent). Quite a substantial proportion (22.8 per cent) of the fathers were currently unemployed and it was therefore not possible to determine their occupational status.

The subjects rated four concepts on 20 semantic differential scales. The concepts were a typical Indian girl who has lived all her life in India, a typical English girl, a typical Indian girl who has lived all her life in England (these will be referred to as Asians, henceforth), and self. It was thought necessary to choose a specific age and sex of the target person in order to make the task more meaningful. Thus, subjects were asked to rate a typical female from each of the three cultural groups who was of the same age as the subjects themselves. The instructions were similar to those suggested by Osgood *et al.* (1957), except that they were modified slightly to refer to ethnic groups. This was done in order to accommodate the Pakistanis, East African Indians, and Afro-Caribbeans in the class who were instructed to rate a typical girl from their own particular cultural background in place of a typical Indian girl. The bi-polar adjectives were chosen after careful pilot work. This involved eliciting self-descriptions from 20 Indian girls in India, 20 second generation Indian girls resident in Britain, and 20 English girls ($n = 60$). The 'Who am I?' protocols used in Chapter 7 were utilized for this purpose. The five most frequently used self-descriptions were chosen for each cultural group and finally the five most frequently used self-descriptions *across* the three groups were chosen. This yielded a total of 20 adjectives, which were then paired with their bi-polar opposites. Where the adjectives were identical to ones suggested by

Table 9.3 *t*-Tests between favourability ratings of Indians, English, and Asians assessed by the total sample of subjects

Pairs	$\bar{X}$	s.d.	*t*-test	d.f.	2-tailed probability (*p*)
Typical Indian	5.57	0.71	6.44	95	< 0.000
Typical English	4.87	0.98			
Typical Indian	5.57	0.71	−2.88	95	< 0.005
Typical Asian	5.29	0.95			
Typical Asian	5.29	0.95	4.38	95	< 0.0000
Typical English	4.87	0.98			

$\bar{X}$, mean; s.d., standard deviation.

Osgood *et al.* (1957), opposites were chosen according to those given by the authors. This gave rise to scales such as pleasant–unpleasant, kind–unkind, honest–dishonest, good–bad, etc. For adjectives not covered by Osgood, the pair was completed by adding the phrase 'Not at all . . .' to the adjective (Weinreich 1980). This yielded scales, such as: racially prejudiced–not at all racially prejudiced; frank–not at all frank; studious–not at all studious; etc. All adjective pairs were to be rated on a seven-point scale.

Table 9.3 reveals several important features of the favourability ratings of this sample of South Asian subjects. First of all, the typical Indian girl who has lived all her life in India is rated most favourably, suggesting an idealized image of people on the Indian subcontinent shared by the whole ethnic minority group. This stereotyped image of Indians is significantly more favourable than the ethnic minority's image of itself (the Asians). However, there is little to suggest that the South Asians in Britain rate themselves less favourably than the majority English group. In fact, the reverse is true, suggesting that there is a rejection of any deleterious images of the ethnic minority group as a whole. However, it should be pointed out that although English people are rated significantly less favourably than Indians and Asians, the mean rating ($\bar{X} = 4.87$) is on the positive pole of the scale. Thus, although English people are rated *less* favourably they are not rated *un*favourably.

Three separate factor analyses were then computed in order to determine the adjectives that contributed to these stereotypical images of Indians, English people, and Asians. A factor analytic approach to stereotyping has been used previously by several authors (Gardner *et al.* 1968, 1970; Triandis *et al.* 1982) and has been found to identify stereotypes effectively.

The 'Indian' stereotype comprised two main factors after Varimax rotation of the axes accounting for a total variance of 67.2 per cent at the stop-criterion of an eigen-value of unity. The first factor, claiming 55.0 per cent of the variance loaded highly on four adjective scales: good (0.71); loving (0.70); honest (0.66); and generous (0.60). The second factor, accounting for a further 12.2 per cent of the variance, loaded highly on two adjective scales: clever (0.64); and studious (0.60).

The 'English' stereotype consisted of three factors after Varimax rotation of the axes, accounting for a total of 88.1 per cent of the variance. The first factor, accounting for 66.8 per cent of the variance, loaded highly on: helpful (0.76); friendly (0.74); kind (0.65); obedient (0.63); and good (0.58). The second factor, claiming a further 11.2 per cent of the variance, loaded highly on honest (0.64); pleasant (0.63); generous (0.59); good (0.59); and not at all racially prejudiced (0.57). The third factor of the English stereotype accounting for a further 10.2 per cent of the variance loaded highly on only one scale, optimistic (0.56).

The 'Asian' stereotype also comprised three factors (after rotation), claiming 78.7 per cent of the total variance. The first factor loaded highly on: clever (0.84); good (0.80); honest (0.68); and loving (0.58). The second factor, accounting for a further 10.9 per cent of the variance, loaded highly on: generous (0.77); friendly (0.64); a hard worker (0.61); and respects her elders (0.53). The third factor of the Asian stereotype, accounting for another 8.9 per cent of the variance, loaded on: not at all violent (0.67); and sincere (0.63).

Next, the data on ratings of self were factor anaylsed. Again, three factors emerged after Varimax rotation of the axes, accounting for 69.2 per cent of the total variance. On the first factor (42.9 per cent of the variance), the following adjectives obtained high loadings: kind (0.72); generous (0.54); and loving (0.52). On the second factor, which accounted for another 14.7 per cent of the variance, high loadings were obtained for: not at all racially prejudiced (0.66); unselfish (0.53); and sincere (0.53). The third factor, accounting for a further 11.6 per cent of the variance, loaded highly on: good-tempered (0.70); and friendly (0.55).

What becomes immediately obvious is the similarity between the Indian stereotype and the Asian stereotype. Indians are seen to be good, loving, honest, generous, clever, and studious; Asians are also seen to be good, loving, honest, generous, clever, and hard-working, although, in addition, they are seen to be friendly, respectful of elders, sincere, and not at all violent.

The Asian stereotype also has quite a lot in common with the English stereotype—both are seen to be good, honest, generous, and friendly. Interestingly, the subjects see English people as not at all racially prejudiced. They see themselves (self-ratings) also as not at all racially prejudiced, friendly, and kind, and these attributes are held in common with

English people, but not with Indians or with Asians (with the exception of friendly, which is also an Asian attribute). Only two attributes on the self-ratings are held in common with Indians and Asians, namely, loving and generous, although generous is also an important English attribute. Together with the above, self is seen as sincere, unselfish, and good-tempered.

Studies using factor analysis to investigate the content of ethnic minority self-stereotypes are limited by the fact that this statistical technique reveals little about the cognitive organization of the stereotype in question. Rosch (1978) has suggested that cognitive categories are organized hierarchically. Thus, there may be an initial classification of persons into broad racial groups: blacks; whites; Asians. With increasing experience of each of these groups, the perceiver will develop subordinate categories. For the super-ordinate category Asians, for example, there may be sub-types representing traditional Asians and modern Asians, middle class Asians and working class Asians, etc. Nested within super-ordinate categories are lower-order sub-categories. When rating out-groups, analysis at super-ordinate levels may be appropriate if only because the perceiver has little basis to make differentiations between the sub-categories of the group. However, when rating a group with which the perceiver is familiar, tapping stereotypes at a super-ordinate level of analysis may be less of a meaningful task. Brewer (1979) studying stereotypes of the elderly, proposed that 'old person' is a super-ordinate category and that people store information in more meaningful units (grandmothers, senior citizens, etc.) A free-sort cluster analysis revealed that subjects did not perceive stimulus photographs of elderly people simply in terms of 'old people' but in terms of three meaningful sub-categories of the elderly. Brewer's (1988) more recent writing on the subject suggests that subordinate categories (business women) are often distinct from super-ordinate categories (women) and even perhaps from super-ordinate categories that are logically adjacent, such as women and business executives. Thus, as Hamilton (1981) cautions, a researcher's analysis based on measures reflecting only super-ordinate categories is likely to lead to inappropriate conclusions if the subject is using a well-defined system of sub-categories. In addition, inferences about the nature of inter-personal interaction will depend not only upon a knowledge of the super-ordinate category to which the target person belongs, but also upon an understanding of the subordinate level categories and the beliefs associated with each one.

Social cognition techniques using response times as a dependent variable are quickly superseding more traditional methods of eliciting stereotypes. The technique has the advantage of being relatively non-reactive. Subjects are asked to make simple responses or, in some experiments, evaluative judgements about trait words, such as 'ambitious', 'lazy', which are displayed after the presentation of a category label (whites, blacks). Faster response times are meant to indicate greater associative strength between category labels and traits (Gaertner and McLaughlin 1983; Dovidio *et al.* 1986). Using these techniques the authors were able to demonstrate that in spite of recent survey evidence suggesting that white American stereotypes of blacks are becoming less prejudiced (see Dovidio and Gaertner 1986), attitudes and beliefs have not changed substantially. Gaertner and Dovidio (1986) have shown that white attitudes towards blacks are marked by a conflict between egalitarian values and unacknowledged negative feelings. Kinder (1986) and McConohay (1986) suggest that Americans are torn between the belief that racism is bad and the belief that most inequalities have been addressed and blacks are now making unfair demands.

Several questions remain to be addressed, for example, How are stereotypes formed? Once formed can they be changed (and if so, how)? What are some of the effects of stereotypes on social interaction, and what is the relationship of social identity theory to social stereotyping? There is an impressive body of research that has been accumulated in answer to these questions. However, a detailed analysis is beyond the scope of this book (see Hamilton 1981; Hamilton and Trolier 1986, for comprehensive reviews).

Stereotypes are formed through the process of socialization (this will be discussed later). From a cognitive perspective stereotypes develop around stimuli that are salient or distinctive in the social environment. A stimulus may be salient because of the value system of the perceiver. Thus, a black person's race may always constitute a salient stimulus for a person who is racially prejudiced. A study by Scodel and Austrin (1957) showed that anti-Semites: (1) were more accurate in identifying photographs of Jews than were non-prejudiced subjects; and (2) assigned a significantly larger number of photographs to the Jewish category. Tajfel (1981) interprets such over-exclusion (some non-Jews were categorized as Jews) as less risky to the value systems of prejudiced subjects than the inclusion in the non-Jew category of those that may well be Jews. Distinctiveness may be based on the context in which it occurs. The stimulus may be novel or unusual and may therefore siphon off a disproportionate amount of attention. This is a social psychological equivalent of the Von Restorff effect. Taylor's (1981) studies on context-based distinctiveness (see Chapter 7) show that a black person when he was the only black in the group was perceived as more active and talkative during discussion periods, having more influence on the group discussion, and was rated more extremely on personality characteristics, than when the same person was part of a mixed race group in which there were also two other blacks.

According to Hamilton *et al.* (1985) stereotypes are formed by the development of an illusory correlation between distinctive group membership and distinctive behaviour. White people, they maintain, have relatively infrequent exposure to blacks, making black people salient to the white perceiver. Certain forms of undesirable behaviour also occur with relative infrequency and therefore become distinctive. Thus, the co-occurence of a black person exhibiting an undesirable behaviour would have the effect of being doubly salient to the white perceiver. This illusory correlation would then constitute the nucleus for the growth of a stereo-type of blacks. Thus group level information is assumed to be acquired from social learning experiences with individual members of a particular category, about whom information is not stored.

Prototype models of social stereotypes have been widely used. However, more recently it has been realized that people also make estimates about how variable a group is and thus prototype models have been overtaken by mixed models and pure exemplar models. Mixed models (Estes 1986) postulate that both central tendency (stereotypical) and frequency information (variability) are stored. Pure exemplar models (Hintzman 1986) suggest that information about individual category members is stored. Linville's (Linville *et al.* 1986, 1989) multiple exemplar model suggests that judgements about a group as a whole are made by retrieving and integrating information from several exemplars as well as abstracted sub-types. (For a discussion of these models see Messick and Mackie 1989.)

The interest in sub-types gains its impetus from the hope that increasing specification results in the individualization of the target and that indivi-dualization of the target will ultimately lead to reduced prejudice and improved inter-group relations. Rothbart and John (1985) and Sears (1983) found that individual members of a group are reacted to more favourably than groups as a whole, suggesting that there are benefits to the individualizing process. However, Pettigrew's (1979) work on the ultimate attribution error highlights the fact that mere individualization may not lead to any shift in stereotypic beliefs about the groups as a whole. Instead, the individual may be classified as an exception to the rule.

Once formed, *can* stereotypes be changed? Synder and Swann (1978) viewed stereotypes as a number of hypotheses concerning people of different social categories and found that their subjects actively sought out information that confirmed their hypotheses rather than information that would disconfirm their hypotheses. Taylor (1981) also shares the same pessimism about the invulnerability of stereotypes, once formed. Viewing stereotypes as multi-level configurations, hierarchically arranged, Taylor points out that disconfirmation of stereotypes is difficult because the stereotyped individual can be perceived as belonging to one or another sub-category. If no appropriate category exists, a new sub-type may be established. However, two models of stereotype change have been sug-gested: the book-keeping model; and the conversion model. According to the book-keeping model the individual keeps accurate accounts of confirming and disconfirming evidence of stereotypic beliefs. As disconfirming evidence is accumulated stereotypes gradually change. According to the conversion model, change is more catastrophic than gradual. A few highly salient instances play a critical role in disconfirming the stereotype. Empirical evidence for these two models is still sketchy and awaits further research.

The effects of stereotyping on social interaction are far-reaching. Racial stereotypes often become self-fulfilling prophecies. Research by Word *et al.* (1974) showed that black job applicants were given shorter interviews and were responded to less positively than white job applicants, even though both black and white applicants were confederates of the experimenter and had been trained to respond similarly to the interviewers (subjects). Furthermore, in a subsequent study they found that a negative interviewing style actually produced different levels of performance in subjects. Thus, the perceiver's stereotype influences how s/he will interact with members of the stereotyped group, and also affects the stereotyped person in such a way as to confirm the already existing stereotypes.

Having said this, however, it is not uncommon to find friendships flourishing across stereotyped group boundaries. A white person may enjoy, and solicit the company of a black person. Yet his stereotype of blacks as a group may remain unchanged. That is, there may be a certain non-correspondence between stereotypes and actual interactions. This is most true when there is a discrepancy between the inter-personal–inter-group level of analysis. When the target person (black friend who also happens to be a member of the stereotyped group) is being perceived primarily from the inter-personal pole of the inter-personal–inter-group continuum, then the individuation of the out-group member can highlight his/her heterogeneity and thus lead to a reduction in in-group–out-group bias. As soon as perception snaps back into the inter-group pole, and the target person is seen primarily as a representative of the stereotyped group, there is likely to be an increase in correspondence between stereotypic beliefs and modes of interaction.

Thus, contact *per se* is an insufficient predictor of the course of inter-group relations. The contact hypothesis which proposed that direct inter-personal contact between members of antagonistic groups will bring about a reduction in prejudiced attitudes and discriminatory behaviour has been extensively explored by Hewstone and Brown (1986). Pettigrew (1986), in his summary of the Hewstone and Brown volume, has highlighted the theoretical frailty of the hypothesis, suggesting that it is 'logically loose, narrowly cognitive, statically focused on isolated rather than cumulative impacts, and mute about generality'. Hewstone and Brown (1986) place great emphasis, instead, on whether the contact is inter-personal or inter-group. They further examine the actors' perceptions and attributions regarding the contact and the implications of the hypothesis for social identity theory.

This then brings us to the final question. What is the relationship between social identity theory and stereotyping? We have seen that stereotyping has its roots in social categorization and social categorization is the process by which the individual organizes and interprets the world. The differentiation of the social environment into groups provides the individual with a basis for self-categorization. That is, individuals derive important aspects of their self-concepts from the different social groups to which they belong. As people are driven by the need to achieve a positive social identity, they choose to construe their own groups in positive terms. Group evaluations are determined always in reference to other social groups and are therefore inherently comparative and this process of social comparison, motivated as it is by the drive towards psychological distinctiveness, results in in-group favouritism.

More recently, self-categorization theory (SCT) put forward by Turner (1987), has emerged as a new direction for those originally interested in social identity theory. Self-categorization theory seems to place the focus of attention upon categorization processes *per se*. According to Turner (1987), people perceive themselves to be members of their various groups and these groups are arranged in a hierarchical structure of organization. The act of categorization and, in particular, self-categorization leads to perceptual distortion such that intra-category similarities are accentuated and inter-category differences are maximized. This aspect of self-categorization theory is reminiscent of Tajfel's earlier studies in perception (Tajfel and Wilkes 1963). Categories that contain the self are not only easily accessible, they are also positively regarded, i.e. they contain positive distinctiveness. Individuals therefore become ethnocentric by the act of self-categorization.

Once self-categorization has been accomplished and individuals have applied to themselves the labels of a particular group, the way is open for referent informational influence to occur (Hogg and Turner 1987). The process of referent informational influence occurs in three stages (Hogg and Abrams 1988). First, as mentioned above, people assign themselves a particular social category. They then learn the stereotypic norms of that social category and finally they assign the stereotypes to themselves (self-stereotyping). Their behaviour will then be in accord with their cognitive representation of the stereotypes of the in-group. Thus, conformity to the group of one's self-categorization can be expected (see Abrams *et al.* 1990).

The preceding analysis draws us to the rather dismal conclusion that stereotyping (and the associated prejudices that stereotypes carry) cannot be eliminated. First, stereotyping fulfils a basic need for order and predictability. Secondly, the need for a positive social identity creates a vested interest in maintaining the stereotypic inferiority of relevant out-groups. Hogg and Abrams (1988), however, do not see things as pessimis-tically as this. They remind us that these needs should not be considered to be mechanical causes with a one-to-one relationship with behavioural outcome. Rather, they suggest that the question of eliminating stereotyp-ing be recast: stereotyping is essential, the question is how can we modify stereotypes so that they do not oppress others and result in discriminatory behaviour.

A first clue to this dilemma may be found in the results of Vanbeselaere's (1987) study. Messick and Mackie (1989) account for Vanbeselaere's findings: they suggest that cross-categorization on two dimensions at once reduces or eliminates the perceptual distortion that accompanies single categorization and without perceptual distortion the gradient between the two comparison groups disappears, eliminating, thereby, inter-group dis-crimination. Thus, by looking for multiple categories that emphasize the commonalities between groups we may be able to reduce and perhaps even eliminate prejudice and discrimination.

For the ethnic minority individual, multiple categories are readily available. Whether they are used, of course, is a matter of individual choice. Much depends upon the dynamic of the experiences of the individual with members of the ethnic minority group and members of the majority group. Over time, individuals abstract from these experiences kernels of perceived truth which then become the nuclei for the growth of stereotypes—Indians are . . . the English are . . . Depending upon the nature of these abstractions, they will then place themselves at a self-chosen distance from the ethnic minority group and the majority group. In other words, the individual consciously articulates a stance towards each group and thus develops a strategy of self-categorization. Although not yet borne out by research, there should be a high degree of corres-pondence between the individual's stereotypes and his/her strategy of self-categorization. For example if the individual has a favourable stereotype of the ethnic minority group and an unfavourable stereotype of the majority group, then it is likely that s/he will use the ethnic minority label for self-categorization rather than the majority group label, i.e. the dissociative strategy will be used. Or, if the individual has equally favourable stereotypes of both groups then it is likely that the acculturative strategy will be used, i.e. the individual will use both group identities for self-categorization. And so for individuals who have favourable stereo-types of the out-group and unfavourable stereotypes of the ethnic minority group, self-categorization will be in terms of assimilation. The marginal person is either indifferent to or chooses to transcend ethnic group identities, defining him/herself in terms of other parameters. The role of stereotyping (if any) for this person remains unclear. Indeed, all the above hypotheses await further clarification and research.

Thus, we can anticipate a merging of social identity theory with the research findings arising out of a social cognition perspective. By empirically pursuing the interfaces between these two approaches we may be able to establish the foundation for a more integrated theoretical framework.

10.

Conclusion: towards a new perspective on ethnic minority identity

The aim of this book has been to bring together a diverse and scattered literature on ethnic minority identity. This review, of both the theory and the empirical research related to the field, has raised as many questions as it has answered and it is clear that there are many unresolved issues still to be tackled. However, the effort of this enquiry has been to clarify conceptual difficulties and to establish a number of empirical generalizations regarding the antecedent and consequent factors underlying ethnic minority identity.

In this chapter an attempt will be made to sift through and integrate some of the ideas that have arisen from previous theory and research into a new perspective on ethnic minority identity. This new model will be put forward, therefore, as a framework for further research. The propositions are tentative, requiring refinement and greater precision. However, Festinger (1950b) has argued that the premature precision of a theory can lead to sterility. None the less an attempt will be made to avoid unnecessary ambiguity. Thus, the theory is presented formally only to facilitate verification or falsification in future studies.

A brief review

Historically, we have seen that many of the conceptualizations of ethnic minority identity were assimilationist in essence. The trend, both in terms of theorizing and in terms of public policy, was to view ethnic minority groups as inferior, and to expect them therefore to shed the bulk of their cultural traditions and customs, in other words, their ethnicity, in order that they become as much like the majority as possible. The norm for conformity was thus Anglo-Saxon. This assimilationist trend took a change in direction when it was observed that ethnicity persisted over many generations in spite of governmental policy to keep it in check. The new direction repudiated the superiority of the Anglo-Saxon norm, but saw ethnicity as eventually disappearing into the melting-pot of a new cultural identity. Thus, for the first time ethnic minority groups were seen as having something positive to contribute to national life. However, the melting-pot philosophy predicted the gradual but inevitable decline of ethnicity.

These sociological theories found their parallel in psychological thought. Early psychologies assumed that true integration was equivalent to complete assimilation, that the annihilation of difference between the minority and the majority was vital to the healthy functioning both of the nation and of the individual. Ethnic minorities who could not 'disappear', i.e. who were racially distinct from the majority, were expected to manifest low levels of self-esteem, and high levels of self-hatred.

In recent decades, however, both the sociological and psychological theories of ethnic minority identity have been called into question, first, by the observation that ethnicity persisted in spite of more than adequate opportunity to assimilate (as amongst white ethnics), and secondly, by the observation that high levels of self-hatred were conspicuously absent even among those ethnic minority individuals who were racially distinct.

In fact, a trend in the opposite direction is manifest: there has been an upsurge of ethnicity in many multi-ethnic societies such that ethnic minority individuals have made concerted attempts to rediscover their roots. Once again, therefore, a new philosophy of ethnicity has emerged: that of ethnic pluralism. Ethnic (or cultural) pluralism acknowledges the increasingly heterogeneous nature of life in the Western world. It also acknowledges the persistence of ethnicity and sees ethnic minority groups as an essential and edifying part of the mosaic of national life. The implications of this shift in philosophy have been far-reaching. The philosophy of ethnic pluralism has called for changes in public policy with regard to law, policing, education, housing, and employment opportunities for ethnic minority individuals. It expresses itself in a concern that ethnic minority individuals be protected from discrimination and enjoy equal opportunity in all spheres of life (see Glazer and Young 1983, for the summary of a conference on ethnic pluralism and public policy). The emphasis has thus shifted from an annihilation of difference to a celebration of difference.

Thus, the theories that have made self-hatred and the impetus to assimilate the primary dynamic underlying ethnic minority identity have been found wanting, both by sociological observation and psychological investigation. This is perhaps due to the fact that assimilation is only one of several options available to the ethnic minority individual. In fact, there are a variety of identity options available to the ethnic minority child. In the doll studies (Clarke and Clarke 1939) which have been used to measure ethnic identification in black American children (and more recently in black British children), children were presented with one black doll and one white doll and then asked to express their preference for one or the other. This then was used as index of ethnic identification. Yet to force the child into choosing a black or a white doll fails to uncover the real issues underlying ethnic identification. The question is not so much whether the child *can* identify him/herself as belonging to an ethnic group (recent studies have shown that identification as seen in this light is not unduly problematic to the black child), nor is it a question of whether the child wishes to identify with one group as opposed to another. The key question is the *degree* to which the child *wishes* to identify with the ethnic group or the majority group, with both groups, or with neither group. When posed in this way, it becomes clear that the issue of ethnic identification is not a simple either/or matter. In most cases, it is not a simple preference for one group to the exclusion of the other; it is a delicately graded balance of identification with both the ethnic minority group and the majority group.

The issue becomes even more clear when considering the case of mixed-race children, where the child is racially part of two or more cultures, in some cases accepted by both, in other cases accepted by neither. There has been a gradual awakening to the fact that researchers have been confronting the child with a ready-built model of society in which the racial structure is strictly dichotomous. When presented with photographs indicating gradations of skin colour, Wilson (1981) reported that only two children of a sample of 51 mixed-race children spontaneously grouped the photographs into two groups of white and non-white. That is, in a situation in which children were given the freedom to categorize photographs spontaneously, only a very small percentage of mixed-race children used the strictly dichotomous scheme of racial categorization that psychologists have persistently presented to their subjects. In fact, many children, about one-third of Wilson's sample, do not use colour at all, but nationality and culture components to describe themselves. Greenwald and Oppenheim (1968) found that when black children were presented with black, white, and mulatto dolls, a significant proportion chose the mulatto doll. This is interpreted by the authors to mean that previous studies had presented children with dolls that were too dark to be perceived as Negroid. However, an alternative explanation might be that in choosing a mulatto doll, black children were expressing an unwillingness to indicate a preference for either the black doll or the white doll. In other words, the choice of a mulatto doll may indicate some degree of identification with both black and white groups, or even perhaps a lack of it with either group.

A new model of ethnic minority identity

If racial categorization is more complex a phenomenon than a black or white dichotomy then the spill-over effect into other areas of ethnic identification may be considerable. Essentially the same question may be posed of (say) the second generation Indian immigrant who is at once a

British citizen *and* of Indian origin. Might not s/he, if asked the right questions, display an equally varied array of identity options? In an insightful expose on identity options, Wallman (1983, p.8) suggested that the possession of an array of identity options is in itself a healthy choice.

It is not difficult to imagine that a child, say, born in England of one (white) Scottish and one (black) Jamaican parent now living in South London could when asked 'What are you?' define himself as English, Black English, West Indian, Scots, a Londoner or a South Londoner in turn depending who asked him the question, why they asked it, and what else was happening at the time. Equally, it is not hard to imagine the same child 'claiming' all those identities, not because he lacks a single identity focus and is (therefore) 'in crisis' but because multiple identity is itself a healthy choice.

Thus, ethnic minority identity is not necessarily a singular, fixed, inflexible given but may be constituted of hyphenated identities that indicate varying degrees of identification with both the ethnic minority group and the majority group. In order to tap the subjective sense of ethnic identity, the traditional bi-polar model which asks questions such as 'Are you Aboriginal *or* Australian?' (Sommerlad and Berry 1970), needs to be abandoned for a more attentuated model in which the questions tap the balance of subjective identification with both groups. For example, to a French Canadian, the question may be posed as follows: 'To what extent do you *feel* French? To what degree do you feel Canadian?'

Using pairs of questions to measure ethnic identification, it is possible to determine the ethnic individual's strategy of self-categorization. Figure 10.1 indicates that there are at least four such strategies. In the light of the scheme shown in Fig. 10.1, the acculturative individual categorizes him/herself with a hyphenated identity: Indian-British, Greek-Australian, Spanish-American. The assimilative individual concentrates on the major-ity group label of his/her identity: a second generation adolescent of Indian origin may choose to see him/herself as entirely British. The dissociative individual defines him/herself entirely within the bounds of the ethnic minority group, and the marginal individual is indifferent to ethnic group identifications *or chooses* to identify with neither group.

The theories and the research arising from the theories have tended to confuse two different aspects of ethnic minority identity, namely, that ethnic minority identity is composed of two distinct and not necessarily related components: (1) a consciously articulated stance or strategy of self-categorization; and (2) an underlying system or body of beliefs, attitudes, values, and behaviour—or a style of cultural adaptation. Both components are developed in relation to the ethnic minority group *and* the majority group in conjunction with each other.

The same model (Fig. 10.1) may be used to measure styles of cultural adaptation. Most measures have assumed that ethnic minority identity is

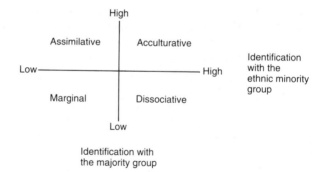

Fig. 10.1. A quadri-polar model for the study of ethnic minority identity.

uni-dimensional, i.e. one has more or less of it, and that identification with the minority group assumes a corresponding lack of identification with the majority group. Attempts at quantifying cultural adaptation have therefore measured either the degree of identification with the ethnic group *or* the degree of assimilation into the majority group. One example of this, the Ethnic Identity Questionnaire (Masuda *et al.* 1973) measures liking for Japanese food, movies, etc. The implicit assumption here is that high identification with the minority group precludes high identification with the majority group. Such measures tell only a partial, truncated story of cultural adaptation. According to the model I have presented, both the acculturative and the dissociative individual should show high levels of identification with the ethnic minority. It is their pattern of identification with the majority that makes the crucial difference in their style of cultural adaptation. The two dimensions—ethnic minority identification and majority group identification—*must* be used in conjunction with each other, in order to arrive at an accurate understanding of the various styles of cultural adaptation.

This model is similar to one presented by Bochner (1982) in his analysis of the psychological outcomes for individuals who are in contact with people from other cultures. His four types are the 'passing' (or assimilative), the chauvinistic (or dissociative), the mediating (or acculturative), and the marginal individual. The individual who adopts a style of cultural adaptation that is assimilative rejects the culture of his/her origin and embraces the cultural norms and practices of the majority group. In the dissociative style, cultural norms of the ethnic group increase in salience, while those of the majority group are spurned. The marginal individual vacillates between the two groups; the norms of both cultures are perceived as salient but somewhat incompatible, and the result is a low level of identification with both groups. For the individual who adopts an acculturative style, norms of both cultures are perceived as salient and as capable of being synthesized or integrated. Although it may be possible to classify individuals as consistently manifesting more of one style than another, the four styles should not be seen as static, but dynamic in nature.

It has been generally assumed that there is a one-to-one correspondence between one's strategy of self-categorization and the style of cultural adaptation one adopts for oneself. That is, if a second generation adolescent of Indian origin categorizes him/herself as British, then his behaviour and attitudes will be consistent with this categorization. This assumption has been so widespread that most studies have measured the one as an index of the other. However, a close study of the literature seems to indicate that self-categorization, particularly of the dissociative type, persists long after the individual has made the necessary cultural adaptations for effective living. Gordon (1964), as long as 25 years ago, suggested that cultural assimilation may precede and even occur independently of identificational assimilation. That is, ethnic individuals, should they choose the assimilative style of cultural adaptation, may become indistinguishable from their majority group contemporaries in terms of their behaviour, attitudes, and language, while yet retaining a subjective sense of belonging to the ethnic group at the level of self-categorization. Conversely, Banks and Gay (1978) observe that although fourth generation Irish-Americans, Polish-Americans, and Italian-Americans may not identify socially or psychologically with their original ethnic groups and have little or no consciousness of their ethnic culture, their 'Irishness', 'Polishness', or 'Italianness' is still very much a part of their lives.

This, perhaps, is the most important aspect of the current model: that self-categorizations may be relatively independent of styles of cultural adaptation and that eventually they may acquire functional autonomy. The notion of the functional autonomy of self-categorization from cultural adaptation suggests that the ethnic minority individual may feel strongly Indian (say) but be very British in his/her behaviour and other attitudes.

It is for this reason that definitions of ethnic identity which refer to a 'shared sense of peoplehood', a 'common cultural tradition', etc. are inadequate. They are unable to embrace second, third, and successive generations of ethnic minority individuals, who may be well acculturated or even assimilated into the surrounding culture, but who may nevertheless feel very strongly identified with their ethnic minority group in terms of their self-categorization.

In using the model presented here, not all ethnic minority individuals have an 'ethnic identity', in that they may eschew the cultural traditions of their group. However, all have a method of ethnic identification which is manifest in a strategy of self-categorization and a style of cultural adaptation. Thus, the concept of ethnic minority identity must be sharpened so that a distinction is made between self-categorization strategies and styles of cultural adaptation. The notion of functional autonomy would then account for the upsurge of ethnicity that we have seen in recent years. The trend is an upsurge of dissociative self-categorization in spite of more than adequate acculturation into the ways of the country of adoption.

The question then is what is it that makes a particular self-categorization salient? A partial answer has been sought and found in the annals of social cognition, and social identity theory in particular. When the ethnic minority exists in a substantial proportion in the immediate social environment, and conditions are favourable for group entitivity to occur, ethnicity increases in salience. This is true because a numerically preponderant ethnic minority group is able to develop a forum for asserting its positive distinctiveness, thereby to re-evaluate aspects of a negatively valued ethnic identity or to create positive components. Whether a salient ethnicity, produced by numerical preponderance in the social environment, is conducive to further national integration or merely spawns separatist movements is a question that bears further investigation. This issue will be discussed later.

Little is known about the personality correlates of the various patterns of ethnic minority identification, nor will any be suggested here. The most consistent finding is that the mediating person (the acculturative individual) exhibits a high degree of cognitive flexibility (Taft 1981) and field independence (Berry and Annis 1974). Marginality is equated with insecurity, self-pity, sensitivity (Mann 1957), whereas assimilation is associated with low self-esteem (Lefley 1974). Dissociation (ethnocentrism) has been traditionally associated with high authoritarianism (Adorno *et al.* 1950). Although explorations in this area may prove valuable, the more immediate concern of this work was to determine the key social psychological factors that might give rise to the four types of social self-categorization. In other words, how does the ethnic minority individual come to choose for him/herself one stategy of social self-categorization over the others?

It would seem that social comparison is a fundamental process in the choice of strategy. Previously, it had been assumed that the only really salient group for social comparison for ethnic minority individuals is the high status majority group. Rosenberg (1979) has argued the opposite, that social comparison occurs with people who are most similar to oneself and that the ethnic minority child compares him/herself with other children from the ethnic minority group. In contrast to Tajfel's emphasis, it would seem that when a minority group is an ethnic minority group, social comparisons may be made with other members of the group in order to achieve a positive social identity. With reference to Rosenberg it might be argued that although in childhood one may be protected from making social comparisons with the majority group by virtue of a relatively confined environment, this is unlikely in adolescence and adulthood. It is far more reasonable to believe that the ethnic minority adolescent makes social comparisons between *both* the majority group and the ethnic minority group and locates him/herself somewhere within the framework of these comparisons.

The outcomes of the social comparison process are rooted in the dynamic of the experiences of the individual with members of both groups over time. Thus, if their experiences with the ethnic minority and the majority are predominantly positive, it is likely that they will categorize themselves with labels characteristic of both groups, for example, Indian-British. That is, they will choose the acculturative strategy. If, on the other hand, their experiences with the majority group are predominantly negative, whereas those with the ethnic minority are generally positive, their strategy of self-categorization will be essentially dissociative in nature. Assimilation occurs only if experiences with the majority are more favourable than those with the ethnic minority. Individuals who have negative outcomes with both groups are likely to be marginal. It may be that such individuals will use self- rather than group-identity as primary reference points.

Initially, 'experience' with the ethnic minority and the majority group consists in interactions with significant others who are representatives of the two groups. As transmitters of culture, parents and teachers are important identificands for the primary schoolchild. Later, the peer group, depending upon its ethnic composition, will be the harbinger of experience with people from different cultural backgrounds.

The term 'experience' is deliberately broad; it is meant to encompass not only direct social interactions with significant others but also introjected aspirations, reflected appraisals (Rosenberg 1979), ideals and values and attitudes of world-mindedness (Bochner 1982), or prejudice (Allport 1954) communicated by these significant others. Also, the balance of the individual's experiences with the two groups is not a simple sum or the difference of the positive or negative experiences that accrue to the individual. A single experience depending on its salience to the individual may have the power dramatically to reverse or disproportionately to enhance the ongoing process. Thus, the individual is not to be seen as a *tabula rasa* upon which the hand of experience writes, not a simple stimulus–response mechanism that is easily shaped or moulded by a simple manipulation of good or bad experiences. S/he brings to each situation his/her own idiosyncratic response.

The concept of 'culture clash' is based on the assumption that as the ethnic minority adolescent comes into increasing contact with his/her Western peers' values and norms (which are often at variance with the ethnic minority culture), they become increasingly attractive, and violent conflict ensues between the individual and his/her parents. A study by Brittain (1963) on parent–peer cross pressures indicated that adolescents have a well worked-out non-conflicted system of reference: choices in favour of parents were made when an option involved long-term consequences and stable value conditions, such as vocational decisions, etc. Adolescents tended to follow their peers when status or identity needs were to be gratified, when excommunication from the peer group was imminent, or where the option provided similarity to peers on issues such as choice of clothes, etc. A further study by Burret and Hutnik (1982) found that Indian adolescent girls with a low level of self-acceptance showed significantly more conformity to parents than peers when the values under consideration involved long-term consequences (i.e. where stable). Adolescents with a high level of self-acceptance showed no significant differences in the number of parent-oriented, peer-oriented, and self-determined choices they made when values were stable. When the value options offered were in a transitional stage (for example, emancipation of women), adolescents with a high level of self-acceptance indicated a significant peer-orientation, while those with a low level of self-acceptance showed no difference in the number of parent- and peer-oriented responses they made. With reference to the ethnic minority individual, such studies suggest that a high level of self-acceptance would predispose the individual to be more 'open' to experiences with peers from the majority culture as well as from the ethnic minority. Individuals with a low level of self-acceptance would show greater parent conformity. If parents are keen to perpetuate the ethnic group culture, then the adolescent chooses almost by default to be relatively 'closed' to experiences, positive or negative, from the majority. Thus, what the individual brings to each situation will play an important role in determining the outcome of his/her experience with the majority and the ethnic minority.

Gradually, individuals come to abstract from these experiences kernels of perceived truth, which become internal representations to them of the whole group. The English are . . . , Indians are . . . . Depending upon the content of these abstractions, or images, they will place themselves at a self-chosen distance with regard to the ethnic minority group and the majority. This exemplifies Chun's (1983) conception of ethnic identity as being a process of socio-epistemic self-emplacement. In terms of social identity theory, the individual consciously articulates a stance towards each group and develops a strategy of self-categorization. Thus, the individual who has had positive experiences with both groups and has therefore developed internal representations of both groups that are equally favourable, will use social self-categorizations that are typical of both the minority group ('I am Indian') and the majority group ('I am also British'). For the person who has received much in the way of prejudice and discrimination at the hands of the majority group, the internal representations of this group are likely to be negative. If their internal representations of the ethnic minority are positive they will be able to achieve a sense of positive social identity by articulating a dissociative stance ('I am Indian . . . , 'I am not British'); if negative they will be propelled in the direction of marginality ('I identify neither as Indian, nor as British'). Assimilation, in this paradigm, occurs when the negative connotations of minority group membership far outweigh the positive benefits, and when the internal representations of the majority are highly favourable.

When assimilative individuals who categorize themselves as British and not Indian find that access into various aspects of majority group life is closed to them, one of several options becomes possible. If the history of their experiences with the ethnic minority group is irredeemably negative they may then choose to be marginal, i.e. they choose to identify neither with the group nor the other. Another option, as suggested by Taylor and McKirnan (1984) and Tajfel (1978), may be that these individuals are propelled in the direction of dissociation and may attempt to rediscover or create dimensions of social comparison in order to achieve a positive social identity, defined in apposition to the majority group. A dissociative stance will produce attempts at consciousness-raising, especially if the system of social relations is moderately unequal and is perceived as illegitimate and the stance is born out of failed attempts at assimilation. However, in the current model, consciousness-raising and social action may also arise from people who are acculturative. Such individuals, while identifying with the majority group, have also developed a sense of ethnic dignity and an awareness of the rights of the minority group living within the context of the majority culture. Thus, social action that arises from a strategy of acculturation is likely to be less defensive, less violent, and more effective, because the acculturative individual serves as a mediator between cultures, narrowing rather than widening the gap.

There are many assumptions implicit in this model, not the least of which is that the ethnic minority group exists within the context of a society in which mediation in the form of acculturation is possible, and cultural pluralism (as opposed to cultural assimilation or separatism) is increasingly valued. In rigidly stratified societies, such as those in Northern Ireland or South Africa, cross-cutting identity labels are not always available to the ethnic minority, usually because the dominant majority does not want to encourage dimensions of identity that might bring unification. Thus, the black in South Africa cannot categorize him/herself as white, and the 'South African identity' which is equally applicable to both blacks and whites is not encouraged.

Having pointed out the limitations of this perspective with regard to the various strategies of self-categorization, it is important to say that this model will hold with regard to styles of cultural adaptation, whichever type of society the ethnic minority exists within. A black in South Africa may not be able to categorize him/herself as white, but s/he can (although s/he may not want to) develop attitudes and behaviours that emulate the whites. Thus, assimilation is possible in one's style of cultural adaptation, even if it is not possible in one's self-categorization. It is for this reason that a separation between the two components of ethnic minority identity is necessary. Efforts towards national integration will then look for and emphasize the value of super-ordinate levels of self-categorization that transcend immediate group boundaries and that emphasize essential commonalities.

One further question remains to be addressed. If indeed one's self-categorizations eventually become functionally autonomous from cultural adaptation, then what role do they play in mediating one's social identity? It would seem that they act as 'switches' that turn on (or off) aspects of social identity. According to the Tajfelian tradition, all behaviour can be arranged in a continuum from inter-personal to inter-group. Consider a situation in which a white person is chatting with a black friend about college admissions. Both are 'individuated' in that they are discussing their individual performance in the college entrance exams. Both have performed extraordinarily well and admission is certain. Both are relating on an inter-personal level and the conversation is easy and without tension. Then the white person says, 'The trouble with the admissions procedure is that there is such an unreasonably large quota for blacks in this college.' Such a statement, however factually based, holds the seeds of an attack on 'blacks'. The conversation is now ripe for a switch to the inter-group level of behaviour and, depending on his/her strategy of self-categorization, the black person in question may take the bait or may chose to ignore it. If s/he chooses to ignore it, it is likely that the conversation will continue on an inter-personal level. If the bait is taken then the two friends 'switch' into being representatives each of their own racial group and a 'mini-war' may begin. Thus, self-categorizations potentially produce racial spirals of attack and defence which may be vicious or benign (Sherwood 1980) depending on the actors' strategies of coping.

The 'switch' function of self-categorizations is merely offered here as a suggestion for further research and needs to be verified by empirical evidence. However, some studies do point to the validity of the hypothesis. Brown and Ross (1982) hypothesized that levels of in-group bias and feelings of antipathy towards the out-group should increase in proportion to the degree of threat to identity implied by communication from the out-group. Subjects were randomly assigned to two minimal and anonymous groups X and Y and were told that they would be participating in a study on reasoning ability. After the reasoning task was completed the subjects' test sheets were returned to them after being scored. Each subject was also given predetermined information about his/her group's performance relative to the other group. Thus, a superior group (Y) and an inferior group (X) were created. Threat was manipulated by conveying contrived information to each group about what the out-group thought about their ability. The threat condition enhanced the in-group bias in the inferior group but did not affect bias shown by the superior group. Expressed antipathy towards out-group members, however, increased in high threat conditions for both superior and inferior groups.

In a similar vein, Schiffmann and Wagner (1985) hypothesized that threat to social identity would lead to greater inter-group differentiation and greater devaluation of the out-group. Their study was conducted on three groups of psychiatric health workers: lay helpers; psychology students; and physicians. The results showed that psychology students denigrated the lay helper's competence more when the psychology in-group identity was threatened by the physicians.

The relevance of social identity to the individual is important in determining reactions to threat. A study by Turner *et al.* (1984) demonstrated that public threat to a personally relevant social identity results in greater in-group cohesiveness as a means to increase inter-group differentiation and to salvage self-esteem. Turner *et al.* pitted social exchange theory against social identity theory, insisting that need satisfaction (rewards) is not essential to group identification. In conditions where personal responsibility is accepted for group failure, failure will actually lead to defensive enhancement of group identification. Here, personal responsibility was operationalized in terms of choice about continuing with the group task. As predicted, group members with high choice scores became more cohesive after failure than after success, whereas people with low choice scores showed less group cohesiveness after failure. Thus, commitment to group membership determines reactions to failure or success. It thus seems plausible to conceptualize self-categorization as a 'switch' that sets into motion spirals of attack and defence.

Some concluding remarks

We now live in the aftermath of assimilationist theory. However, the tentacles of assimilationism are slow to loose their hold. Even respected research continues to correlate various factors with the ethnic minority individual's degree of assimilation (see, for example, Stopes-Roe and Cochrane 1987, 1990). Particularly in the less cosmopolitan areas of our society, ethnic minority individuals are consistently aware of a certain dualism that exists within them. In a personal communication to the author an Indian woman now living in the United States wrote:

Michael says your theory is that I don't feel accepted as an Indian and that is why I don't wear Indian clothes. Well, you are darn right! That and the hassle of having to wash them separately and then iron them (no dhobi hanging at the gate waiting to iron). I have always had this massive grudge about Buffalo, and altho' I am better adjusted here than I have been in years, I still feel like that. I am *not* accepted as an Indian! Never was, never will be! Buffalo is simply not made up of the educated elitist independent free thinking type American to whom your ethnicity would be a challenge, something exciting. Buffalo recoils in horror if you wear salwar kameez—the immediate mental decision is 'I cannot trust you'. Lets face it, Buffalonians are incredibly small town and incredibly blue collar. Not that I care about the color of their collars, but they have had very little exposure to other ethnic groups, and because of this unbelievable narrowness of experience simply do not know how to handle something which is, in their eyes, strange! Which is my primary reason for wanting to move to a more 'broad horizons' type place—unfortunately such places invariably cost a lot more just to live! Still, we will work it out. In the mean time my 'acceptability factor' is at an all time high— but for all the wrong reasons! Namely because I talk English well—better than 90% of them in fact—because I can adopt an American accent at will, because I dress like them, am incredibly funny, and because in general I fit in! I must admit it makes me mad. There is such a big part of me that is denied on a regular basis. Fortunately, a big part of me is also western. I strongly doubt if I would have been confined only to Indian clothes even if I lived in India.

The necessity of having to deny a significant part of oneself in order to fit in is perhaps the tragedy of the immigrant experience in the West.

Even though many people have now repudiated the notion that Anglo-Saxon culture is intrinsically superior, assimilationism has assumed a more subtle garb (Sue 1983). Rather than referring to intrinsic superiority, assimilationists use the argument that encouraging the expression of certain aspects of ethnicity is simply not functional or practical. Thus, bilingual education has been attacked in the United States as being a handicap in classroom learning, which hinders 'mainstreaming' and pro-duces little of real benefit. In fact, it merely heightens the salience of ethnicity.

Usually, a salient ethnicity has been interpreted to debilitate integration because it tends to perpetuate a sense of being 'different'. This argument has been used by opponents of transracial adoption (McGuire *et al.* 1978). As Tizard and Phoenix (1989) suggest, transracially adopted children are likely to have a different identity from that of children growing up in a black family, but there are no well-grounded reasons for believing the practice is damaging to children. The model I have proposed suggests (and this awaits confirmation) that heightened ethnic salience may be actually beneficial to further integration. When ethnicity is salient and holds a positive valence for the individual, there is little suppression of inherent and unavoidable racial differences (even if only with regard to physical features). Therefore it is likely that individuals can develop adequate mechanisms to cope with the societal consequences of these differences. If ethnicity is not at all salient or if the psychologically salient self-categori-zation is 'British only and not Indian' (the assimilative strategy), then this denial of difference may not be met with similar categorizations from members of the majority group, i.e. the individual may categorize him/

herself as British, but in the eyes of others may be perceived and treated as Indian. Such speculations suggest that it would be beneficial for the psychological well-being of the ethnic minority individual to be aware of his/her ethnic origins in order that s/he may acquire adequate psychological strategies to cope with prejudice and discrimination.

Certainly, the issue of housing is very complex and is direct related to whether a consonant situation (which tends to heighten the salience of ethnicity) is more or less beneficial to integration than a dissonant situation. Some housing policies have led to the formation of ghettos (a consonant situation) in which the percentage of a particular ethnic minority group is so high as to perpetuate within the group a feeling of dissociation and separatism. Parts of East London exemplify such a situation. Others have attempted to achieve a 'random racial distribution' (Pettigrew 1985), such that the ethnic minority is scattered according to the proportion of the ethnic minority within the larger population (a dissonant situation). The Vietnamese in Britain are a case in point. It is obvious that neither of these two alternatives is ideal: the one encourages dissociation and separation and therefore inter-group conflict; the other deprives the ethnic minority group of opportunities to perpetuate its culture and the ethnic minority individual of a sense of group-belonging and a secure social identity and makes assimilation the only available option.

Assimilation is not a 'happy' option, perhaps even for those who choose it. Certainly, the history of ethnic groups in North America and elsewhere indicates that assimilation is not a pragmatic social solution to the problems of a culturally heterogeneous society. Acculturation (as opposed to assimilation) merits consideration as being the goal to be reached in striving for the integration of ethnic minorities within the larger society. The studies considered in this book have suggested that acculturation is not only a viable, but also a frequently chosen solution for cultural adaptation. From the point of view of social policy, acculturation would require of the ethnic minority individual a level of competence only in the cultural norms of the majority in order to function appropriately in the context of British society. At the same time, it would accord the ethnic group the freedom to explore, maintain, reject, or rediscover its ethnicity.

In education, this would mean providing opportunities for ethnic minority individuals to learn their ethnic language as part of the school curriculum (not outside it). Britain today is irrevocably multi-ethnic, and it might even be worth encouraging white adolescents to take up Hindi, Punjabi, or Urdu as a second language. However, this is *not* to imply that education for ethnic minority children should be conducted entirely in the ethnic language. To institutionalize such a policy would be to encourage dissociation, and further ethnic segregation rather than integration. The consequences of such policies have been far-reaching in the United States.

Of the escalating violence in New York City, Terry Coleman in *The Guardian* (1985, 9 August, p. 13) writes:

The whole dreadful situation is being compounded by the insistence of these immigrants on their own separate identity and separate language. Many Hispanics in New York (and in other cities like Miami, Houston, Los Angeles), having a legal right to be taught at school in their own language, do not speak enough English to hold down a decent job. They, then, naturally resent the consequences of this incapacity. So much for the American melting pot. If this separation were being forced upon them by the federal or state governments it would be condemned by all libertarians and by the *New York Times*. But they are demanding it themselves.

With a similar situation here in Britain, it is essential that South Asians be at least equally conversant in English as their peers in order to be eligible for as wide a range of jobs. Thus, it would be necessary, at the risk of appearing 'assimilationist' or even 'racist', for educational institutions to resist the pressure from within sections of the South Asian minority, particularly the Muslim minority, to provide separate language schools for their children. At the same time, it would be important to provide every opportunity for ethnic minority children to learn or maintain their ethnic language within the normal school curriculum, and as mentioned before, to encourage majority group children to do the same, in order to facilitate appreciation of their cultures. Shahwar Sadeque, the first Asian governor of the BBC, provides a model for new directions in race relations in Britain. She has produced a pamphlet against the segregation of Muslim children in separate schools. In a recent interview with the *Sunday Telegraph* (9 September, 1990, p. 3), she said,

I am a Muslim. I am a British Muslim. I am a Bangladeshi.

However, even the Commission of Racial Equality seems relatively insensitive to the multiplicity of ethnic identities which are available to ethnic minority individuals for self-categorization. Their recommendations for the 1991 Census are as follows (Anwar 1990):

White
Black-Caribbean
Black-African
Black-other
Indian
Pakistani
Bangladeshi
Chinese
Other

This classification system disallows the hypenated British identity to its ethnic minorities. Thus Black British and Asian British are not available as self-categorization strategies. Also, the category 'white' assumes complete assimilation by British Ukrainians, Poles, and Italians. The psychological and political significance of this insensitivity is, with regard to the research reported in this monograph, far-reaching. Rather than forcing labels upon ethnic minority individuals, is it not feasible to devise questions such that people are able to categorize themselves along the dimensions that they find most meaningful? It would then be the task of the Census Office to cluster people according to their ethnicity.

With the benefit of hindsight, it is abundantly evident that the assimilationist philosophies that pervaded the course of immigration history in the United States are inappropriate for Britain. But neither is the emerging tendency to resist all discussion regarding ethnic differences as reflected in an over-sensitivity on the part of some authorities to address questions regarding ethnic background. Intolerance often takes one of two forms: an over-emphasis of difference; or a complete denial of difference. The one plays upon the diversity inherent in a society of many ethnic and racial groups to the exclusion of any essential unity among them; the other highlights the unity while ignoring the diversity. Peace among the peoples of a nation is never easily won, but the road to peace is clear. The people of Latin America, amidst and perhaps because of the ethnic strife so prevalent there, have declared (*Transformation*, 1985, **2**, p. 25) that peace:

. . . is the result of a reconciliation of disparate elements in society, without their losing their identity or eliminating their heterogeneity. Peace is real and lasting only when it proceeds from a pluralism in which unity is confirmed in diversity. Responsible political action will seek to develop a pluralism which, in its wealth of variety, enriches the body of society and offers everyone the opportunity to make his unique contribution to the general welfare.

The path of pluralism, true pluralism where each is accorded equal dignity, equal opportunity, and equal rights, is as yet untried and mistakes will inevitably be many. But, in an increasingly multi-ethnic society, a concerted effort needs to be made, not merely to accept or tolerate cultural heterogeneity but to appreciate and affirm it, while always maintaining a sense of the essential unity among people of various ethnicities.

Appendix 1:

Biographical information regarding the subjects of studies 1–5

Table 1 Distribution of participants according to ethnic background

	South Asian	Afro-Caribbean	English	Other	Total no. interviewed	Total no. used
Number	43	33	34	28	138	110
Per cent	39.1	30.0	30.9	–	–	100.00

Table 2 presents a breakdown of the South Asian subjects according to their country of origin.

Table 2 Distribution of South Asian participants according to country of origin

	India	Pakistan	Bangladesh	East Africa
Number	23	12	4	4
Per cent	53.5	27.9	9.3	9.3

Most of the South Asian subjects were born in Britain, although a few were born in the country of their origin. Table 3 presents a breakdown of the South Asian subjects according to their place of birth. Only two South Asian subjects were born outside Britain.

Table 3 Distribution of South Asian participants according to place of birth

Place of birth	Britain	India	Pakistan	Bangladesh	East Africa
Number	27	5	4	3	4
Per cent	62.8	11.6	9.3	7.0	9.3

The great majority of South Asian subjects had come to Britain before they were four years old, and were thus truly second generation in that they had received their primary socialization in Britain and not in their country of origin.

Table 4 Distribution of South Asian participants according to the age of arrival in Britain

Age of arrival	0–4 yrs	5–9 yrs	10–14 yrs	Not ascertained
Number	33	5	4	1
Per cent	76.7	11.6	9.3	2.4

In Table 4, the South Asian subjects are distributed according to their religious background. The Afro-Caribbean and English subjects all originated from Christian backgrounds.

Table 5 Distribution of South Asian participants according to their religious background

Religious background	Hinduism	Islam	Sikhism	Christianity	Not ascertained
Number	7	15	15	4	2
Per cent	16.3	34.9	34.9	9.3	4.6

Appendix 2:

Gordon's (1968) coding categories for the 'Who am I?' test

Category	I am . . .	I am not . . .
A. *Ascribed characteristics*		
Sex	man, boy, son	not a girl
Age	15 years old, a girl, a teenager	not an adult not a child
Name	Mark Puddy, Clare Noronha, etc.	–
Race	black, white, coloured	not black, not white
Nationality	Indian, Pakistani, English	not a Paki, not English
Religious categorization (specific religious denomination)	Hindu, Muslim Sikh, Catholic	not a Christian not a Muslim
B. *Roles and membership*		
Kinship role	a son, a sister, an only child	not yet a parent, not married
Occupational role	a worker in my father's shop	not going to be a teacher
Student role	a student, in the 4th form at St. Alban's	not very studious
Political affiliation	a Labour Party supporter, SDP	not Liberal, not Conservative
Social status	from a poor family, middle class	not from a rich family, not from a poor family
Territoriality, citizenship	a British citizen, living in Handsworth	not an Indian citizen
Membership in an actual interacting group	an Aston Villa supporter	not a skinhead

C. *Abstract identifications*

Existential, individuating	me, myself	not a stranger, I don't know
Membership in an abstract category	a person, a foreigner, a human being	not an alien
Ideological and belief references	a Marxist, a Christian, for CND	not against cruise missiles coming to Britain, not in favour of unrestricted immigration

D. *Interests and activities*

Judgements, tastes	one who likes jazz, a fan of Michael Jackson	not interested in golf
Intellectual concerns	fond of reading, interested in science	not keen on poetry
Artistic activities	a singer, a ballet dancer	not a movie-goer
Other activities	a tennis player, an athlete	not keen on sports

E. *Material references*

Possessions, resources	rich, I have enough to get by on	not poor, not a person who has a lot of clothes
Physical self	good-looking, tall, fashionable, too thin, 5′2½″	not fat, not fashion-conscious

F. *Major senses of self*

Moral worth	honest, good, bad, wicked, trustworthy	not a liar, not always obedient to my parents, not a good person
Self-determination	ambitious, hard-working, going to do well at school	not hard-working, not lazy
Unity	a whole person, mixed up	not in harmony with myself
Competence	intelligent, talented, creative, good at maths	not good at English, not stupid

G. *Personal characteristics*

Inter-personal style	friendly, good with children	not hard to get on with, not selfish, not greedy
Psychic style	optimistic, happy, sad, introverted	not reserved, not always objective

Judgements imputed to others	popular, respected, a good laugh	not thought to be talkative

H. *External references*

Situational references	tired, bored hungry, in love with Abigail	not going out with Irene yet
Ideological frame of reference towards other groups in society	a bit biased against immigrants, a Paki-hater	not prejudiced, not racist
Uncodeable response	a drop in the ocean	not a star

A few comments: the above coding system contains 32 categories. The racial and national heritage categories are here considered as two separate categories rather than one, as in Gordon's scheme. Also category 31—ideological frame of reference towards other groups in society—is a further specialization of category 16, which is peculiar to this sample of data. The 'I am not . . .' data were coded under the same categories.

Appendix 3:

Study 4: sample characteristics of South Asian adolescents from schools S and H

		School S (n = 30)	School H (n = 40)
I.	*Whether father is currently employed*		
	Yes	70.0	55.0
	No	20.0	40.0
	Not ascertained	10.0	5.0
II.	*Class background*		
	1. Professionally qualified and high administrative	0.0	0.0
	2. Managerial and executive	3.3	0.0
	3. Inspectional, supervisory and other non-manual (high grade)	13.3	2.5
	4. Inspectional, supervisory, and other non-manual (low grade)	3.3	2.5
	5(a). Routine grades of non-manual work	3.3	5.0
	5(b). Skilled manual	23.3	20.0
	6. Manual semi-skilled	20.3	20.0
	7. Manual routine	3.3	2.5
	Not ascertained	10.0	45.0
III.	*Country of origin*		
	India	30.0	97.5
	Pakistan	56.7	0.0
	East Africa	13.3	2.5
IV.	*Place of birth*		
	Within Britain	86.7	100.0
	Outside Britain	13.3	0.0
V.	*Age of entry into Britain*		
	0–4 years	96.7	100.0
	5–9 years	3.3	0.0

		School S ($n = 30$)	School H ($n = 40$)
VI.	*Religious affiliation*		
	Hindu	13.3	42.5
	Muslim	76.7	0.0
	Sikh	10.0	47.5
	Other	0.0	5.0
	Not ascertained	0.0	5.0
VII.	*Mean age of subjects* (years)	14.67	15.25
	Standard deviation	0.48	0.4

All figures except where otherwise indicated represent percentages. The class background of the subjects was ascertained by using the Hall–Jones Scale of Occupational Prestige and is only a rough estimate.

Appendix 4:

Study 6: class distribution of subjects using the Hall–Jones scale of occupational prestige

Class		Frequency	Percentage
1.	Professionally qualified and high administrative	1	1.0
2.	Managerial and executive	0	0.0
3.	Inspectional, supervisory, and other non-manual (high grade)	4	3.9
4.	Inspectional, supervisory, and other non-manual (low grade)	3	2.9
5(a).	Routine grades of non-manual work	11	10.7
5(b).	Skilled manual	13	12.6
6.	Manual semi-skilled	9	8.7
7.	Manual routine	15	14.6
	Unemployed	37	35.9
	Not ascertained	8	7.8

Of the sample, 69 per cent speak a mixture of English and the ethnic group language in their homes, 26 per cent speak only the ethnic language at home, and 4 per cent speak English only.

References

Aboud, F. E. and Mitchell, F. G. (1977). Ethnic role-taking: The effects of preference and self-identification. *International Journal of Psychology*, **12**, 1–17.

Aboud, F. E. and Skerry S. A. (1984). The development of ethnic attitudes: A critical review. *Journal of Cross-Cultural Psychology*, **15**(1), 3–34.

Abrams, D., Wetherell, M., Cochrane, S., Hogg, M. A., and Turner J. C. (1990). Knowing what to think by knowing who you are: self-categorisation and the nature of norm formation, conformity and group polarisation. *British Journal of Social Psychology*, **29**, 97–119.

Adelson, J. A. (1953). A study of minority group of authoritarianism. *Journal of Abnormal and Social Psychology*, **48**, 477–85.

Adorno, T. W., Frenkel-Brunswick, E., Levinson, D., and Sanford, R. N. (1950). *The authoritarian personality*. Harper & Row, New York.

Aellen, C. and Lambert, W. E. (1969). Ethnic identification and personality adjustment of Canadian adolescents of mixed English–French parentage. *Canadian Journal of Behavioural Science*, **1**(2), 69–86.

Allport, G. W. (1945). Introduction. In *Resolving social conflicts: Selected papers on group dynamics* (ed. K. Lewin), p. vii. Harper and Brothers, New York.

Allport, G. W. (1954). *The nature of prejudice*. Addison-Wesley, Cambridge, Mass.

Anisfield, M., Bogo, N., and Lambert, W. E. (1962). Evaluational reactions to accented speech. *Journal of Abnormal and Social Psychology*, **65**, 223–231.

Anwar, M. (1982). *Young people and the job market*. Commission for Racial Equality, London.

Anwar, M. (1986). Redressive action policies in the United Kingdom. In *XI World Congress of Sociology*. Research Committee on Ethnic, Race and Minority Relations. 18–22 August New Delhi.

Anwar, M. (1990). Debates: Ethnic classifications, ethnic monitoring and the 1991 Census. *New Community*, **16**(4), 607–15.

Apter, M. J. (1983). Negativism and the sense of identity. In *Threatened identities* (ed. G. Breakwell). John Wiley, Chichester.

Argyle, M. (1967). *The psychology of interpersonal behaviour*. Penguin, Harmondsworth, Middlesex.

Argyle, M. and Kendon, A. (1967). The experimental analysis of social performance. In *Advances in experimental social psychology* (ed. L. Berkowitz), vol. 3. Academic Press, New York.

Ashmore, R. D. and Del Boca, F. K. (1981). Conceptual approaches to stereotypes and stereotyping. In *Cognitive process in stereotyping and inter-group behaviour* (ed. D. L. Hamilton). Lawrence Erlbaum, Hillsdale, NJ.

Bachman, J. G. (1970) The impact of family background and intelligence on tenth-grade boys. In *Youth in transition*, Vol. 2. Survey Research Centre, Institute for Social Research, Ann Arbor, Michigan.

Ballard, C. (1979). Conflict, continuity and change: Second generation South Asians. In *Minority families in Britain* (ed. V. S. Khan). Macmillan, London.

Banks, J. A. and Gay, G. (1978). Ethnicity in contemporary American society: Toward the development of a typology. *Ethnicity*, **5**(3), 238–52.

Banks, W. C. (1976). White preference in blacks: A paradigm in search of a phenomenon. *Psychological Bulletin*, **83**, 1179–86.

Banks, W. C. and Rompf, W. J. (1973). Evaluative bias and preference in black and white children. *Child Development*, **44**, 776–83.

Barth, F. (ed.) (1969). Ethnic groups and boundaries. In *The social organisation of culture difference*. George Allen and Unwin, London.

Berry, J. W. and Annis, R. C. (1974). Acculturative stress: The role of ecology, culture and differentiation. *Journal of Cross-Cultural Psychology*, **5**(4), 383–405.

Bianchi, G. N., Cawte, J. E., and Kiloh, L. G. (1973). Culture, identity and mental health. In *The psychology of Aboriginal Australians* (ed. G. Kearney, P. de Lacey, and G. Davidson). John Wiley, Sidney.

Billig, M. (1976). *Social psychology and intergroup relations*. Academic Press, London.

Bochner, S. (1976). Religious role differentiation as an aspect of subjective culture. *Journal of Cross-Cultural Psychology*, **7**(1), 3–19.

Bochner, S. (ed.) (1982). The social psychology of cross-cultural relations. In *Cultures in contact: Studies in cross-cultural interaction*. Pergamon Press, Oxford.

Bochner, S., Hutnik, N., and Furnham, A. (1985). Friendship patterns of overseas and host students in an Oxford student residence. *Journal of Social Psychology*, **125**, 689–94.

Bochner, S., McLeod, B. M., and Lin, A. (1977). Friendship patterns of overseas students: A functional model. *International Journal of Psychology*, **12**, 277–94.

Bond, M. and Cheung, T. S. (1983). College students' spontaneous self-concept: The effect of culture among respondents in Hong Kong, Japan and the United States. *Journal of Cross-Cultural Psychology*, **14**(2), 153–71.

Brah, A. (1978). South Asian teenagers in Southall: Their perceptions of marriage, family and ethnic identity. *New Community*, **6**(3), 197–206.

Brah, A. (1979). Inter-generational and inter-ethnic perceptions: A comparative study of South Asian and English adolescents and their parents in Southall. Unpublished D.Phil. thesis, University of Bristol.

Branch, C. and Newcombe, N. (1980). Racial attitudes of Black pre-schoolers as related to parental civil rights activism. *Merrill-Palmer Quarterly*, **26**, 425–8.

Brand, E. S., Ruiz, R. A., and Padilla, A. M. (1974). Ethnic identification and preference: A review. *Psychological Bulletin*, **81**(II), 860–90.

Brennan, J. and McGeevor, P. (1987). *The employment of graduates from ethnic minorities: A research report*. Commission for Racial Equality, London.

Breton, R. (1964). Institutional completeness of ethnic communities and personal relations to immigrants. *American Journal of Sociology*, **70**, 193–205.

Brewer, M. B. (1979). A cognitive model of stereotypes of the elderly. In *Symposium on Perceptions of the Aged: Basic Studies and Institutional Implications*. American Psychological Association Convention, New York.

Brewer, M. B. (1988). A dual process modal of impression formation. *Advanced Social Cognition*, **1**, 1–36.

Brigham, J. C. (1971). Ethnic stereotypes. *Psychological Bulletin*, **76**, 15–38.

Brittain, C. V. (1963). Adolescent and parent–peer cross pressures. *American Sociological Review*, **28**, 385–91.

Brown, C. (1984). *Black and white in Britain*. Policy Studies Institute, London.

Brown, C. and Gay, P. (1985). *Racial discrimination 17 years after the Act*. Policy Studies Institute, London.

Brown, R. J. and Ross, G. F. (1982). The battle for acceptance: An investigation into the dynamics of intergroup behaviour. In *Social identity and intergroup relations* (ed. H. Tajfel), pp. 155–78. Cambridge University Press.

Brown, R. J. and Turner, J. C. (1979). The criss-cross categorisation effect in intergroup discrimination. *British Journal of Social and Clinical Psychology*, **18**, 371–83.

Burrett, G. and Hutnik, N. (1982). A study of parent–peer cross pressures and self-determination experienced by adolescents as a function of the stability of societal values and the level of self-acceptance. Presented at the *All-India UGC Conference. Stress in Contemporary Life, Strategies of Coping*, April, Department of Psychology, Lady Shri Ram College, Lajpat Nagar, New Delhi.

Cairns, E. and Mercer, G. W. (1978). Adolescent social identity in Northern Ireland: The importance of denominational identity. Unpublished MS, New University of Ulster. Mentioned in H. Tajfel (ed.) (1982). *Social identity and intergroup relations*. Cambridge University Press.

Callan, V. G. and Gallois, C. (1983). Ethnic stereotypes: Australian and southern European youth. *Journal of Social Psychology*, **119**, 287–8.

Cantor, G. N. (1972). Use of a conflict paradigm to study race awareness in children. *Child Development*, **43**, 1437–42.

Cantor, G. N. and Patternite, C. E. (1973). A follow-up study of race awareness using a conflict paradigm. *Child Development*, **44**, 859–61.

Cartwright, D. and Zander, A. (1968). *Group dynamics: Research and theory*. Harper & Row, New York.

Chance, N. (1965). Acculturation, self-identification and personality adjustment. *American Anthropologist*, **67**, 372–93.

Chun Ki-Taek (1983). Ethnicity and ethnic identity: taming the untamed. In *Studies in social identity* (ed. T. R. Sarbin and K. E. Schiebe). Praeger, New York.

Clark, K. (1965). *Dark ghetto: Dilemmas of social power*. Harper & Row, New York.

Clark, K. B. and Clark, M. P. (1939). The development of consciousness of self and the emergence of racial identification in Negro pre-school children. *Journal of Social Psychology*, **10**, 591–9.

Clark, K. B. and Clark, M. P. (1940). Skin colour as a factor in racial identification of Negro pre-school children. *Journal of Social Psychology*, **11**, 159–69.

Clark, K. B. and Clark, M. P. (1947). Racial identification and preference in negro children. In *Readings in social psychology* (ed. T. M. Newcombe and E. L. Harley). Holt, New York.

Cochrane R. (1983). *The social creation of mental illness*. Longman, Harlow, Essex.

Cochrane, R. and Stopes-Roe, M. (1980). The mental health of immigrants. *New Community*, **8**(1,2), 123–8.

Cochrane R. and Stopes-Roe, M. (1981*a*). Psychological and social adjustment of Asian immigrants in Britain. *Social Psychiatry*, **12**, 195–206.

Cochrane R. and Stopes-Roe, M. (1981*b*). Psychological symptom levels in Indian immigrants in England: A comparison with native English. *Psychological Medicine*, **11**, 319–27.

Coelho, G. V. (1958). *Changing images of America*. Free Press, Glencoe, I11.

Coelho, G. V. (ed.) (1972). *Mental health and social change: An annotated bibliography*. National Institute of Mental Health. Government Printing Office, Washington D.C.

Commins, B. and Lockwood, J. (1978). The effects on inter-group relations of mixing Roman Catholics and Protestants: An experimental investigation. *European Journal of Social Psychology*, **8**, 383–6.

Commission for Racial Equality (1984). *Race and housing in Hackney* and *Race and Housing in Liverpool. A research report*. CRE, London.

Commission for Racial Equality (1985). *Race and mortgage lendings in Rochdale*. CRE, London.

Cope, R. (1989). The compulsory detention of Afro-Caribbeans under the Mental Health Act. *New Community*, **15**(3), 343–56.

Cota, A. A. and Dion, K. L. (1986). Salience of gender and sex composition of ad hoc groups: An experiemental test of distinctiveness theory. *Journal of Personality and Social Psychology*, **50**(4), 770–6.

Crocker, J. and Luhtanen, R. (1990). Collective self-esteem and ingroup bias *Journal of Personality and Social Psychology*, **58**(1), 60–7.

Crocker, J, McGraw, K. M., Thompson, L. L., and Ingerman, C. (1987). Downward comparison, prejudice and evaluations of others: Effects of self-esteem and threat. *Journal of Personality and Social Psychology*, **52**(5), 907–16.

Crooks, R. C. (1970). The effects of an inter-racial pre-school program upon racial preference, knowledge of racial differences and racial identification. *Journal of Social Issues*, **26**(4), 137–44.

Crowley, M. (1978). The other side of the integration coin: Level of worldmindedness of third generation Australian children as a function of ethnic composition of friendship group, age, ethnic density of school and sex. Unpublished Honours thesis, School of Psychology, University of New South Wales. Mentioned in S. Bochner (ed.) (1982). *Cultures in contact: Studies in cross-cultural interaction*. Pergamon Press, Oxford.

Cubberly, E. P. (1929). *Changing conceptions of education*. Houghton and Mifflin, Boston.

Dahya, B. (1973). Pakistanis in Britain: Transients or settlers?. *Race*, **14**, 3.

Danziger, K. (1974). The acculturation of Italian immigrant girls in Canada. *International Journal of Psychology*, **9**(2), 129–37.

Davey, A. G. and Mullin, P. N. (1980). Ethnic identification and preference of British primary school children. *Journal of Child Psychology and Psychiatry*, **21**, 241–51.

Deschamps, J. C. and Doise, W. (1978). Crossed category memberships in intergroup relations In *Differentiation between social groups* (ed. H. Tajfel). Academic Press, London.

Deutsch, S. E. and Won, G. Y. M. (1963). Some factors in the adjustment of foreign nationals in the United States. *Journal of Social Issues*, **19**(3), 115–22.

Doke, L. A. and V. Risley T. R. (1972). Some discriminative properties of race and sex for children from an all-Negro neighbourhood. *Child Development*, **43**, 677–81.

Dove, L. A. (1974). Racial awareness among adolescents in London comprehensive schools. *New Community*, **3**(3), 255–61.

Dovidio, J. F. and Gaertner, S. L. (ed.) (1986). *Prejudice, discrimination, racism: Theory and research*. Academic Press, New York.

Dovidio, J. F., Evans, J., and Tyler, R. B. (1986). Racial stereotypes: The concepts of their cognitive representation. *Journal of Experimental Social Psychology*, **22**, 22–37.

Dreidger, L. (1975). In search of cultural identity factors: A comparison of ethnic students. *Canadian Review of Sociology and Anthropology*, **12**, 150–62.

Dreidger, L. (1976). Ethnic self-identity: A comparison of ingroup evaluations. *Sociometry*, **39**(2), 131–41.

Drew, D. and Clough, E. (1985). *The future in black and white*. City Polytechnic, Sheffield.

Epstein, Y. M., Krupat, E., and Obudho, C. (1976). Clean is beautiful: Identification and preference as a function of race and cleanliness. *Journal of Social Issues*, **32**, 109–18.

Erikson, E. H. (1950). *Childhood and society*. Penguin, London.

Erikson, E. H. (1958). *Young man Luther*. Norton, New York.

Erikson, E. H. (1959). Identity and the life cycle: Selected papers. *Psychological Issues*, **1**(1), 23 ff.

Erikson, E. H. (1964). Memorandum on identity and Negro youth. *Journal of Social Issues*, **20**(4), 29–42.

Erikson, E. H. (1968). *Identity: Youth and crisis*. Faber and Faber, London.

Erikson, E. H. (1970). *Gandhi's truth: On the origins of militant non-violence*. Faber and Faber, London.

Estes, W. K. (1986). Array models for category learning. *Cognitive Psychology*, **18**, 500–49.

Fairchild, H. P. (1926). *The melting pot mistake*. Little, Brown, Boston.

Feminella, F. X. (1973). The immigrant and the melting pot. In *Perspectives in urban American* (ed. M. Urofsky). Doubleday, New York.

Fernando, S. (1988). *Race and culture in psychiatry*. Routledge, London.

Festinger, L. (1950a). Laboratory experiments: The role of group belongings. In *Experiments in social process* (ed. J. G. Miller). McGraw-Hill, New York.

Festinger, L. (1950b). Informal social communication. *Psychological Review*, **57**, 271–82.

Foster, D. and Finchilescu, G. (1986). Contact in a 'non-contact' society: The case of South Africa. In *Contact and conflict in intergroup encounters* (ed. M. Hewstone and R. Brown), pp. 119–36. Basil Blackwell, Oxford.

Foster-Carter, O. (1986). Insiders, outsiders, and anamolies: A review of studies of identity. *New Community*, **8**(2), 224–34.

Fox, D. J. and Jordan, V. B. (1973). Racial preference and identification of Black, American, Chinese and White children. *Genetic Psychology Monographs*, **88**, 229–86.

Francis, E. K. (1947). The nature of the ethnic group. *American Journal of*

Sociology, **52**, 393–400. As mentioned in W. W. Isajiw (1974). Definitions of ethnicity. *Ethnicity*, **1**(2), 111–24.

Furnham, A. and Bochner, S. (1986). *Culture shock: Psychological reactions to unfamiliar environments*. Methuen, London.

Furnham, A. and Kirris, R. (1983). Self-image disparity, ethnic identity and sex-role stereotypes in British and Cypriot adolescents. *Journal of Adolescence*, **6**, 275–92.

Gaertner, S. L. and Dovidio, J. F. (1986). The aversive form of racism In *Prejudice, discrimination, racism: Theory and research* (ed. J. F. Dovidio and S. L. Gaertner) pp. 61–89. Academic Press, New York.

Gaertner, S. L. and McLaughlin, J. P. (1983). Racial stereotypes: Associations and ascriptions of positive and negative characteristics. *Social Psychological Quarterly*, **46**, 23–30.

Gamble, R. (1982). Investigation within an integrated school. Unpublished M.Sc. thesis. Queen's University of Belfast.

Gardner, R. C., Wonnacot, E. J., and Taylor, D. M. (1968). Ethnic stereotypes: A factor analytic investigation. *Canadian Journal of Psychology*, **22**(1), 35–44.

Gardner, R. C., Taylor, D. M., and Feenstra, H. J. (1970). Ethnic stereotypes: Attitudes or beliefs. *Canadian Journal of Psychology*, **24**(5), 321–39.

Gaskell, G. and Smith, P. (1981). 'Alienated' black youth: An investigation of 'conventional wisdom' explanations. *New Community*, **9**, 182–93.

Gerard, H. B. and Hoyt, M. F. (1974). Distinctiveness of social categorisation and attitude toward ingroup members. *Journal of Personality and Social Psychology*, **29**(6), 836–42.

Gilbert, G. M. (1951). Stereotype persistence and change among college students. *Journal of Abnormal and Social Psychology*, 245–54.

Ginsberg, A. M. and Gioelli, M. M. (1979). A comparative study of acculturation and adaptation of descendants of Japanese born in Brazil (Nissei) compared with Japanese and Brazilians. *Human Development*, **22**(5), 340–57.

Gitter, A. G. and Satow, Y. (1969). Colour and physiognomy as variables in racial misidentification among children. *Proceedings of the 77th Annual Convention of the American Psychological Association*, vol. 4, Part 2, pp. 677–8. APA.

Gitter, A. G., Mostofsky, D. I., and Satow, Y. (1972). The effect of skin colour and physiognomy on racial misidentification. *Journal of Social Psychology*, **88**, 139–43.

Glazer, N. and Moynihan, D. (1970). *Beyond the melting pot*. MIT Press, Cambridge, Mass.

Glazer, N. and Moynihan, D. P. (ed.) (1975). *Ethnicity: Theory and experience*. Harvard University Press, Cambridge, Mass.

Glazer, N. and Young, K. (ed.) (1983). *Ethnic pluralism and public policy: Achieving equality in the United States and Britain*. Heinemann Educational Books, London.

Goodman, M. E. (1946). Evidence concerning the genesis of inter-racial attitudes. *American Anthropology*, **48**, 624–30.

Goodman, M. E. (1952). *Race awareness in young children*. Addison-Wesley, Reading, Mass.

Gordon, C. (1963). Self-conception and social achievement. Unpublished D.Phil.

thesis. University of California at Los Angeles. University Microfilms, Ann Arbor.

Gordon, C. (1968). Configurations of content. In *The self in social interaction* (ed. C. Gordon and K. J. Gergen), vol. 1. John Wiley, New York.

Gordon, M. (1964). *Assimilation in American life*. Oxford University Press.

Grant, M. (1916). *The passing of the great race*. Scribner, New York.

Greenwald, H. G. and Oppenheim, D. B. (1968). Reported magnitude of self misidentification—Artefact? *Journal of Personality and Social Psychology*, **8**(1), 49–52.

Gregor, A. J. and McPherson, D. A. (1966*a*). Racial preferences and ego-identity among white and Bantu children in the Republic of South Africa. *Genetic Psychology Monographs*, **73**, 217–53.

Gregor, A. J. and McPherson, D. A. (1966*b*). Racial attitudes among white and Negro children in a deep South metropolitan area. *Journal of Social Psychology*, **68**, 95–106.

Hall, C. S. and Lindzey, G. (ed.) (1978). *Theories of personality* (3rd edn). John Wiley, New York.

Hamilton, D. L. (1981). Stereotyping and intergroup behaviour: Some thoughts on the cognitive approach. In *Cognitive processes in stereotyping and intergroup behaviour*, (ed. D. L. Hamilton). Lawrence Erlbaum, Hillsdale, NJ.

Hamilton, D. L. and Trolier, T. K. (1986). Stereotypes and stereotyping: An overview of the cognitive approach. In *Prejudice, discrimination and racism* (ed. J. F. Dovidio and S. L. Gaertner). Academic Press, Orlando.

Hamilton, D. L., Dugan, P. M., and Trolier, T. K. (1985). The formation of stereotype beliefs: Further evidence for distinctiveness-based illusory correlations. *Journal of Personality and Social Psychology*, **39**, 832–45.

Harrison, J., Owens, D., Holton, A., Neilson, D., and Boot, D. (1988). A prospective study of severe mental disorder in Afro-Caribbean patients. *Psychological Medicine*, **18**(3), 543–657.

Hauser, S. T. (1971). *Black and White identity formation*. John Wiley, New York. Mentioned in A. S. Waterman (1982). Identity development from adolescence to adulthood: An extension theory, a review of research. *Developmental Psychology*, **18**(3), 341–58.

Hewstone, M. and Brown, R. (ed.) (1986). *Contact and conflict in intergroup encounters*. Blackwell, Oxford.

Hill, H. C. (1919). The Americanization movement. *American Journal of Sociology*, **24**(6), 609–42.

Himmelfarb, H. S. (1979). Patterns of assimilation: Identification among American Jews. *Ethnicity*, **6**, 249–67.

Hintzman, D. L. (1986). 'Schema abstraction' in a multiple-trace memory model. *Psychological Review*, **93**, 411–28.

Hoetker, J. and Siegel, C. (1970). Three studies of the preferences of students of different races for actors in inter-racial theatre productions. *Journal of Social Issues*, **26**(4), 87–103.

Hofman, J. E. (1983). Social identity and inter-group conflict: A conspectus. In *The Conference of European and Israeli Social Psychologists*. 13–16 October, Shefayun, Israel.

Hofman, J. E. and Rouhana, N. (1976). Young Arabs in Israel: Some aspects of a conflicted social identity. *Journal of Social Psychology*, **99**, 75–86.

Hofman, J. E., Brit-Hallahmi, B., and Hertz-Lazarowitz, R. (1982). Self-concept of Jewish and Arab adolescents in Israel. *Journal of Personality and Social Psychology*, **43**, 786–92.

Hogg, M. A. and Abrams, D. (1988). *Social identifications: A social psychology of intergroup relations and group processes*. London: Routledge.

Hogg, M. A. and Turner, J. C. (1987). Social identity and conformity: A theory of referent informational influence. In *Current issues in European social psychology* (ed. W. Doise and S. Moscovici), vol. 2. Cambridge University Press.

Home Affairs Committee (1986). *Racial attacks and harassment*. HMSO, London.

Home Office (1981). *Racial attacks: A report of a Home Office study*. HMSO, London.

Horowitz, R. E. (1939). Racial aspects of self-identification in nursery school children. *Journal of Psychology*, **7**, 91–9.

Howard, J. W. and Rothbart, M. (1980). Social categorisation and memory for in-group and out-group behaviour. *Journal of Personality and Social Psychology*, **38**, 301–10.

Hraba, J. and Grant, G. (1970). Black is beautiful: A re-examination of racial preference and identification. *Journal of Personality and Social Psychology*, **16**, 398–402.

Hunt, D. E. and Hardt, R. H. (1969). The effects of upward bound programs on the attitudes, motivation and academic achievements of Negro students. *Journal of Social Issues*, **25**, 122–4.

Hunt, L. L. and Hunt, J. G. (1975). A religious factor in secular achievement among Blacks: The case of Catholicism. *Social Forces*, **53**, 595–606.

Hutnik, N. (1985*a*). Ethnic minority identity: The case of second generation South Asians in Britain. Unpublished D.Phil Thesis. University of Oxford.

Hutnik, N. (1985*b*). Aspects of identity in a multi-ethnic society. *New Community*, **12**(1), 298–309.

Hutnik, N. (1986). Patterns of ethnic minority identification and modes of social adaptation. *Ethnic and Racial Studies*, **9**(2), 150–67.

Ineichen, B. (1987). The mental health of Asians in Britain: A research note. *New Community*, **14**(1/2), 136–41.

Ineichen, B. (1989). Afro-Caribbeans and the incidence of schizophrenia: a review. *New Community*, **15**, 335–41.

Inkeles, A. and Smith, D. H. (1970). The fate of personal adjustment in the process of modernisation. *International Journal of Comparative Sociology*, **11**, 81–114.

Isaacs, H. (1974). Basic group identity: The idols of the tribe. *Ethnicity*, **1**, 15–41.

Jaspars, J. M. F. and Warnaen, S. (1982). Inter-group relations, ethnic identity and self-evaluation in Indonesia. In *Social identity and intergroup relations* (ed. H. Tajfel). Cambridge University Press.

Jowell, R. and Airey, C. (ed.) (1984). *British social attitudes: The 1984 report*. Gower, London.

Kallen, H. (1925). *Culture and democracy in the United States*. Arno Press, New York, 1970. Mentioned in G. A. Postiglione (1983). *Ethnicity and American social theory: Toward critical pluralism*. University Press of America, Lanham, New York.

Karlins, M., Coffman, T. L. and Walters, G. (1969). On the fading of social stereotypes: Studies in three generations of college students. *Journal of Personality and Social Psychology*, **28**, 280–90.

Katz, D. and Brayly, K. (1933). Racial stereotypes in one hundred college students. *Journal of Abnormal and Social Psychology*, **28**, 280–90.

Katz, P. A. and Zalk, S. R. (1974). Doll preferences: An index of racial attitudes. *Journal of Educational Psychology*, **66**, 663–8.

Katz, P. A. and Zalk, S. R. (1978). Modification of children's racial attitudes. *Developmental Psychology*, **14**, 447–61.

Kelly, G. A. (1955). *The psychology of personal constructs*. Norton, New York.

Khan, V. S. (1979a). Migration and social stress. In *Minority families in Britain* (ed. V. S. Khan). Macmillan, London.

Khan, V. S. (ed.) (1979b). Mirpuris in Bradford. In *Minority families in Britain*. Macmillan, London.

Kinder, D. R. (1986). The continuing American dilemma: White resistance to racial change 40 years after Myrdal. *Journal of Social Issues*, **42**, 151–71.

Kitwood, T. (1983). Self-conception among young British–Asian Muslims: Confutation of a stereotype. In *Threatened Identities* (ed. G. Breakwell). John Wiley, London.

Kitwood, T. M. and Borrill, C. S. (1980). The significance of schooling for an ethnic minority. *Oxford Review of Education*, **6**, 241–53.

Kline, H. K. (1970). An exploration of racism in ego-ideal formation. *Smith College Studies in Social Work*, **40**, 211–15. Mentioned in E. Brand, R. Ruiz, and A. M. Padilla (1974). Ethnic identification and preference: A review. *Psychological Bulletin*, **81**(11), 860–90.

Krishna, G. (1990). Salience of minority group identity: A social identity approach. Unpublished Honours thesis, University of Delhi.

Kuhn, M. K. and McPartland, S. (1954). An empirical investigation of self-attitudes. *American Sociological Review*, **19**, 68–76.

Lambert, W. E., Libman, E., and Poser, E. G. (1960). The effect of increased salience of a membership group on pain tolerance. *Journal of Personality*, **28**, 350–7.

Landreth, C. and Johnson, B. C. (1953). Young children's response to picture and inset test design to reveal reactions to persons of different skin colour. *Child Development*, **24**, 63–79.

Lawrence, D. (1987). Racial violence in Britain: Trends and a perspective. *New Community*, **14**(1/2), 151–60.

Leavitt, H. J. (1951). Some effects of certain communication patterns on group performance. *Journal of Abnormal and Social Psychology*, **46**, 38–50.

Lefley, H. (1974). Effects of a cultural heritage program on the self-concept of Miccosukee Indian children. *Journal of Educational Research*, **67**, 462–4.

Lemaine, G., Kastersztein, J., and Personnaz, B. (1978). Social differentiation. In *Differentiation between social groups: Studies in the social psychology of intergroup relations* (ed. H. Tajfel). Academic Press, London.

Levine, R. A. and Campbell, D. T. (1972). *Ethnocentrism: Theories of conflict, ethnic attitudes and group behaviour*. John Wiley, New York.

Lewin, K. (1935). Psycho-sociological problems of a minority group. *Character and Personality*, **3**, 175–87.

Lewin, K. (1936). *Principles of topological psychology*. McGraw-Hill, New York. Mentioned in C. S. Hall and G. Lindzey (ed.) (1978). *Theories of personality* (3rd edn). John Wiley, New York.

Lewin, K. (1948). *Resolving social conflicts*. Harper and Brothers, New York.

Lewin, K. (1952). *Field theory in social science: Selected theoretical papers*. Tavistock, London.

Lewin, K., Lippit, R., and White, R. K. (1939). Patterns of aggressive behaviour in experimentally created 'social climates'. *Journal of Social Psychology*, **10**, 271–99.

Liebkind, K. (1983). Identity in multiple group allegiance. In *Identity: Personal and socio-cultural—A symposium* (ed. A. Jacobson-Widding). Almquist and Wiksell, Stockholm.

Liebkind, K. (ed.). (1989). *New identities in Europe: Immigrant ancestry and the ethnic identity of youth*. Avebury, Aldershot.

Linville, P. W. (1982). The complexity–extremity effect and age-based stereotyping. *Journal of Personality and Social Psychology*, **42**, 193–211.

Linville, P. W., Salovey, P., and Fischer, G. W. (1986). Stereotyping and perceived distribution of social characteristics: An application to ingroup-outgroup perception. In *Prejudice, discrimination, racism: Theory and research* (ed. J. F. Dovidio and S. L. Gaertner), pp. 165–208. Academic Press, New York.

Linville, P. W., Fischer, G. W., and Salovey, P. (1989). Perceived distributions of the characteristics of ingroup and outgroup members: Empirical evidence and a computer simulation. *Journal of Personality and Social Psychology* **57**, 165–88.

Littlewood, R. and Lipsedge, M. (1982). *Aliens and alienists. Ethnic minorities and psychiatry*. Penguin, Harmondsworth, Middlesex.

London, H. (1967). Liberalising the White Australia policy: Integration, assimilation or cultural pluralism. *Australian Outlook*, **21**, 338–46.

London, M. (1986). Mental illness among ethnic minorities in the United Kingdom. *British Journal of Psychiatry*, **149**, 265–73.

Lott, A. J. and Lott, B. E. (1961). Group cohesiveness, communication level, and conformity. *Journal of Abnormal and Social Psychology*, **62**, 408–12.

Louden, D. M. (1978a). Self-esteem and locus of control: Some findings on immigrant adolescents in Britain. *New Community*, **6**(3), 218–34.

Louden, D. M. (1978b). Self-esteem and locus of control in minority group adolescents. *Ethnic and Racial Studies*, **1**, 196–217.

Lyon, M. (1972). Race and ethnicity in pluralistic societies: A comparison of minorities in the UK and USA. *New Community*, **1**(4), 256–62.

Lyon, M. (1973). Ethnicity in Britain: The Gujarati tradition. *New Community*, **2**(1), 1–11.

Majeed, A. and Ghosh, E. S. K. (1982). A Study of social identity in three ethnic groups in India. *International Journal of Psychology*, **17**, 455–63.

Mann, J. W. (1957). The problem of the marginal personality: A psychological study of a coloured group. Unpublished D.Phil. thesis. University of Natal.

Mann, J. W. (1963). Rivals of different rank. *Journal of Social Psychology*, **61**(1), 11–27.

Mann, J. F. and Taylor, D. M. (1974). Attribution of causality: Role of ethnicity and social class. *Journal of Social Psychology*, **94**, 3–13.

Masuda, M., Matsumoto, J. H., and Meredith, J. M. (1970). Ethnic identity in three generations of Japanese Americans. *Journal of Social Psychology*, **81**, 199–207.

Masuda, M., Hasegawa, R. S., and Matsumoto, G. (1973). The Ethnic Identity Questionnaire: A comparison of three Japanese age groups in Tachikawa, Japan, Honolulu and Seattle. *Journal of Cross-Cultural Psychology*, **4**(2), 229–45.

McConahay, J. B. (1986). Modern racism, ambivalence, and the modern racism scale. In *Prejudice, discrimination, racism: Theory and research* (ed. J. F. Dovidio and S. L. Gaertner), pp. 91–126. Academic Press, New York.

McCready, W. (ed.) (1983). *Culture, ethnicity and identity: Current issues in research*. Academic Press, London.

McDonald, R. L. and Gynther, M. D. (1965). Relationship of self and ideal-self description with sex, race and class of Southern adolescents. *Journal of Personality and Social Psychology*, **36**, 511–20.

McGovern, D. and Cope, R. V. (1987). First psychiatric admission rates of first and second generation Afro-Caribbeans. *Social Psychiatry*, **22**(3), 139–49.

McGuire, W. J., McGuire, C. V., Child, P., and Fujioka, T. (1978). Salience of ethnicity in the spontaneous self-concept as a function of one's ethnic distinctiveness in the social environment. *Journal of Personality and Social Psychology*, **36**(5), 511–20.

McGuire, W. J., McGuire, C. V., and Winton, W. (1979). Effects of household sex composition on the salience of one's gender in the spontaneous self-concept. *Journal of Experimental Social Psychology*, **15**, 77–90.

Messick, D. M. and Mackie, D. M. (1989). Intergroup relations. *Annual Review of Psychology*, **40**, 45–81.

Milner, D. (1975). *Children and race*. Penguin, London.

Milner, D. (1983). *Children and race: Ten years on*. Ward Lock Educational, London.

Montemayor, R. and Eisen, M. (1977). The development of self-conceptions from childhood to adolescence. *Developmental Psychology*, **13**, 314–19.

Morland, J. K. (1958). Racial recognition by nursery school children in Lynchburg, Virginia. *Social Forces*, **37**, 132–7.

Morland, J. K. (1962). Racial acceptance and preference of nursery school children in a Southern city. *Merrill-Palmer Quarterly*, **8**, 271–80.

Morland, J. K. (1963). Racial self-identification: A study of nursery school children. *American Catholic Sociological Review*, **24**, 231–42.

Morland, J. K. and Hwang, C. H. (1981). Racial ethnic identity of pre-school children: Comparing Taiwan, Hong Kong and the United States. *Journal of Cross-Cultural Psychology*, **12**(4), 409–24.

Morris, H. S. (1968). Ethnic groups. In *International Encyclopedia of the Social Sciences*, Vol. 5. Macmillan and the Free Press, New York.

Moscovici, S. and Paicheler, G. (1978). Social comparison and social recognition: Two complementary processes of identification. In *Differentiation between social groups: Studies in the social psychology of intergroup behaviour* (ed. H. Tajfel). Academic Press, London.

Mullan, E. (1981). Theoretical investigation of the salience of religion and national identity in Northern Ireland. Unpublished B.A. thesis. Queen's University of Belfast.

Narroll, R. (1964). Ethnic unit classification. *Current Anthropology*, **5**(4). Mentioned in F. Barth (ed.) (1969). *Ethnic groups and boundaries: The social organisation of cultural differences*. George Allen and Unwin, London.

Novakovic, J. (1977). The assimilation myth revisited: Rejection of home culture by second generation Yugoslav immigrant children as a function of age, friendship group and sex. Unpublished Honours thesis. School of Psychology, University of New South Wales. In S. Boucher (ed.) (1982). *Cultures in contact: Studies in cross-culture interaction*. Pergamon Press, Oxford.

Oakes, P. (1987). The salience of social categories. In *Rediscovering the social group: A self-categorisation theory* (ed. J. C. Turner). Basil Blackwell, Oxford.

Oberg, K. (1960). Culture shock: Adjustment to new cultural environments. *Practical Anthropology*, **7**, 177–82.

Office of Population Censuses and Surveys (1983). *Census 1981: Country of birth*, HMSO, London.

Osgood, C. E., Suci G. J., and Tannebaum, P. H. (1957). *The measurement of meaning*. University of Illinois Press, Urbana.

Parekh, B. (1986). Racism and anti-racism: A study in the contradictory profile of the British State. In *The XIth World Congress of Sociology, Research Committee on Ethnic, Race and Minority Relations*. 18–22 August, New Delhi.

Park, P. and Rothbart, M. (1982). Perception of out-group homogeneity and levels of social categorisation: Memory for the subordinate attributes of in-group and out-group members. *Journal of Personality and Social Psychology*, **42**, 1051–68.

Park, R. E. (1928). Human migration and the marginal men. *American Journal of Sociology*, **33**, 881–93.

Peres, Y. and Yuval-Davis, N. (1969). Some observations on the national identity of the Israeli Arab. *Human Relations*, **22**(3), 219–33.

Pettigrew, T. F. (1979). The ultimate attribution error: Extending Allport's cognitive analysis of prejudice. *Personality and Social Psychology Bulletin*, **5**, 461–76.

Pettigrew, T. F. (1985). New patterns of racism: US Black–White relations since the 1960s. In *Seminar on Ethnic, Cultural and Racial Studies*. 7 May, St. Antony's College, Oxford.

Pettigrew, T. F. (1986). The intergroup contact hypothesis reconsidered. In *Contact and conflict in intergroup encounters* (ed. M. Hewstone and R. Brown), pp. 169–95. Basil Blackwell, Oxford.

Pienkos, D. (1974). Foreign affairs perceptions of ethnics: The Polish–Americans of Milwaukee. *Ethnicity*, **1**, pp. 223–35.

Porter, J. (1971). *Black child, White child: The development of racial attitudes*. Harvard University Press, Cambridge, Mass.

Porter, J. D. R. and Washington, R. E. (1979). Black identity and self-esteem: A review of studies of Black self-concept, 1968–1978. *Annual Review of Sociology*, **5**, 53–74.

Postiglione, G. A. (1983). *Ethnicity and American social theory: Toward critical pluralism*. University Press of America, Lanham, New York.

Powell, G. J. and Fuller, M. (1973). *Black Monday's children*. Appleton-Century-Crofts, New York.

Proshansky, H. and Newton, P. (1968). The nature and meaning of Negro self-identity. In *Social class, race and psychological development* (ed. M. Deutsch, I. Katz, and A. R. Jensen). Holt, Rinehart and Winston, New York.

Radke, M. and Trager, H. G. (1950). Children's perceptions of the social roles of Negroes and Whites. *Journal of Psychology*, **29**, 3–33.

Radke-Yarrow, M. and Lande, B. (1953). Personality correlates of differential reactions to minority group belonging. *Journal of Social Psychology*, **38**, 253–72.

Rice, A. S., Ruiz, R. G. and Padilla, A. M. (1974). Person perception, self-identity and ethnic group preference in Anglo, Black and Chicano pre-school and third-grade children. *Journal of Cross-Cultural Psychology*, **5**(1), 100–7.

Riesman, D. (1953). Some observations on intellectual freedom. *American Scholar*, Winter, 9–25.

Rosch, E. (1978). Principles of categorisation. In *Cognition and categorisation*, (ed. E. Rosch and B. B. Lloyd), pp. 27–48. Lawrence Erlbaum, Hillsdale, NJ.

Rosenberg, M. (1965). *Society and the adolescent self-image*. Princeton University Press.

Rosenberg, M. (1977). Contextual dissonance effects: Nature and causes. *Psychiatry*, **40**, 205–17.

Rosenberg, M. (1979). *Conceiving the self*. Basic Books, New York.

Rothbart, M. and John, O. P. (1985). Social categorisation and behavioural episodes: A cognitive analysis of the effects of intergroup contact. *Journal of Social Issues*, **41**, 81–104.

Rothman, J. (1960). In-group identification and out-group association: A theoretical and experimental study. *Journal of Jewish Communal Service*, **37**, 81–93.

Sagar, H. A. and Schofield, J. W. (1980). Racial and behavioural cues in Black and White children's perceptions of ambiguously aggressive acts. *Journal of Personality and Social Psychology*, **39**, 590–8.

Sapru, S. (1989). A study on the salience of ethnicity among minority group individuals. Unpublished Honours thesis. University of Delhi.

Sarnoff, I. (1951). Identification with the aggressor: Some personality correlates of anti-Semitism in Jews. *Journal of Personality*, **20**, 199–218.

Schermerhorn, R. A. (1971). *Comparative ethnic relations: A framework for theory and research*. Random House, New York.

Schiffman, R. and Wagner, U. (1985). How is the problem between the groups going? (in German). *Gruppendynamik*, **16**(1), 43–52.

Scodel, A. and Austrin, H. (1957). The perception of Jewish photographs by non-Jews and Jews. *Journal of Abnormal and Social Psychology*, **54**, 278–80.

Sears, D. O. (1983). The person-positivity bias. *Journal of Personality and Social Psychology*, **44**, 233–50.

Seelye, N. H. and Brewer, M. B. (1970). Ethnocentrism and acculturation of North Americans in Guatemala. *Journal of Social Psychology*, **80**(2), 147–55.

Shaw, M. E. (1932). A comparison of individuals and small groups in the rational solution of complex problems. *American Journal of Psychology*, **44**, 491–504.

Sherif, M. (1966). *In common predicament: Social psychology of inter-group conflict and co-operation*. Houghton-Mifflin, Boston, Mass.

Sherwood, R. (1980). *The psychodynamics of race*. Harvester Press, Sussex.

Shibutani, T. and Kwan, K. M. (1965). *Ethnic stratification: A comparative approach*. Macmillan, New York.

Shomer, R. W. and Centers, R. (1970). Differences in attitudinal responses under conditions of implicitly manipulated group salience. *Journal of Personality and Social Psychology*, **15**(2), 125–32.

Shorter Oxford English Dictionary (1980). Vol. 2 (rev. edn). Clarendon Press, Oxford.

Simpson, G. E. (1968). Assimilation. In *International encyclopedia of the social sciences*, Vol. 1. Macmillan and the Free Press, New York.

Slugoski, B. (1984). Ego identity and explanatory speech. In *International conference on self and identity, for the Symposium on Social Construction of Selves*. 9–13 July, Cardiff.

Snyder, M. and Swann, W. B. Jr. (1978). Hypothesis-testing processes in social interaction. *Journal of Personality and Social Psychology*, **36**, 1202–12.

Sommerlad, E. and Berry, J. D. (1970). The role of ethnic identification in distinguishing between attitudes of assimilation and integration of a minority racial group. *Human Relations*, **23**, 23–9.

Spencer, M. B. and Horowitz, F. D. (1973). Effects of systematic social and token reinforcement on the modification of racial and colour concept attitudes in Black and White pre-school children. *Developmental Psychology*, **9**, 246–54.

Stevenson, H. W. and Stewart, E. C. (1958). A developmental study of racial awareness in young children. *Child Development*, **29**, 399–409.

Stonequist, E. V. (1937). *The marginal man*. Scribner, New York.

Stopes-Roe, M. and Cochrane, R. (1986). Prejudice: Asian and British views on its present occurence. *New Community*, **13**(2), 235–49.

Stopes-Roe, M. and Cochrane, R. (1987). The process of assimilation in Asians in Britain: A study of Hindu, Muslim and Sikh immigrants and their young children. *International Journal of Comparative Sociology*, **28**(1–2), 43–56.

Stopes-Roe, M. and Cochrane, R. (1990). The child-rearing values of Asians and British parents and young people: An inter-ethnic and inter-generational comparison in the Evaluation of Kohn's 13 Qualities. *British Journal of Social Psychology*, **29**, 149–60.

Sue, S. (1983). Ethnic minority issues in psychology, *American Psychologist*, May, 583–92.

Sue, S., Ito, J., and Bradshaw, C. (1982). Ethnic minority research: trends and directions. In *Minority mental health* (ed. E. E. Jones and S. J. Korchin). Praeger, New York.

Sumner, G. A. (1906). *Folkways*. Ginn, New York.

Taft, R. (1973). Migration: Problems of adjustment and assimilation in immigrants. In *Psychology and race* (ed. P. Watson). Penguin Educational, London.

Taft, R. (1981). The role and personality of the mediator. In *The mediating person: Bridges between cultures* (ed. S. Bochner). Schenkman, Cambridge, Mass.

Tajfel, H. (1972). Social categorisation. In *Introduction à la psychologie sociale* (ed. S. Moscovici), Vol. 1. Larousse, Paris.

Tajfel, H. (1978). *The social psychology of minorities*. Minority Rights Group, London.

Tajfel, H. (1981). *Human groups and social categories: Studies in social psychology*. Cambridge University Press.

Tajfel, H. (1982). Social psychology of inter-group relations. *Annual Review of Psychology*, **33**, 1–39.

Tajfel, H. and Dawson, J. L. (eds) (1965). *Disappointed guests*. Oxford University Press.

Tajfel, H. and Wilkes, A. L. (1963). Classification and quantitative judgement. *British Journal of Psychology*, **54**, 101–14.

Tajfel, H., Flament, C., Billig, M., and Bundy, R. P. (1971). Social categorisation and inter-group behaviour. *European Journal of Social Psychology*, **1**, 149–78.

Tajfel, H., Sheikh, A. A., and Gardner, R. C. (1964). Contexts of stereotypes and the inference of similarity between members of stereotyped groups. *Acta Psychologia*, **22**, 191–201.

Taylor, D. M. and Jaggi, V. (1974). Ethnocentrism and causal attribution in a South Indian context. *Journal of Cross-Cultural Psychology*, **5**, 162–71.

Taylor, D. M. and McKirnan, D. J. (1984). Theoretical contributions: A five-stage model of intergroup relations. *British Journal of Social Psychology*, **23**, 291–300.

Taylor, D. M. and Simard, L. M. (1979). Ethnic identity and intergroup relations. In *Emerging ethnic boudaries* (ed. D. J. Lee). University of Ottawa Press.

Taylor, S. E. (1981). A categorisation approach to stereotyping. In *Cognitive processes in stereotyping and intergroup behaviour* (ed. D. L. Hamilton), pp. 83–114. Lawrence Erlbaum, Hillsdale, NJ.

Taylor, S. E., Fiske, S. T., Close, M., Anderson, C., and Ruderman, A. (1977). Solo status as a psychological variable: The power of being distinctive. Mentioned in S. E. Taylor *et al.* (1979). The generalizability of salience effects. *Journal of Personality and Social Psychology*, **37**(3), 357–68.

Taylor, S. E., Crocker, J., Fiske, S. T., Sprinzen, M., and Winkler, J. D. (1979). The generalizability of salience effects. *Journal of Personality and Social Psychology*, **37**(3), 357–68.

Theodorson, G. A. and Theodorson, A. G. (1969). *A modern dictionary of sociology*. Thomas & Crowell, New York.

Thompson, M. (1974). The second generation: Punjabi or English? *New Community*, **3**, 242–54.

Tizard, B. and Phoenix, A. (1989). Black identity and transracial adoption. *New Community*, **15**(3), 427–37.

Trew, K. (1981*a*). Social identity and group membership. In *Annual Conference of the BPS: Northern Ireland Branch*; *Symposium, Intergroup Relations in Northern Ireland*. May, Rosapenna.

Trew, K. (1981*b*). Intergroup relations and social identity in Northren Ireland. In *British Psychological Society, Social Psychology Section, Annual Conference*. 18–20 September, University of Oxford.

Trew, K. (1982*a*). Group identification in a divided society. In *The International Association of Child and Adolescent Psychiatry and Allied Professions: 10th International Congress*; *Symposium, Children in a Society in Turmoil*. July, Dublin.

Trew, K. (1982*b*). A sense of national identity? *Annual Conference of the Psychological Society of Ireland*; *Symposium, Growing up in a Troubled Society: Children in Northern Ireland*. November, Sligo.

Triandis, H. C., Lisansky, J., Setiadi, B., Chang, B. H., Martin, G., and Betancourt, H. (1982). Stereotyping among Hispanics and Anglos: The uniformity, intensity, direction and quality of auto- and heterostereotypes. *Journal of Cross-Cultural Psychology*, **13**, 409–26.

Turner, F. (1920). *The frontier in American history*. Holt & Co, New York.

Turner, J. C. (1982). Towards a cognitive redefinition of the social group. In *Social identity and intergroup relations* (ed. H. Tajfel). Cambridge University Press.

Turner, J. C. (1985). Social categorisation and the self-concept: A social cognitive theory of group behaviour. *Advances in Group Processes*, **2**, 77–121.

Turner, J. C. (1987). *Rediscovering the social group: A self-categorisation theory*. Basil Blackwell, New York.

Turner, J. C., Hogg, M. A., Oakes, P. J., and Smith P. M. (1984). Failure and defeat as determinants of group cohesiveness. *British Journal of Social Psychology*, **23**, 97–111.

Tyson, G. A. (1985). Children's racial attitudes: A review. Unpublished Human Science Research Council Report, Pretoria.

Vanbeselaere, N. (1987). The effects of dichotomous and crossed social categorization upon intergroup discrimination. *European Journal of Social Psychology*, **17**, 143–56.

Vaughan, G. M. (1964). The development of ethnic attitudes in New Zealand school children. *Genetic Psychology Monographs*, **70**, 135–75.

Verna, G. B. (1982). A study of the nature of children's race preferences using a modified conflict paradigm. *Child Development*, **53**, 437–45.

Wadell, N. and Cairns, E. (1984). Situational ethnicity in Northern Ireland. In *British Psychological Society, Social Psychology Section, Annual Conference*. 14–16 September, University College, Oxford.

Wagley, C. and Harris, M. (1958). Minorities in the New World, Columbia, p. 10. Mentioned in G. E. Simpson and J. M. Yinger (1965). *Racial and cultural minorities: An analysis of prejudice and discrimination*. Harper & Row, New York.

Wallman, S. (1983). Identity options. In *Minorities: Community and identity* (ed. C. Fried). Springer, New York.

Ward, S. H. and Braun, J. H. (1972). Self-esteem and racial preference in Black children. *American Journal of Orthopsychiatry*, **42**, 644–7.

Weinreich, P. (1980). *Manual for identity exploration using personal constructs*. SSRC Research Unit on Ethnic Relations, University of Aston in Birmingham.

Weinreich, P. (1982). A conceptual framework for exploring identity development: Identity structure analysis and Idex. In *Symposium, Identity Exploration using IDEX. 10th International Congress of the International Association for Child and Adolescent Psychiatry and Allied Professions*. 25–30 July, Dublin.

Weinreich, P. (1983a). Emerging from threatened identities: Ethnicity and gender in redefinitions of ethnic identity. In *Threatened Identities* (ed. G. Breakwell). John Wiley, London.

Weinreich, P. (1983b). Psychodynamics of personal and social identity: Theoretical concepts and their measurement in adolescents from Belfast sectarian and Bristol ethnic minority groups. In *Identity: Personal and socio-cultural—A symposium* (ed. A. Jacobson-Widding). Almquist and Wiksell, Stockholm.

Williams, J. E., Best, D. L., and Boswell, D. A. (1975). The measurement of children's racial attitudes in the early school years. *Child Development*, **46**, 494–500.

Williams-Burns, W. (1980). Self-esteem and skin colour perception of advantaged Afro-American children. *Journal of Negro Education*, **49**, 385–97.

Wills, T. A. (1981). Downward comparison principles in social psychology. *Psychological Bulletin*, **90**, 245–71.

Wilson, A. (1981). Mixed race children: An exploratory study of racial categorisation and identity. *New Community*, **9**(1), 36–43.

Wishart, D. (1982). *Clustan user manual*. Program Library Unit, Edinburgh University.

Worchel, P. (1957). Adaptability-screening of flying personnel: Development of a self-concept inventory for predicting maladjustment. Texas: Randolph Air Force Base, USAF. Mentioned in Leo Dreidger (1976). Ethnic self-identity: A comparison of in-group evaluations. *Sociometry*, **39**(2), 131–41.

Word, C. O., Zanna, M. P., and Cooper, J. (1974). The non-verbal mediation of self-fulfilling prophecies in interracial interaction. *Journal of Experimental Social Psychology*, **10**, 109–20.

Wright, S. C., Taylor, D. M., and Moghaddam, F. M. (1990). Responding to membership in a disadvantaged group: From acceptance to collective protest. *Journal of Personality and Social Psychology*, **58**(6), 994–1003.

Wylie, R. (1978). *The self-concept: Theory and research on selected topics*, Vol. 2 (rev. edn). University of Nebraska Press, Lincoln.

Young, L. and Bagley, C. (1979). Identity, self-esteem and evaluation of colour and ethnicity in young children in Jamaica and London. *New Community*, **7**(2), 154–70.

Zangwill, I. (1929). *The melting pot*. Macmillan, New York.

Index